MW00860608

TIEBREAKER:
TOWER OF SECRETS II

Victor Sheymov

TIEBREAKER

Copyright 2013 Victor Sheymov

ISBN: 0985893036
ISBN 13: 978-0-9858930-3-3
Library of Congress Control Number: 2013920169
Cyber Books Publishing, Vienna, VA

http://www.cyberbookspublishing.com

What they said about Victor Sheymov's earlier books:

Tower of Secrets: A Real Life Spy Thriller

Superlative...a breathtaking true story...a towering book, fascinating and hair-raising...far more exciting than the most exciting accomplished fiction of the spy genre.

– Associated Press

For Americans who hear daily of former communists changing their political coats and leading new republics in the former Soviet Union, Sheymov's revelations will cause sober reflections about the future of relations between the United States and these new nations.

– Richard Helms, former Director of the CIA

Victor Sheymov is the real thing–a former KGB officer who had access to the most secret Soviet intelligence. The story of Sheymov's flight... is a memorable final chapter to the Cold War saga. Tower of Secrets gives readers their first real look into the KGB's most tightly held information–how it protected its own communications around the world. Sheymov knew the secrets that spy services die to protect.

– David Ignatius, Associate Editor
of The Washington Post, author of
Agents of Innocence, Body of Lies

Sheymov was a senior manager and troubleshooter in the communications division of the KGB, a position affording him a comprehensive overview of the organization. In this suspenseful third-person narrative, he reveals how he was recruited and trained, gives details of his most interesting assignments and describes the gradual disillusionment that led to his defection. How, in 1980, the CIA smuggled him out of the Soviet Union with his wife and five-year-old daughter into the United States forms the core of this exciting story. The KGB, fooled into thinking Sheymov was dead, did not learn of his defection for 10 years.

– Publishers Weekly

The suspenseful, eye-opening memoir of a Soviet spy who came in from the cold. Writing in the third person, Sheymov offers a riveting account of his upwardly mobile career with the KGB and the factors that led him to defect to the West in 1980. In 1969, after graduating with an engineering degree from Moscow's prestigious Technical University, the author joined a Defense Ministry institute that was researching military uses of space. Recruited by the state's intelligence service in 1971, at age 25, Sheymov eventually became the Eighth Chief Directorate's principal troubleshooter. In this sensitive capacity, he traveled far afield, ensuring the security of enciphered KGB communications throughout the world....But the higher Sheymov climbed, the more disillusioned he became with Communism and the Kremlin elite's corruption. Resolved to inflict as much damage as he could on the system, the author made contact with the CIA.... The exfiltration was so skillfully executed that the author's erstwhile masters long believed that he and his family were dead. While the story ends abruptly with Sheymov's escorted arrival in N.Y.C., it seems likely that the information he subsequently furnished American officials hastened the Cold War's end. A top-level insider's dramatic, stranger-than-fiction disclosures in the great game of espionage.

– Kirkus Reviews

What the experts say about Victor Sheymov's new breakthrough book

Cyberspace and Security:
A Fundamentally New Approach

CYBERSPACE and SECURITY by Victor Sheymov does a wonderful job in discussing the differences between man-made cyberspace and the natural world in which we live. Sheymov uses these differences to explain how securing cyberspace is vastly different from traditional information security. The book is written so that readers without a deep computer science background can readily understand the subject, and readers with a security background will find the concepts informative and thought provoking. I know of no other author who has the real-life experience that Victor Sheymov brings to this subject, and would recommend the book to everyone as an easy and entertaining reading experience.

– Dickie George
Former Technical Director,
Information Assurance Directorate,
National Security Agency

Drawing on his decades of experience with two of the world's premier spy agencies, Victor Sheymov offers penetrating and compelling insights into the challenges–and opportunities–involved in securing cyberspace. A must-read for all–from IT professionals and techno-nerds to policy makers and corporate executives.

– Dr. Sujeet Shenoi
F.P. Walter Professor of Computer Science
University of Tulsa.

In an era when everyone is applying techniques to secure cyberspace that have repeatedly failed, it is refreshing to see an approach that goes to the core of the problem. Victor Sheymov introduces security concepts to the cyberspace arena that he has gleaned from decades of working with national intelligence agencies. The result is a work of proven principles that is a must read for cyber security specialists, researchers and IT professionals.

– Dr. Jonathan Butts, USAir Force Major
Assistant Professor of Computer Science
Air Force Institute of Technology
[Note that these views do not necessarily
reflect the official position of the
United States Air Force or Department of Defense.]

And look for Victor Sheymov's

Party Gold: A Cyrus Grant Novel of Suspense

To Olga and Elena

CONTENTS

FOREWORD

Some of the events described in this book may not be particularly flattering to the CIA. The author would like to make it clear that if any government organization publicly challenges the factual events described in this book, he will feel compelled to publish relevant particulars and details of the challenged facts, such as exact places and real names of the participants, so that the descriptions can be conclusively verified.

V.S.

INTRODUCTION

I never wanted to be an intelligence officer. I always wanted to be a scientist. In fact, my first degree was in aerospace engineering. However, I was born in a country where one did not choose one's job after graduation—the government decided it for you.

Fueled by Communist ideology, the Cold War engulfed most of the world in the second half of the last century and spilled over to this one. It also created a very powerful intelligence vortex. By virtue, or vice, of my fate I was drawn into that vortex. I tried to escape it, but could not—until the end of that war. I happened to be close to the center of many critical moments of the intelligence battles of the war, and worked with many of the key participants.

I published my first book, *Tower of Secrets*, in 1993. It described my experience in Communist Russia and the KGB that ended with our family's arrival in the United States in 1980. I was pleasantly surprised by the number and sincerity of the letters from readers. These letters were one of the most gratifying experiences of my life, and I felt somewhat obligated to answer the question raised in most of the letters: what happened afterwards? No less important, I had a unique perspective to offer: during my career in intelligence I got to know the inner workings of the KGB intimately, I had a good experience working with the NSA, and I had numerous encounters with the CIA. Furthermore, while my expertise was in technical security, I also had first-hand experience and understanding of human intelligence. All these factors contributed to my decision to publish this book.

Our family was exfiltrated from the Soviet Union by the CIA, and, naturally, we felt deep appreciation for the performance of those who actually carried out the operation, especially the courageous couple who took us through the extremely heavily fortified Soviet border. When we came to the United States we knew very little about this country. Being a dedicated anti-communist, my attitude was simple: the enemy of my enemy was my ally. Upon arrival we faced many challenges, learning English being just one of them. We were extremely impressed and deeply touched by the natural hospitality and friendliness of the American people. People helped us just for the sake of helping. Ironically, all our seriously negative experiences were related to the CIA. We soon concluded that we came from a big bad country with a few good people to a big great country with a few bad people. And we came to love this country.

To say that my encounters with the CIA in the United States were surprising would be a gross understatement. I had heard about their obsession with control of defectors and their bad treatment of them. Professionally, I also understood that how people are treated by an intelligence service is highly dependent on their value. Given my background and level of expertise in highly secret areas, I understood that after my arrival my continuing value in United States intelligence was significant. This was confirmed by the CIA's Distinguished Service medal that I was awarded, and my extended work with the NSA. So if I was treated badly, sometimes clearly illegally, I could only imagine how badly defectors were treated who had lost their value.

I did not want to fight the CIA, I just wanted to be left alone. So I felt personally disappointed and even angry, particularly at the treatment of my family. But besides being disappointed personally, professionally I could not understand what was going on. Indeed, what the CIA was doing was entirely contrary to the objective interests of the United States. Why? I felt compelled to research the reason for this CIA hostility, not just toward me personally, but as a trend,. The results of that research are presented in this book.

In yet another twist of my fate, The FBI appointed Robert Hanssen as my FBI liaison. At the time of our introduction Hanssen was a high level FBI Special Agent with top level security clearances. Our families were on friendly terms, and we frequently socialized together. This gave me a unique vantage point for observing Bob Hanssen outside of his office environment. It was really ironic that amongst thousands of its agents the FBI chose Hanssen, who later would be revealed as a longtime KGB mole who had achieved the most damaging penetration of the FBI ever.

I either participated in, or observed directly, most of the events described in this book. Many of these events are related to intelligence, so some names, places and times have necessarily been altered. In the interest of readability I have tried to avoid bothering the reader with overly-detailed particulars. However, these events indeed took place and the descriptions are accurate. I have tried to avoid making explicit judgments except where the judgment is obvious. I would like to urge the reader to draw his own conclusions and I fully understand that they may be different from mine.

Overall, this book reflects my personal experience in intelligence from an unusual vantage point. I hope it will help the American general public to understand some not readily apparent processes. I also still harbor a hope that it can help professionals understand and improve American intelligence services, particularly the CIA. Alas, I am not particularly optimistic that the CIA culture will change. Stripped from the elaborate semantics, their perpetual response seems to be: it never happened, but if it did, it was a long time ago and we have already corrected all the shortcomings of the past.

Acknowledgments

I was again fortunate to have the talent and experience of my editor, Roger Jellinek, contributing to this book.
I am grateful to Olga Sheymov who applied her talent to designing this book's cover.

PART I

May 1980. Victor opened his eyes. That was all he needed to fully awaken. He knew exactly where he was—in a CIA safe house near Vienna, Austria. Olga and Elena were still sleeping. He dressed quietly and went downstairs to the kitchen.

Bob Elwood was already there, sipping coffee. "Good morning," he said in Russian. "Want some breakfast?" Victor guessed why Elwood didn't ask how he'd slept; Elwood knew that Victor, like everybody else in the safe house, had dozed fitfully at best, with his senses tuned acutely to the surroundings, sensitive to any suspicious sound. Probably only Elena, unaware of the danger, had found peaceful slumber.

"Good morning. I'll just join you for coffee for now."

06:45. *08:45 in Moscow. The show at KGB Headquarters will begin shortly after nine, when my absence is noticed. That is, if everything went well. If not, a different show will begin here, in Vienna, when they try to intercept us and either kidnap or kill me at the airport.*

Victor poured himself a cup of coffee and sat at the table opposite Elwood. Though Elwood was in his early fifties, his narrow face, creased with deep wrinkles, made him appear older. His jutting jaw and ever-present pipe, clinched by crooked teeth, only enhanced this impression. About five-nine and wiry, Elwood was nevertheless fit; his energetic, sure movements were that of a person much younger.

"I talked to our guy on the phone ten minutes ago. He bought the tickets, and he'll be here in less than an hour. Bought on the spot to avoid reservations, of course. I think we're home free."

"Yeah," said Victor, "if the KGB hasn't picked up our trail and caught up overnight. It's unlikely, but there's still a chance."

"True," said Elwood, re-lighting his pipe. "We'll have the airport covered, just in case."

"You've taken all the precautions anyone could think of."

"Of course. We don't snatch a KGB officer out from under the KGB's nose every day." Elwood chuckled. "Especially with his family. This operation is as high-level as it gets. Don't see how in the world the KGB could've gotten wind of it."

"Oh, a leak of some sort, maybe. Information flows in mysterious ways..,"

"Don't think there's a chance of that here. It's so hushed-up. Even I don't know who you really are. All I know is you're a KGB officer. Others don't even know that." Elwood puffed on his pipe. "What's your rank anyway?"

"Major."

"Not bad for your age, particularly in the KGB, huh?"

Victor smiled. "Not too bad." That was true. One of the youngest majors in the KGB, Victor had been heading for the top. But this wasn't what made him special to both the KGB and the Americans. Rather, it was his position. He was a senior officer of the Eighth Chief Directorate, the highly secret inner sanctum of KGB crypto communications. Consequently, he knew more about KGB operations than most officers senior to him ever would. Victor worked directly for "Boss," Colonel Alexey Bosik, First Deputy Chief of Directorate A.

07:00. *09:00 in Moscow. Boss will arrive at his office any minute now, expecting to find a report from me on his desk. Not finding one, Boss will start looking for me immediately. If not for that damned report, I'd have at least another six hours before Boss raised a fuss.*

A local CIA man pulled up to the house. Judging by the dark circles around his eyes, Victor figured the guy had spent a sleepless night.

The man put an envelope on the table and poured himself some coffee. "Well, we're all set, docs and tickets are here." He glanced at the envelope. "Everything's in perfect order. Your flight leaves at ten."

Elwood translated this for Victor, who acknowledged with a nod.

Laura, a CIA officer, entered the kitchen accompanied by Olga. After greetings all around, Laura began preparing a breakfast of eggs and ham. Tall, with blond hair and a solid, athletic-looking body, Laura provided a contrast to Olga, who was dark-haired, slim, and still graceful from her girlhood ballet training.

Elwood took papers out of the envelope: Olga and Victor's foreign passports with U. S. entry visas, international driver's licenses, and airplane tickets for five. Elwood and Victor carefully examined the documents on the table, and found everything in order. After Victor and Olga memorized their names and particulars Elwood put the papers back in the envelope, which he stuck in his light bag.

With almost an hour before they needed to leave for the airport, Victor, Olga, and Elena, accompanied by Laura, went out the back door of the picturesque country house to look around and inhale some fresh, cool morning air. Around the perimeter of the home, which sat on nearly an acre of land, stood a tall hedge so dense that one could not see through it. In the spacious rear yard Victor and Olga remarked on the beauty of the large and meticulously manicured garden, which skillfully used every square foot of the grounds. Victor wondered about the identity of the owner, who obviously took considerable pride in the property.

Elena spotted a swing set for children, and delightedly scampered towards it. Laura, whose assignments normally didn't include dealing with five-year-olds, seemed to be happy with the deviation and was enthusiastically pushing Elena on the swing, higher and higher.

Elwood joined Victor and Olga, but the serenity of the scene before them, punctuated by Elena's joyful shouts, did not ease their growing tension over the final phase of the operation. They spoke little.

08:30. *10:30 in Moscow. All attempts to locate me on that Monday morning would have failed. No one answered at our home number, Olga was not at her job at the museum, and Elena had not been dropped off at kindergarten. Boss would now be cursing me, making use of his vast arsenal. He would dial up my section, demanding that I be found immediately, "dead or alive." Somebody would remember that I said we planned to spend the weekend at a friend's dacha. But nobody would recall the name of the friend, nor the location of the dacha.*

There could be many innocent explanations for our absence. Perhaps some-one fell ill or, maybe we had a transportation problem. Perhaps we were involved in an accident, or stranded at the dacha with no phone.

Elwood glanced at his watch automatically, surely knowing the exact time before doing so. He sighed, and said: "Well, it's time. Let's go." It was important that they not arrive too early, but neither could they miss the plane, because time hadn't been allowed for a silly mishap. The CIA guy returned to his car, brought over two stuffed toy monkeys, and gave them to Elena. For her it was love at first sight. She no longer insisted on carrying her own bag—the monkeys were much more important.

The cars they rode in the day before had been taken away. The Sheymovs, Elwood, and Laura got into a dark blue Mercedes and a gray Volvo, both with diplomatic license plates. The man who had brought the documents drove the Volvo, with Elwood and Victor inside. Another CIA man was behind the wheel of the Mercedes, which carried Olga, Laura, and Elena. A back-up car followed a short distance behind.

The procession followed a narrow country road that led to the main highway. After several more miles, they arrived in the vicinity of Schwechat airport. Having twenty minutes to spare, they circled the airport a few times before approaching the terminal.

09.25. The cars pulled up to the departure area of the airport. The five travelers got out of the cars and walked into the terminal, which was not very crowded, making it easier to maintain security.

Because they had no bags to check in and their seats were already assigned, they didn't need to stand in line at the ticket counter. *The positive side of traveling light.* The Sheymovs, along with Elwood, Laura, and two CIA men walked quickly toward the international departures entrance. Nobody in the group said a word. Victor knew that if something had gone wrong he would be the focal point of the ensuing drama. *Would they start shooting here? Probably. They'd know that now is their best opportunity.* He moved away from Elena and Olga, to the other side of the group. He could think of nothing else to minimize the danger to them.

Victor looked around. Nothing suspicious: a moderate-sized crowd, a few policemen, and three men who were obviously plain-clothes airport security officers. Then Victor noticed a couple standing a few steps up the stairs in one corner of the terminal—a strategically located observation point. Then he spotted a man in another corner who suddenly got up, put his newspaper on the seat, and began following the group at thirty feet. When Victor looked at Elwood, he smiled with his eyes only. His meaning was clear: CIA.

Having gone through the security gates, Victor felt some relief. The most opportune moment for a KGB ambush had passed. Several minutes later Victor heard an announcement in two languages, neither of which he understood. Elwood translated: "Our flight is delayed. All first-class passengers are invited to the restaurant in the international part of the terminal."

Victor didn't like it. "What do you think?" He knew that Elwood would also be suspicious of a possible KGB setup.

With a frown Elwood replied: "It's probably okay."

Elwood gave a long look at a man at the far side of the lounge. The man folded his magazine and walked away, probably to verify that the delay was legitimate. Laura got up from her chair and went to get more information. In a few minutes the man returned, passed slowly by Laura, who then returned to the group. "The delay's for weather. A thunderstorm on the departure path not far from the airport. All flights are delayed."

Elwood nodded and turned to Victor. "Looks okay to me. I think we can just enjoy the hospitality of the airline."

"Sure."

The group walked to the restaurant. Although Victor and Olga much preferred being on the plane to sitting down to a meal, they were hungry nevertheless.

In just over an hour an announcement was made that the flight to New York was now boarding. Olga knelt and said to Elena: "Let's go, darling, our flight is ready." Elena was happy to get moving.

The Sheymovs, Elwood, and Laura proceeded through the gate. The Boeing 747 was barely half-full, which made seating pleasant for everybody. In the upstairs first-class lounge Elena was quite proud to have her own seat, which she climbed into firmly hugging her two beloved monkeys; they became her favorite toys for years to come. Besides the Sheymov group, the only other occupants of the upper-deck lounge were four young American businessmen and two heavy-set men sitting in the rear. Judging by Elwood's unconcerned glance at them, Victor figured that they were their bodyguards. After another thirty minutes, the large Boeing airliner pulled away from the gate.

Through his window Victor saw two CIA men—the one who gave Elena the monkeys, and the one who checked on the delay—at the window of the boarding area. He knew they'd choose a spot where they could actually see the Boeing 747 taking off. Only then would they leave for the embassy, where they'd fire off a cable to Washington.

13:00. *15:00 in Moscow. Now Boss is not swearing anymore. He knows that something serious has happened. But he doesn't know how serious and I hope he won't know for a long time. But my disappearance is a grave enough matter that he must inform General Andreyev, the Head of the Chief Directorate. By five o'clock it'll be a full-blown emergency and a National Search will be declared, involving the KGB, the police, and the military.*

With a long sigh Victor reclined his seat. *Did I make any errors back in Moscow?*

2

The Sheymovs had been whisked in the CIA Director's personal plane from Kennedy International to Washington's National

Airport. Now, flanked by their security entourage, Victor, Olga, and Elena, exhausted from tension and back-to-back flights, were being driven through the gate of the safe house. They noticed the spacious grounds of the property, which were enclosed by tall thick shrubs; someone passing by would find it impossible to see the house and its immediate surroundings.

Several people were waiting outside the house. Robert Monsanto, the jolly man with wide-spaced front teeth who'd shouted an exuberant welcome to the Sheymovs upon their arrival at Kennedy International, introduced Victor to Jack Decker, a short man in his late fifties with a receding hairline. "Jack will be your primary point of contact. If you have any questions or requests, ask Jack. He'll take care of it."

Although Jack's accented Russian sometimes produced amusing errors, it was not bad at all. "Sorry we didn't have a chance to prepare properly for your arrival. The whole thing was so secret—we didn't know about you until your plane was about to land in New York."

"Everything's just fine. As a matter of fact, all we need now is sleep."

"How about dinner first? It's ready."

Victor looked at Olga, who smiled. "I want to sleep, but I'm hungry, too."

The split-level house was commodious. A large room above the garage contained a huge TV set, and was furnished with several coffee tables and a sofa along each wall. The wide windows enhanced the perception of roominess. Adjacent was a large formal dining room with a long table and heavy drapes. On the upper level were four bedrooms. The lower level contained a fully equipped conference room and the housekeepers' quarters. The two housekeepers, along with two sociable dogs, were permanent residents of the facility.

Olga put Elena to bed, who fell asleep instantly. In their bedroom, Olga was greeted by a huge bouquet of red roses, at least four dozen. "Victor, look. They're so beautiful. I don't think I ever had roses like that in Russia."

At the delicious, rather formal dinner, served by the housekeepers, Victor went over to Elwood. "I don't know who is who around here, and I don't want to offend anyone. But I have some urgent and very important information to pass on. I would like to meet with someone at the highest level in the CIA to discuss it. The sooner, the better,"

"All right. I think it can be done tomorrow. Meanwhile, we all need a good rest, especially you."

Elwood and Robert Monsanto left, but Laura stayed in the house. After their departure Olga noted that everyone had seemed quite curious about the Sheymovs, but nobody had asked any questions. Agreeing with Olga's observation, Victor concluded that strict orders had been given to ask none.

In the middle of the night Victor woke up—the eight-hour time difference with Moscow was making itself felt. He went downstairs and outside, where he heard the bodyguards in the house communicating with those on the grounds using walkie-talkies. After a fifteen-minute walk in the garden, where the air was humid and still, he returned to the house and joined the bodyguards in the large living room for a cup of coffee. But the language barrier prevented chitchat, and Victor went back to bed.

In the morning Victor was awakened from a sound sleep by Olga's voice. She was telling him how lovely it was outside. Feeling rested for the first time in a week, Victor and Olga sat down to a big breakfast in the dining room. Afterwards they strolled outside where Elena was racing around with her new friend, the safe house dog.

Olga said: "I still can't believe that we're alive, here, and safe."

Victor shared the feeling, yet he understood the uncertainty of their situation. He was dealing with people he did not know in a country totally unfamiliar to him. But, regardless of what lay ahead, he knew that his strength would reside in his unique expertise.

Elwood showed up in the middle of the afternoon, and took Victor aside. "Victor, I was asked to pass on all appropriate congratulations as well as expressions of admiration for your courage and professional skills. And, of course, welcome to our country."

Victor said only: "Thank you."

"That comes from the highest level, Victor."

"Oh, you mean the President?"

After looking aside as if Victor had said something inappropriate, Elwood did not answer.

"In return, I have to express my appreciation of the President's political courage to authorize this kind of operation under the current circumstances, especially with the Iran hostage crisis going on, and the upcoming elections."

For some reason Elwood became uncomfortable. "Who told you that this operation was authorized by the President?"

Victor smiled. "Come on, Bob. Do you mean to tell me that this kind of exfiltration could be authorized by anyone else?"

Elwood looked at Victor quizzically, and then managed a laugh. "Of course not. You understand too well how things are done. Anyway, congratulations and the warmest welcome."

"Thank you very much. I hope that I can do a lot of good here."

Robert Monsanto arrived about an hour later, and invited Victor into the conference room along with Jack and an interpreter. After everybody was seated, Monsanto began:

"Well, Victor, once again, welcome to the United States. I understand that you asked to discuss something very important and urgent with a high-ranking official. I'm listening."

"I didn't realize that you're the one. May I ask your position?"

"I'm a special assistant to the Director of the CIA."

"All right." Victor paused. "The matter concerns Brezhnev's successor as head of state. We all know that Brezhnev is in a poor heath. I have information that his successor will be Yuri Andropov."

Victor knew that this was a gem for intelligence professionals and foreign-policy decision-makers. Intelligence organizations around the globe were trying to figure out who would succeed Brezhnev. Victor also knew that practically all Western reporters, 'Kremlinologists,' and other observers had written Andropov off, having concluded that he couldn't possibly be a contender because he was tainted by being the head of the KGB. This faulty assessment arose from transposing western political standards to the Soviet system—an exercise that was naïve at best. Victor also realized that the CIA would be startled that he possessed this information, since very few people knew about Andropov's future elevation, even in Moscow.

Robert replied: "Oh, really? Is there anybody else that you might see as a successor?"

Shocked by the response, Victor said quickly: "And what's wrong with Andropov?"

"Well, we all know that with his background as head of the KGB, it's impossible. He's compromised beyond repair."

Victor was about to say that the Soviets didn't regard Andropov as a compromised man—a point so obvious that Victor would consider it offensive to suggest it to anyone even remotely familiar with Russian politics. Before he opened his mouth, Robert closed the subject: "Is there any other Brezhnev successor you want to discuss?"

Victor said softly: "No."

"Good. Let's discuss your future here. One of my superiors said that the reward for what you've done should be heaven, and—"

"Actually, I'd prefer to stay on earth for a while."

Everybody laughed, Robert much louder than the others. "Good, good. You know what I mean." He cleared his throat. "So, what are you going to do? You can retire right now—I mean right after the debriefings—and you're entitled to a very good retirement."

"I want to work. I didn't come here to die slowly. I believe that I can do a lot of useful things." Victor had heard lots of stories about defectors drinking themselves into permanent stupors, or committing suicide.

"Well said, well said. Good. We'll arrange everything. Meanwhile, you'll be living in this safe house. For a few months. Then, we'll see."

"Robert, I don't like to be dependent on anybody. So, first of all, I'd like to start studying English immediately. Secondly, I would like to buy my own place and live independently. Then, as soon as my English permits, I would like to go to a university to get an American degree."

"Well, that's a very ambitious program. Let's take a look at it. First, arranging English lessons is the easy part. When do you want to start?"

"Tomorrow. Both for my wife and me."

Robert laughed. "You're really in a hurry. All right. On the second point, what's wrong with living in a safe house? Don't you like it here? We can't provide the same level of security if you live independently."

"The KGB will conclude in a short while that we're dead. So, they won't even be looking for us."

"Do you really believe that with some little tricks you've fooled the KGB?"

"Yes, there's a good chance of that."

Robert's reaction was a smirk. "Well, we'll see. In a few weeks it should be obvious."

In a very even voice Victor said: "Sure. But I still want to live independently. I'd like it to be arranged as soon as possible."

A trace of irritation showed in Robert's face. "All right. We'll rent something for you. How about a townhouse?"

"What's that?"

"See, you don't even know what a townhouse is, and you want to live on your own?"

"Yes."

"Jack will explain it to you." After a pause, Monsanto went on. "On your third point, a university, let's wait and see. When your English is good enough for that. If ever."

Victor had no other choice but to smile. "All right. By the way, one more point. I'm not sure what our status is here, and who is paying for everything. Since we made a financial agreement in Moscow, I'd like to settle it soon."

"Well, that will take a while. All the paperwork will take at least a month."

"What paperwork? I was assured that we already had an agreement."

"We do. But there's still a lot of paperwork involved. Jack will explain that too. But you have nothing to worry about, really. If you need anything, we'll buy it for you. Just enjoy our hospitality. By the way, any one of us would like to live in this house—the longer the better. It's free. No worries about food or household chores. You'll have a car and a driver. Think about it."

After the meeting Jack and Victor strolled around the property. Jack explained to Victor what a townhouse was, and promised to show him one.

"But why rent, Jack? I'd prefer to buy."

Jack smiled. "You really are a man in a hurry. Slow down, enjoy life." Then he added: "You see, you've got to be around Washington during the debriefing. After that, you're better off somewhere else. Too dangerous for you here. The embassy and all. Two other bad spots are New York and San Francisco, with the Soviet diplomatic missions there. Other than those places, you can settle anywhere. So, for now it makes no sense for you to buy a place here. Besides, we'll pay the rent, since you're going to work for us. But I would still urge you to stay in this safe house."

"I'd rather not."

"Well, living up to your reputation? A man with nerves of steel. I don't even know who you really are, but I was told a few things about you. The point is, you have a wife and a child."

"Jack, I've already discussed it with my wife."

Jack laughed. "OK, OK, I give up. You're stubborn, too."

"By the way, how long will we need to stay around Washington?"

"Nobody knows. Surely for a couple of years, maybe more, that's the current consensus. In the course of the debriefing it will become much clearer."

"All right. Let's make it rent for now, and then we'll see."

On an after-dinner walk, while Elena was horsing around, Olga turned to Victor. "You're upset about something. What happened?"

"Is it that obvious?"

Olga smiled. "To me. Nobody else noticed, I'm sure. What is it?"

"Well, I told them that Andropov is going to replace Brezhnev. They just laughed."

"Andropov? I wouldn't have imagined that. But so what?" It was a very closely held secret in Moscow, known only to a few in the KGB, so it was natural that Olga did not know it.

"It's a pretty important piece of information for any intelligence service."

"I understand. But what's upset you?"

"That Robert Monsanto refused to even listen to my information about that. He simply dismissed it as if it were lunacy."

"Why?"

"That's precisely the point. He said that Andropov was compromised beyond repair by being head of the KGB, and thus can't be a contender."

"What nonsense! This Robert obviously doesn't know what he's talking about." Anyone in Russia understood the fallacy of the assumption by common Western "experts" that being linked to the KGB could be a political impediment.

"Well, you understand it, but they don't. The big deal is that what he said shows a fundamental misunderstanding of the basics of Soviet reality. And he seems to be speaking for others in American intelligence. I could understand if a casual Western observer said that, but not an intelligence professional. I bet that what I told him won't even be reported as 'raw intelligence'."

"Well, don't get upset about it. You told them, the rest is their problem."

"I have to find out who I'm really dealing with, and quickly. I'm getting mixed signals."

The next morning brought an exciting meeting. Two men came over to visit Victor at the safe house, Donald and Scott. Donald was Victor's age, Scott was a little older, both spoke good Russian, worked for the Soviet division, and were desk officers—Donald for Moscow, and Scott for Leningrad. That told Victor a lot. To hold positions as important as these at a young age, one had to be a star.

At last Victor had the chance of meeting the man who ran the entire exfiltration operation from its beginning on Halloween day 1979—Donald. Scott oversaw the Soviet border crossing. Victor was most grateful to them both.

Victor asked Donald: "Do you have an uncle in the Politburo?" – a common Russian reference to high-level connections.

Donald chuckled. "No."

"Well, then, you must really be some kind of super performer."

Donald seemed to blush. "No, not really. Just had some luck."

The three were amazed at how quickly they found common interests; they established a close rapport during three hours of enthusiastic discussion and they parted fast friends.

After the two men left, Victor told Olga: "You know, these two guys are the first I've met here that I really feel comfortable with. They're smart and natural, they don't try to pretend about anything."

"I liked them too."

Victor and Olga took a walk in the garden. They walked in silence, enjoying the fine weather. Then Olga said: "You know, Victor, it feels great to be alive and free. Especially after that terrible period when we didn't know whether we'd face a disaster the next day, or whether we'd be alive a week later."

"I know how you feel." Victor gazed at the bright Virginia sky. "It seems like we've been through a lifelong ordeal. Just eighteen months ago everything looked very different for us."

After strolling for several minutes, Olga said: "By the way, you never could tell me what your business was in the KGB. Can you tell me now? What was so special about it? Why does everyone treat you like some sort of superstar?"

Victor laughed. "Sure. Now I can. But it might take a while."

"We have all the time in the world now. And I'm really curious. Have been for a long time, as a matter of fact."

They sat on a bench, and Victor began. "I worked in the Eighth Chief Directorate of the KGB. That's the most secret part of it. That directorate covers everything connected to cipher communications in the country. It used also to cover the intercepts—the eavesdropping—by the KGB all over the world. Not long ago the directorate was split, and the intercepts part became independent, the Sixteenth Directorate."

"That's why all you did was so secret."

"Yes. When I first came to work for the KGB, I was trained and worked in different parts of our directorate, Directorate A."

"And what does 'A' do?"

"It maintains the cipher communications of the KGB. I was involved in the communications of the KGB with its stations abroad."

"I see. What did you do there?"

"Oh, they were preparing me for the top, so over the years I got assigned to different parts. Do you remember the time when I worked different shifts?"

"Yes. When we first met, and for about a year afterwards."

"Well, at that time I was directing cable traffic at the Center. It's sort of complicated, but in essence my job was to know who was doing what in KGB intelligence—to know about every major KGB operation abroad. A very interesting vantage point."

"Now I understand why the Americans are so interested in you."

"Not exactly. My last job was even more important. I was dealing with the overall security of KGB cipher communications. I coordinated all aspects of it: technical, human and procedural. In essence, I had the keys to the security of the whole system."

During the first two weeks at the safe house Victor and the debriefers dealt with the most urgent matters—those that represented an imminent danger to U.S. interests, or an immediate opportunity for American intelligence. Victor conferred with representatives from two distinctly different organizations: the NSA—the National Security Agency—and the CIA.

As Victor expected, the NSA's interests were mostly highly technical, and concerned Victor's own area of expertise, computer and communications security. The CIA, on the other hand, was interested in a mixture of operational and some technical issues, but the latter were discussed at a rather primitive level. What perplexed Victor was how little the CIA knew about the KGB and how poorly they understood it.

To Victor's surprise all the NSA debriefing meetings were attended and taped by the CIA. During a coffee break Victor seized a moment alone with an NSA interpreter and asked him: "Why is the CIA always present at our meetings? This is a breach of the cornerstone of security—compartmentalization. Besides, they have no earthly idea what we're talking about anyhow."

"True. But it's a bureaucratic thing, you know. Who's in control, institutionally. If it were up to us, they wouldn't even know where we meet. But there's nothing we can do, they're absolutely adamant about being in control."

"I see."

Most of the time the NSA was represented by one of its top experts, James Dwyer, along with a young whiz-kid named Chuck; occasionally a few others attended. Three NSA translators took turns, making sure that two were present at every meeting. The NSA team created a meeting atmosphere that was always relaxed, cheerful, and productive.

The CIA handled their meetings very differently. They sent quite a few people to confer with Victor, which raised his concerns about security. Because some CIA representatives had scant knowledge of the subjects they brought up, Victor concluded that they regarded talking to him as a prestigious event, and just wanted to "punch their tickets." Most of the questions from these men should have been asked through the CIA supervisor of the meeting since they did not require much discussion, just simple answers.

Victor was also bothered by a seeming furtiveness among some CIA representatives, as if they had hidden agendas. Victor took this in stride, but was irritated by one guy who apparently was trying to impersonate a World-War-II interrogator and treated Victor like a captured enemy soldier.

The CIA supervisor of the meetings who had witnessed the bizarre exchange took Victor aside. "I'm sorry, Victor. I'm ashamed. I apologize for him."

"No need. You're not responsible for him."

The CIA took the matter seriously; from then on every new person Victor met elaborately flattered him before and after each meeting. Sometimes it became absurd. At some meeting one of the NSA guys came to Victor at a coffee break and sincerely apologized for wearing brown trousers. Victor was startled. It turned out that some time before an officer who had accompanied Victor to a clothing store reported that when he suggested a brown jacket, Victor remarked that he didn't like brown in men's clothing. The CIA ordered that no one meeting Victor was to wear brown. Needless to say, Victor's remark was a very casual half-joke. Victor found this both amusing and sad. That evening he bought a pair of brown trousers and wore them the next day.

Jack came to adore Elena. He consistently went out of his way to please her, so much so that Victor and Olga began worrying that he might spoil the five-year-old. Victor and Jack were on friendly terms, but the prevailing feeling was that of strong mutual respect. Another one in Victor and Olga's social circle was David, a blond guy with an open, friendly face and a wholesome character, a security expert who spoke good Russian and helped Victor by tactfully teaching him about life in the United States. Victor also grew friendly with James Dwyer, who possessed one of the finest minds Victor had ever encountered. James displayed brilliant insights and a remarkable range of knowledge during some extremely complicated technical discussions.

3

One morning the normal debriefing meeting with the NSA was canceled to allow for an important event: a visit from Robert Monsanto.

Robert appeared, projecting an aura of self-importance, cracking jokes immediately followed by his own appreciative laughter. He seemed oblivious to the silence of his audience, who squeezed out polite smiles.

"Well, Victor, and Olga, I bring very good news for you." He put a piece of paper on the table in front of him. "I want you to understand something. Usually, this process takes at least a couple of months, but for you we made an exception. We've done it in a couple of weeks. This paper is a Memorandum of Agreement between us. It specifies your payment for what you have done for us, as agreed to in Moscow, and it shows the United States' deep appreciation for your help and your courage. We also realize that you left all your possessions and savings behind." Robert grinned. "Even Olga's jewelry."

Olga smiled. "I will surely miss my lynx coat in winter."

Robert paused significantly, and began talking while referring to the agreement.

"You're going to be very well off, Victor. You've said that you want to buy a house. Okay, you'll receive one hundred thousand dollars for the purchase of a house, and twenty thousand dollars to buy furniture. You'll also receive eight thousand dollars to purchase a car. Of course, all of this is tax free."

Robert stopped, and looked at everybody, as if waiting for a reaction. After several moments, he continued: "On top of this, we'll buy an annuity for you, which will pay you thirty-thousand dollars a year for the rest of your life. While, of course, the annuity purchase is tax free, you'll pay taxes on your income from it." After several moments, he said. "Any questions so far?"

Victor said: "Yes. What is an annuity?"

"That's when we pay a large sum of money to a private company now, and they guarantee to pay you a certain monthly income for years to come."

"I see."

"But that's not all. We'll pay for your university education. That is, if you choose to study as you've said, and if you're able to do so. We'll also pay for Olga's education on the same terms and pay for care of your daughter, if Olga decides to study. This money won't be paid if you don't study. We'll also find a job for both of you if you choose to work."

Robert stopped. Then he raised his hand, and voice: "Victor, nobody was ever paid as much money as you. All this is an expression of our country's gratitude to you, and I'm proud to represent this country."

Olga, unable to resist the temptation, whispered into Victor's ear. "I'm sure Napoleon looked exactly like this when he was about to win a battle." Victor stifled a chuckle. Robert looked at them suspiciously.

Victor felt compelled to respond. "Well, I'm very grateful for so flattering an evaluation of my humble efforts." He took a deep breath. "Please, forgive my ignorance. You have to understand that I've never seen a dollar bill before coming here. Also, I have no idea what the prices are of anything here. So, I'd like to ask a few questions."

"Sure, go ahead," Robert said cheerfully.

"But first, I would like to address the agreement we made in Moscow. I specified three conditions to my coming here and working with you, to which you agreed."

Robert nodded, and Victor continued: "First, immediate citizenship for all of us. Second, a payment of at least one million dollars. Third, full medical coverage for me and my family. I would like you to relate what you've just described in these terms."

Robert cleared his throat. "Well, let me address the citizenship issue first. It's not as easy as you think. We have a democracy here, not a totalitarian state. We have laws that everybody must obey. We're doing everything we can, I can assure you."

"Frankly, I don't see any conflict between democracy and citizenship. In regard to the laws of the United States, I just don't know anything about them. However, in Moscow, I was told that this would be no problem."

"Well, there are two ways to get United States citizenship: by waiting for five years—ten for a former member of a communist party—or by an act of Congress."

"So, I presume that when you agreed to this in Moscow, you meant a special act of Congress."

"Yes. But the situation seems to have changed. We assumed that the KGB would immediately find out that you're here—I know that you thought otherwise. I don't know why, but no matter how unreal it sounds, it looks like you're right. All our monitoring of the situation in Moscow indicates that they don't know you're here, alive and well. And an act of Congress would tip our hand. So, we have a problem."

"First of all, nothing was said in Moscow about any contingencies. Second, an act of Congress would be in my resettlement name, not Sheymov."

"Yes, but we have to disclose the real name and who you are to the sponsor of the bill, and to some other senators. You don't know those people, but believe me, you can't trust them. That's the real problem."

Now Victor was annoyed. "I don't particularly like being a victim of my own success. My instinct tells me to take a chance with the United States Senate. At any rate, I must insist that you fulfill your promise on citizenship."

"We'll see what we can do."

Victor continued: "The second issue discussed in Moscow was a payment of at least one million dollars. We all know the value of the information that I possess. I have difficulty seeing a million dollars in what you've described."

Robert laughed loudly. "Yeah, I know well where you're coming from. After the Soviet system, where everything is based on lies, after the KGB, it's very difficult to trust anybody. Here, we're different. We don't dupe our friends, those who help us. We're here to help them. We're here to help you, to make your life in this country successful. Your success is our success." He took a breath. "Of course, we could've just given you a million or two and said 'buy what you need'. We don't do that; it wouldn't be fair. We want to make sure that you're happy. Actually, we've done much better than that. Let's see. Your life expectancy is about eighty-five. You're now thirty four, right?"

"Right."

"Well, multiply thirty thousand by fifty. The annuity payments come to a million and a half. The other things we're offering make up another big chunk. So, the whole package is closer to two million than one. To be modest, let's call it a million."

"Again, forgive my understandable ignorance, but speaking from a strictly mathematical standpoint there is something that I don't understand. I was told that the inflation rate here is now about fifteen percent. Thirty thousand a year with an inflation rate of fifteen percent factored in should be much less than your figure."

"Oh, Victor, Victor. I know it's hard for you to understand a free-economy system. You may know math, but this is economics. Someday, hopefully, you'll understand it. Meanwhile, let us help you. Just trust us."

Victor felt guilty that he had questioned the good intentions of his benefactors. "All right, if you say so."

"I give you my word that this country, and we as government representatives, are not trying to mislead you. As a matter of fact, it's our obligation to look after your best interests." He sighed, as if to remark on the difficulty of trying to help victims of communist disinformation. Then Robert said: "Well, what else?"

"Another point, agreed to in Moscow, is full medical coverage. I don't know whether or not it's Soviet propaganda, but I had heard all sorts of horror stories, about how expensive medical care is in the United States, and how people are going bankrupt and dying because they can't afford to pay for it. I certainly want to make sure we won't be in that position."

Robert laughed wholeheartedly. "If you're so much a victim of communist propaganda, I hate to imagine what other Russians think about this country." Recovering his composure, Robert went on. "We'll pay all your medical and dental bills, starting now. As a matter of fact, all of us pay for our medical insurance, which covers whatever medical care we need. You'll pay nothing for your insurance; it's part of the package I was going to tell you about.

"So, the payments I described are for what you've already done, in the past. Now, about the future. While you're working for us in Washington, during all the time you're debriefing, you'll be paid one hundred dollars a day for your work. We'll pay for your medical coverage, as I said.

Also, we'll buy you a life-insurance policy, so if anything happens to you, Olga will receive one hundred-fifty thousand dollars."

"I'm sorry, but I don't have any frame of references to appreciate this pay. I'm sure this is very generous."

"Well, it is. But you're very special to us."

"On the other hand, Robert, I'm not sure if it's necessary, really. You just told me that my pay for my work done prior to coming to this country is well over one million dollars, and that I'm a wealthy man now. So, if I don't have to worry about money, I could just work for free as long as necessary."

"Oh no, Victor. Nobody works for free in this country—this is America. We want you to prosper, remember?"

"Well then, thank you."

"You are most welcome. Okay, I guess we've covered it all."

After that meeting Victor, having renewed doubts about the financial package offered by the CIA, asked Donald about it. He had grown to trust Donald; after all, he was running the show when Victor and Olga's lives were hanging in the balance. Donald's answer was brief: "Victor, I know nothing about finances. But I assure you that Robert's word is good."

With this endorsement, Victor put his doubts aside.

4

During the Sheymovs' third week at the safe house, Robert Monsanto and Elwood showed up again to discuss the upcoming move to a townhouse in Oakton and the immediate security concerns. They quickly went over the "legend," the cover story for the Sheymovs.

They became the Schwartz family, with new places and dates of birth, altered educational backgrounds, and different previous residences.

Victor raised a concern. "But what about Elena? She's only five years old, but very bright. She already reads and writes Russian pretty well. Needless to say, she knows her last name, as well as the names of a lot of our relatives and friends. I have no idea how we should deal with this situation."

"Oh, don't worry about that," said Robert. "We have a lot of experience with this sort of thing. Just cut all the references to her past. Completely. In a while she'll remember nothing."

Olga was not convinced. "I'm not sure that's a good idea. She's a very intelligent and curious child. And very persistent too."

"There's nothing to worry about. I realize this is all new to you but, as I said, we know how to deal with it. Just do as we say, and everything will be all right. In a year she won't remember a thing. Not only the names of her grandparents, but even her own."

Olga glanced at Victor. She clearly did not like what she heard. Neither did he.

One day Victor became the target of a conspiracy. Jack came over to Victor's house in the afternoon and declared that Donald had invited him, Olga, and Victor to dinner at a restaurant. "So, you guys have half an hour to get ready."

Victor didn't mind the short notice because Russians are used to getting little warning of things, and nobody takes offense. In fact, Olga and Victor enjoyed spontaneous social events. Ever efficient, Jack even managed to find a baby-sitter.

Then there was another warning. "Oh, Victor, do me a favor, let's go in my car."

"Why?"

"Well, there's a big problem with parking there." Anticipating the next argument, he added: "And your LTD is too big for the narrow spaces." Like many people in the office, Jack frequently changed rental cars.

Forty minutes later, on the way to the restaurant, Jack suddenly recalled: "Oh, my God! I forgot to lock up my safe. Let's stop by headquarters."

Still nothing clicked with Victor. "Sure. It shouldn't take too long." They were riding through McLean.

At Langley Jack entered through the back gate, where he flashed his badge. Instead of going to the parking lot, he turned towards the gated rear entrance to the main building. After displaying his badge once again, Jack drove into the executive garage, where only a few cars were parked.

"Well, since we're here, why don't I show you my office?"

Even that triggered nothing. "All right."

While in the elevator, Jack said: "By the way, this is the Director's elevator."

"I didn't realize that you're that high in this bureaucracy."

"I'm not. He just lets me use it once in a while."

Victor's guard was definitely down that day.

They exited the elevator, went through a corridor, and Jack opened a door. Victor instantly realized that he'd been had. He was in the Director's formal conference room, and it was filled with people. Everybody connected to the operation and some with the debriefings was there. Even Zdenek, their Soviet border crossing driver, and his wife.

Victor's face must have reflected his utter astonishment, for the room erupted into laughter. He looked at Jack, who smiled mischievously.

Soon Robert Monsanto stepped into the room through another door. Donald ceremoniously declared "Ladies and gentlemen, the Special Assistant to the Director."

Everybody stood up. Robert waved his hand, and the attendees found seats and fell silent.

Robert gave an elaborate speech about courage, determination, freedom, democracy, and intelligence. At the end he said: "Victor and

Olga, each of you is being awarded a medal—a very special medal. There are four different grades of it. Victor is being awarded the highest grade, and Olga, the second highest. It is very rare. As a matter of fact, the medal was established more than twenty years ago, and only a very few people have received it. Until now no one has received the highest grade—Victor is the first."

Everyone, except Victor, was delighted that he had fallen for the deception big- time—thanks to Jack's ingenuity.

During this period Victor and Olga grew more friendly with David, the security expert assigned to them. Their conversations became increasingly candid. David was a Vietnam War veteran, a former Army captain, who was still struggling emotionally with the cold reception given to Vietnam vets returning home to the United States. He was a conscientious and sensitive man, and certain things bothered him deeply.

One day David said he was thinking of retiring.

"What? You're not even thirty, are you?"

"Just over."

"What's wrong?"

"I'm not sure I'm right for the job. You see, I don't like some things that the Agency is doing, and I don't want to be a part of it."

"What do you mean?"

"Well, for one, we put the squeeze on people like you, and then throw them to the wolves."

Victor was concerned, but kept his tone light. "Well, they can't afford to do that with me, can they?"

"No, not with you." Still upset, he added: "Don't worry, I just got pissed off at the office this morning."

"Why was that?"

Now David looked uncomfortable. "I do get pissed off sometimes. A strange thing happened a while ago when I was accompanying a defector on a country trip. The guy was very horny, so I gave him a tour of singles bars. Naturally, he kept bringing girls to the hotel."

Victor nodded, and David continued: "Well, my wise bosses demanded that I make a very thorough report. All the details; not only the type of girls he was interested in but who, when, how, what, all the details."

"That's sickening. Why would they need that?"

"Some damn psychologists. They claimed they needed it for their analysis, so they'd know what recommendations to make for future handling of the guy."

"I've met a couple of those psychologists. I must say that both seemed to be total lunatics in dire need of psychiatric treatment."

"That's for sure," said David. "When we came back to Washington, the boss demanded a detailed report. I refused. I wasn't going to put my name under such sleazy crap."

"And then?"

"He insisted. So, I made a normal security report, and stated only that the guy was 'socially active.'"

Victor cracked up. This was so much like David. "Brilliant. What happened next?"

"Well, I never got an assignment like that again. But they remember my 'bad attitude' very well."

"By the way, David, I've heard a lot of stories about defectors going crazy, becoming alcoholics, and so on. How much truth is there in that?"

"A lot. Most of them start drinking pretty heavily soon after they arrive. Many become really unstable later—start doing strange things, going public. But by that time they look awful and nobody listens to them."

"Why?"

"I don't know why, it's just a statistical fact."

"It's very strange. Most defectors are intelligence officers who go through rigorous psychological evaluations before they're accepted in their services, and frequent evaluations after that. How come so many go crazy when most regular immigrants, not brought here by the CIA, are sane and doing well?"

"Come to think of it, you're right. That's a very interesting point."

Some time later, Victor approached Jack. "You know, Jack, I want to buy a house somewhere."

"Why, Victor? You've everything here you need to live comfortably. If you don't, tell me what you want, and it'll be done."

Victor laughed.

"It's true. See, Operations—particularly the Soviet Division—is overseeing everything related to you. Not the Resettlement people, as usual. We have orders to provide you with anything you wish. And this will continue until your debriefing is over."

"And with Resettlement it would be different?"

"Oh, yes. Believe me."

"Well, Jack, I'd still like to have a place of my own, and be independent."

Jack smiled. "You know, Americans admittedly are very independent-minded people, but you are more so than most of us." He sighed. "It's your business, but I have to tell you that it's not very wise. Financially, it doesn't make sense. You live here with hardly any worries. All you have to buy is groceries and clothing. You don't even know what taxes are. Just save your money, and buy a house later on."

"Jack, I want to buy a house now. I'd feel more comfortable."

After several days of evaluating suggestions regarding suitable cities, Victor and Olga traveled out of state to find a place to settle down. A week later they came back with their minds set on Phoenix, West Carolina.

In a few weeks Victor and Olga returned to Phoenix to meet with a real-estate agent and a lawyer selected by the CIA. After house-hunting for three days they decided upon an attractive three-bedroom house in a quiet neighborhood that had a large room over the garage, which would serve as a perfect studio for Olga. A month later, Victor and Olga became real property owners in the United States.

Several days afterwards, Victor received a letter from the lawyer in Phoenix advising him to rent the house. Victor sought Donald's counsel.

"You could spend quite a few years here in Washington; you'd have no problem finding a job in intelligence. As a friend, however, I'm not sure what to advise. You're living an artificial life here. You can only find independence if you live a real life. You have to decide."

"Personally, I don't want to live in Washington, and go through endless debriefings, although I clearly see a need for me here. So, I think we should work out some kind of compromise, and set a definite date for us to move on."

"Talk to Jack about it. I think setting a date in advance is a good idea."

When Victor approached Jack about deciding on a departure date, he said he'd have to check with others in the CIA. A week later Jack had an answer: "Victor, the feeling is that you need to be here several years. If you leave any sooner, there'd be a lot of unhappy campers because of the importance of your work. Why don't you go ahead and rent out the house, and we'll talk about the situation in a year or so?"

"All right."

Not long after, Victor heard that a new chief of the Soviet Division had been appointed. The SE Division was responsible for the Soviet Union and Eastern Europe—the largest, most important, and certainly the most powerful of the CIA's operational divisions. Victor was naturally interested in the news, but didn't give it much thought. Christmas was coming, and holiday preparations in Washington were in full swing. Victor and Olga keenly anticipated their first Christmas in the West.

They decided to spend the holidays in the Poconos, where they'd take Elena skiing. Jack was distressed by their plans. "Victor, your struggle for independence is beginning to wear me out. What am I supposed to do now?"

"Enjoy Christmas."

"You've just created a security nightmare."

"Jack, I don't understand why. There's no security risk."

Moving ahead with preparations for their trip, the Sheymovs went to Oakton to buy skiing equipment. While buying a Christmas tree Victor marveled at the ease of doing so in America. In Moscow, it invariably took a lot of effort, and a bribe, at least a bottle of vodka.

Three days before Christmas the Sheymovs loaded their new skiing equipment and cherished five-foot Christmas tree on top of their LTD. When Jack came to say good-bye, the Sheymovs invited him to breakfast.

Finally, with Jack waving, the Sheymov's embarked on their first independent trip in America.

On the Sunday after New Year's, Victor, Olga, and Elena returned to Washington. Their vacation had been most pleasurable, despite the short slopes and large crowds.

On Monday morning Jack came over with Victor's driver and announced that work would be postponed by two hours.

"Jack, you don't look like you're anxious for me to get back to work."

Jack let the remark go by. "Victor, there's something you need to know."

"What happened?"

"Nothing. You just have to adjust your plans. Did you rent out the house?"

"I presume the lawyer took care of it."

"Let me talk to him. Maybe he hasn't done it yet."

"Sure. Why?"

Jack avoided looking directly at Victor. In a low, regretful voice he said, "Victor, you're leaving this area in three weeks."

Must be a security problem. Have the KGB found out that we are here? "What happened? If we're going to work in another city, it would put a strain on everyone to travel."

"Victor, I can't explain why."

What's going on? This doesn't make sense at all.

Then Jack spoke with forced cheer: "Now you can go to school. That's what you wanted, isn't it?

"Sure."

Jack took the phone and called the lawyer in Phoenix. Victor couldn't understand most of the conversation because Jack spoke rapidly and used a lot of unknown words. But Victor did get the impression that Jack was twisting the lawyer's arm in a pretty forceful way.

Finally, Jack hung up. "It's all settled. The lease is canceled."

When Victor left for the office, Jack stayed to talk to Olga. Just before Victor walked out the door, Jack said: "By the way, don't discuss what I told you with anybody else."

"Okay."

In the office things were normal, except that everyone was jovial after the holiday break. Victor concluded that nobody knew anything about his imminent departure.

When Victor broke the news to Olga that evening, she reacted mildly.

"Well, it's good for us, isn't it? But you seem upset."

"No, I'm not upset. I'm just a bit concerned." He paused. "See, professionally, it doesn't make sense. They still don't have a lot of what I know. Logically, they should keep me here as long as they can. I don't understand what could've caused this drastic change in plans. "

"Are you sure that your assessment of your value to them is correct?"

"Yes. All their experts feel the same way. Besides, I can tell by their questions exactly where they are on a subject; I know and they know that they're far from finished."

Olga was silent for a while. "Well, maybe they just don't trust you for some reason. Maybe they think that you're supplying them with disinformation."

"Out of the question. In the NSA field, at least, you can't lie. Either you know it, or you don't. Everything is so easily verifiable. That's the main reason that double-agent operations are never attempted in the area of cipher communications."

"Perhaps they now have somebody else like you, and feel they don't need you anymore?"

"No way. If that were the case, they'd take a different approach with their questions. They'd be comparing my statements against somebody else's. Besides, if my knowledge of the KGB was unique there, it should certainly be pretty rare here."

"Then, I don't understand it either." Olga hugged Victor. "Oh darling, don't worry. Whatever the reason, it's better for us as a family, right? So, let's just enjoy things for a change."

"Yeah. But I usually worry about things that I don't understand."

Now, more than ever before, Victor needed to talk to Donald and Scott, but both were on temporary duty abroad.

The next day the afternoon session was canceled. Jack brought a man to the safe house, and introduced him. Jack said, "Victor, you've got to take an IQ test."

"What's that?"

"Oh, it's when they objectively measure how smart you are."

"All right, all right. Let's get on with it. I wouldn't rely on the results too much, though."

"Victor, we need it, so we can help you get the right job."

Besides the IQ test one type of test or another was given to Victor almost every other day. Strange people, mainly psychologists, kept visiting him, asking a lot of odd questions. During one visit the questioning struck Victor as inane.

"You said that your father was a vagrant at age five and was raised in an orphanage?"

"Yes."

"So, he was probably pretty harsh to you and your mother?"

"No."

"Are you sure?"

"Absolutely. He was kind to us."

The man paused. "Well, you haven't met you paternal grandfather, have you?"

"How did you guess?"

The man just nodded, remaining quite serious. "What do you think of your maternal grandfather?" Because he had Victor's bio in front of him, he had to know that Victor's maternal grandfather had died in 1918.

"I think he was dead well before I was born." The man nodded again, and asked similar questions.

A few days later David dropped by with his wife, Wendy. While the ladies were chatting, Victor turned to David: "I presume you know that I'm leaving pretty soon."

"What do you mean?"

"I mean that my job here is over and we're leaving for Phoenix in a couple of weeks."

"What's happened, Victor?"

"That's what I'd like to know."

David shook his head, his face grim.

Victor said: "Don't get me wrong, David. Personally, for me and for my family, this is a better alternative. Besides, I'm eager to start a normal life."

"All I can say, Victor, is that I'm baffled. But, based on what I've picked up so far, your being here is beyond anybody's wildest dream." David seemed troubled. "You know, Victor, you need to learn about living in this country. And you'd better do it fast."

"Well, I've learned quite a bit by now."

"Listen to me. You know exactly nothing about living here. You don't know what taxes are, you don't even know how to pay a utility bill, for Christ's sake. All you know is how to write a check. Up to now you've been living in a bubble. Believe me, there are thousands of little things that you'll have to do, and you don't even know what they are." After several moments he said in a low voice : "Boy, I hate what they're going to do to you–cut you loose without any training, just like the others."

"Oh David, we'll manage. We've survived in a much less friendly environment, you know."

"I know, but it'll cost you. You've been so involved in your work that you don't even know the value of money. For example, do you know how much a store manager makes?"

"No."

"How about an engineer, or factory worker?"

"No."

"See what I mean?" He thought a few moments. "Listen, I'll spend at least two hours every day with you, teaching you the survival basics here. And I'll go with you to Phoenix for a few days to help you get settled in."

"Super. Thanks."

Later Victor tried several times to contact David, but no one answered his phone. Concerned, Victor said to Jack: "I can't find David. Can you ask him to call me?"

"David's away on assignment."

"When's he coming back?"

"I don't know."

Victor had a bad feeling that David might have been sacked. "His wife isn't answering the phone either."

"She's probably away, too. I don't know."

To his sincere regret, Victor never saw David again.

On Monday morning Victor was back in the office for a session with the NSA. The NSA top expert Jim Dwyer showed up late, which was unusual.

"Victor, I was just told you're leaving town very soon. I regret it very much, I must say. Is there any way you can stay longer?"

Victor opened his mouth to answer, but the CIA representative present at all the NSA meetings jumped in. "I suggest that this matter not be discussed any further."

From that moment on, Victor was literally shadowed by the CIA man at all the NSA meetings. He obviously had instructions to not leave Victor alone with NSA people, even for a moment. Although the NSA folks were visibly frustrated, they maintained their politeness to avoid upsetting their "host," the CIA.

After Victor's last day in the office, the Sheymovs were ready to leave the following morning. All their possessions had been loaded into two cars, including their skiing gear and a BOSE stereo system, which took up much of the available space. They stuffed in some boxes of books, bed linens, and three suitcases of clothing. Victor drove with Olga and Elena in the front car, their Ford LTD. Jim Brown, Victor's driver for all these months, followed in his Cutlass with his wife beside him. A good-sized potted plant on the back seat, a present from a friend, nicely obstructed Jim's rear view.

5

When the Sheymovs moved to Phoenix they were surrounded by an invisible security circle. Many people think of personal security as bodyguards, armored cars, and fortified residences. While certainly impressive from a public relations point of view, and easy to sell to wealthy clients, this type of security is not very effective. An attacker usually has the advantage of choosing the time, place, and method of attack. If one has a strong bodyguard, there is always a stronger attacker available somewhere. If one has an armored car, there is always an armor-piercing weapon available somewhere. Breaching security becomes a simple proposition: how badly someone wants to harm you, and the resources he has available.

In any case, an attacker has to know a great deal about his target. He has to know where the target resides, or where it is going to be physically, and when. He has to know how to approach that area without being registered or noticed and remembered. He has to know what type of attack would be effective in that environment, and he must consider the target's level of protection. Finally, he has to arrange a reliable escape route. All that information, and more, needs to be collected, and collection itself leaves footprints. The attack depends on everything going perfectly, though in practice usually it doesn't.

There is another type of security, not widely known to the public, invisible but much more effective. Unlike in the movies, a real-life security environment calls for organizing an invisible and comprehensive defense. The defender moves protective barriers forward, but keeps them invisible to the naked eye. Competent security organizations usually can surround a protectee with invisible layers of "jingle bells"; the organization's intelligence capabilities or "connections" make a circle of protection around the target. Information about the protectee's habits and frequently visited places is often readily available to an attacker. So, for instance, in the case of the protectee's bank, an intelligence organization can use its "connection" at the bank to make sure that any inquiry about the protectee, no matter how casual and innocent, is immediately reported to it. If a protectee is a member of a particular club, the organization can use its "connection" in a key position at the club to report any inquiries about him. This list can be extended indefinitely, but the essence is conceptually simple: make sure that the protectee's circle—his job, friends, banks, clubs and other frequented places– is covered. As soon as an outsider asks a question about the protectee in any of these entities, it is immediately reported to the organization, which then follows the lead, learning about attack preparations well before an attacker actually launches the attack itself. But this kind of security comes at a price. Most people do not realize how many limitations it imposes on what the protectee may and may not do.

The two-car procession arrived in Phoenix in late afternoon, and unloading took less than half an hour. Only now did Olga and Victor realize how empty the house was—not a chair to sit in, no table for a meal and, of course no food in the refrigerator.

Jim and his wife admired the Sheymov's new property. Their spacious four-bedroom colonial sat on a wooded three-quarter-acre lot on top of a hill, which provided a commanding view of their pleasant surroundings. The quiet neighborhood was so dense with foliage that one could not see a neighbor's home except from the street, a cul-de-sac where kids could play safely. The branches of two stately old oaks cast shadows over much of the back yard.

After spending the night on cots, the Sheymovs heard a knock on the door. Upon opening it they saw a smiling lady holding a good-sized basket. "Hello. Welcome to our neighborhood. A few ladies here asked me to deliver some food to you. Of course, we cooked it all ourselves."

Olga ushered her in, but there was not even a chair to offer. Nevertheless, they had an enjoyable chat during which the lady offered help if needed, and tactfully left after a few minutes.

Olga and Victor were quite touched. They had never imagined that neighborly hospitality like this existed. In Russia, it took a long time to become friendly with your neighbors, whom one met mostly through inevitable contacts in cramped apartment complexes. By evening, more than a dozen people had showed up to welcome the Sheymovs and to offer help of all kinds—some men even told Victor he could borrow their tools. This totally unexpected kindness and warmth made Olga and Victor's adjustment to their neighborhood much more pleasant than they had anticipated.

Their security circle was laid out just before the Sheymovs' move to Phoenix, and it was completed shortly after their arrival. Once in Phoenix, they were introduced to their bank, to a lawyer, to Elena's school principal, and so on. And they were warned not to venture outside of the protected circle. They were told, "This is your lawyer, and he is the only lawyer you can talk to, no matter what."

Olga had had no problem figuring out what she'd study at her university—art. Excited at the prospect of getting a formal education in her favorite discipline, she looked forward to her classes, which would begin in September. To get Elena to school, Olga joined a carpool with other parents; she found it mildly challenging when it was her turn to drive because she was pressed for time, but valued having the opportunity to interact with Elena's classmates.

Two days after moving into their new home in Phoenix, the Sheymovs were visited by a bald mature man, the Phoenix CIA Station Chief. After a curt greeting he asked if anything urgent was needed. There was: enrolling Elena in a school, and arranging for her care for several hours in the afternoon on those days Victor and Olga couldn't be home because of their university studies. They assumed that Elena would enter a public school.

"Oh, yes," said the station chief. "Jack communicated that to me already. It's a security issue as well. We have to know what's going on around her. So, a public kindergarten is out of the question."

"Yes," said Victor. "But a private school might ask a lot of questions about her background. With our less than perfect cover stories, something unwanted could come out."

"No problem. We have good connections with an excellent private school here. We can place her there with no questions asked, and closely monitor her environment."

"That would be great."

With no other matters to resolve immediately, he said: "You remember Ed—you met him earlier?"

"Yes."

"He'll be your point of contact from now on." The man handed Victor a card with a few phone numbers on it, and left.

Two days later Ed popped in. Victor and Olga sat down with him in the living room; after some small talk, Victor asked for the delivery of Russian newspapers.

"Washington is absolutely against you subscribing directly, even through a post office box. They'll send them through me."

Then, without warning, Ed stood up and started walking around, scrutinizing the furniture. While passing through the dining room, he said: "I see you bought yourselves good furniture. How much did you pay for this china case?"

"I don't remember, we paid for everything in bulk."

"How much did you pay for it all?"

By now Victor knew that this sort of questioning was not acceptable in America. "I don't remember. All the papers are stuffed away somewhere."

Ed was about to go upstairs when Victor blocked him, and coldly asked: "Can I help you?"

Ed was taken aback. "I'm just looking around to see how you've settled in."

"We're comfortable, thank you."

Annoyed, Ed retreated and left a few minutes later. Olga and Victor in their conversations later referred to him as 'Mr. Ed' in a reference to the popular TV show.

It wasn't until June that the delivery of Russian papers began on a biweekly basis. Because they were a month old, and frequently arrived with articles cut out, and some issues were missing altogether, Victor concluded that they came from the CIA library. But it was much better than having no newspapers at all. Wanting to be better informed, Victor bought a fine Sony receiver with double-frequency conversion and a built-in tape recorder with a timer. He was now able to receive many Russian short-wave stations and stay abreast of most news.

For Victor, deciding what to study had not been simple. The CIA, unhappy with the prospect of Victor studying at a university in the first place, pushed him toward enrolling at an engineering school. But Victor was intrigued by the possibility of studying business. He and Jack had disagreed on this, and one day Jack called to discuss it further:

"Victor, you're trained as an engineer. If you're that eager to get an American education, why don't you get an engineering degree here?"

"Jack, I told you, it doesn't make sense. What am I suppose to learn?"

"American engineering, of course. It's clearly superior to Russian."

"Not in every area. First, I graduated from the Russian equivalent of MIT. Second, I work in an area where the Americans definitely don't have superiority—you can ask your friends in the NSA to confirm that. So, the only thing I can possibly learn is terminology, which isn't worth spending all that time on. I'd much rather acquire totally new skills in a practical area, like business."

"Well, Victor, I've talked to a few people about that and we all feel that you should stick to engineering."

"Jack, just tell me honestly, why are you and the CIA pushing me so hard toward engineering?"

"We're not pushing you."

"Yes, you are."

Jack chuckled. "Well, maybe just a little bit. Look, you won't be able to succeed in business. We just don't want you to fail."

"Why can't I succeed in business?"

"You want me to be honest? OK. Because of your background, Victor. It'd probably be the most challenging field for you. You don't even know anything about managing your own finances, and the concept of a free economy is totally unknown to you. Any kid out of high school is immeasurably more knowledgeable about business than you'd be ten years from now. It's just too much, even for you."

"I'd like the challenge."

Victor missed the deadline for entering a university in September, but after searching for business programs in the Southeast he soon found one beginning in January 1982. It was an executive MBA program in Atlanta, Georgia that lasted a year and a half and prepared mid-level managers to go to the top. Victor considered it a plus that this program catered to people of his age or older, though it would surely be even more demanding than a regular MBA program. A prerequisite of the program was ten years of managerial experience.

Victor contacted Jack and asked him to prepare background documents confirming that he met this requirement.

"Victor, how can you even think about it? You wouldn't last a week there, believe me. Besides, they mean managerial experience in American companies; they're assuming that you already know business very well, and only need top-level training."

"I do, in fact, have ten years' managerial experience."

"Where, in the KGB?"

"Yes, and in the space industry."

"Victor, this is a joke."

"No, it's not. In fact, I've managed large and complicated projects, with a lot of people inside and outside the organization involved.

Besides, the program didn't specify the kind of managerial experience required."

"Victor, this is a totally unrealistic proposition."

Victor's voice took on an edge. "Jack, I've listened to your advice, and now I've made my decision. Let's stop discussing this issue right now."

"Okay, okay. I'll see what I can do."

"Jack, is that another promise that'll be hard to keep?"

The CIA relented. Although they provided Victor with no background documentation, they promised to talk to "their people" on the faculty. Somehow the issue was resolved, and Victor was accepted into the program. Fortunately for him, the program offered a month-long "brush-up" course in math. Victor jumped at it. Not to brush up on his math, but to learn new terminology and get used to the American educational environment.

Soon after beginning the brush-up course in late 1981, Victor was overwhelmed. His English was good enough to graduate from an English school for foreign students, but it was not good enough for easily understanding lectures and fast-paced discussions. The specific terminology was killing him. Consequently, he had to work sixteen hours a day just to keep up. The program was designed for people who worked, and was held on weekends, with periodic two-week sessions. But Victor did have some good luck: the professors and students were extraordinarily helpful. Everyone worked hard in an atmosphere of teamwork and camaraderie. To repay the kindness of his peers, Victor relied on his strong math background to help others.

When the long semester ended in July, Victor was exhausted. And so was Olga. She had taken on all the household chores herself. Besides driving in the carpool, she drove Elena to ballet classes and read Russian books to her at night before bed. But Olga was exhilarated by her own studies. Her obvious talent drew the attention of her teachers and she realized, for the first time in her life, that she not only loved art, but had a talent for creating it. It did not come as a huge surprise though. She was the fifth generation of artists in the family.

Victor found accounting unexciting, though he conceded its importance to the world of business. Marketing, on the other hand, fascinated him. In Russia, the game was to *get* something, whether through party privileges, personal connections, or bribes, or a combination thereof. Russians who had something to sell were in the driver's seat, a position of power. In the United States, Victor discovered, the situation was reversed. So it was difficult for Victor psychologically to accept the concept that one has to make an effort to sell something useful.

Perhaps because of his solid background in mathematics, Victor developed a keen interest in business finance; he now considered it his most important subject. His first real-life encounter with finance came from an unexpected direction.

Olga, who handled the family finances, began asking Victor questions about their income; she couldn't reconcile what they'd been told by the CIA—that a large pile of money had been bestowed upon them—with the fact that she saw no such mound of currency.

"Victor, the way we lived in Washington, where everything was paid for by the CIA, there was no way to verify whether the money promised us was really a whole lot. Now I'm much more familiar with what things cost, and with how much money people make here. Based on what I see and hear, we didn't get that much money. The whole thing just doesn't add up."

"I agree. You know what our lawyer, Rusty Diller, told me the other day? He said: 'Victor, your demeanor is that of someone who is pretty well-off. You should realize that what you're getting, thirty thousand a year, is not really a great deal of money. I don't want you to get into financial trouble, thinking you can afford a lot when in fact you can afford very little'."

They took a short vacation on Hilton Head Island. After an early dinner one evening, as they sat on the beach gazing at the ocean while Elena collected seashells, Olga took another sip of her piña colada and asked, "Darling, are you happy?"

Aware that this was a question Olga rarely asked, Victor thought awhile before answering. "Well, I guess I am. Partially, at least."

Olga laughed. "I didn't know there was any such thing as partial happiness."

"Maybe you're right. But I don't think that total happiness is real either."

"That's an interesting point. I guess I'm trying to figure out if you're satisfied with what's happened since we left Moscow."

"I guess it's fair to say that I'm reasonably satisfied. Our primary goal was to inflict as much damage as possible to the KGB and the communist system. On that account we've done quite well. The damage already done is massive and they don't even know it yet. I can assure you that nobody has yet inflicted as much damage to them as we have."

"And we survived, too."

"Absolutely. That was our second priority. We've done pretty well on that account, too."

"What about our life here?"

"I think I'm happy with it—aren't you?"

"Of course. You know, the biggest and most pleasant surprise for me in America is the people. I never imagined that people could be so sincerely kind and helpful to total strangers. Take our neighbors, for example, or our teachers at the language school, or even the people we've met here in Hilton Head. It must be the true nature of Americans."

"You're absolutely right. I'm also very impressed with how seriously Americans take their liberty, their freedom. I used to think they were naive. Like when they get so upset if the government monitors them, or eavesdrops on them. With my background, I assumed this is inevitable, but they insist that proper legal procedures be followed, and they're dead serious about it."

Olga was silent for a while. Then she said: "All right. But what about the downside? Is there something you're dissatisfied with?"

"Yes, a little. I'm disappointed with the CIA."

"You mean some things they've promised us and are dragging their feet on?"

"It goes deeper than that. First, intelligence is the world's oldest profession—despite unsubstantiated claims to the contrary." Olga chuckled, and Victor continued: "Essentially, it's a very honest profession. Regardless of ideological or political differences, there are certain rules. These rules were worked out over many centuries of intelligence and you don't break them. Ever. One of these rules is that you always deliver what you promise. Even to your enemy. Most important deals are made verbally—you give your word, and you'd better keep it."

"I understand."

"I know you do. But, apparently, they don't. Okay, this is what they promised us in Moscow: one, immediate citizenship; two, a payment of at least a million dollars; and three, full medical coverage. Right?"

Olga nodded.

"Well, let's see what has and has not been delivered. One, no. Two, supposedly—three, no." Victor took a deep breath. "They said that they bought health insurance for us, but as soon as we left Washington, they stopped paying for it. Jack said they covered this in the MOA, our Memorandum of Agreement, but I don't even remember it. It was read and signed in such haste, remember? I had it in my hands literally for less than two minutes."

"I don't think the medical coverage is very important, Victor. When you discussed it in Moscow, all we knew about America was the Soviet propaganda about people dying here because they couldn't pay for a hospital. Now we know that this isn't true, and that we can afford insurance. Besides, we hardly ever go to a doctor. Except Elena, of course. She always has cuts and bruises." Elena was a tomboy who'd fallen from every tree in the neighborhood; local emergency-room personnel knew her by first name.

"True, but that's not the point. Whatever they promised, they must deliver. They didn't."

"Yes, I feel bad about that."

"That makes two of us. There's another thing they didn't deliver on: contacting my parents. Which makes me feel very guilty. They're entitled to know that we're alive, at the very least, and not be in agony over the uncertainty. The CIA keeps telling me that the operational risk is too high, but that's crap. There's always a way."

"I totally agree with you. I feel the same way about my mother. But the only way she can find out that we're alive is through your parents."

"So, the CIA's record in keeping promises is dismal. So I've decided I have no choice but to go to Washington and try to make the CIA keep its promises."

Leonid Brezhnev's death in November 1982 caused turmoil in Washington and in the press. Several days of anxious waiting ended with a shocking announcement: Yuri Andropov was the new head of the Soviet Union. Virtually no one was prepared for this turn of events. All the TV anchors and talking heads were competing for who could talk faster. Victor reacted by shrugging his shoulders and saying to Olga: "I hope the CIA does a better job in other areas."

Olga laughed. "Do you want me to send Monsanto a card?"

"No. He should send me one."

6

One of the last passengers off the flight from Phoenix to Washington National, Victor casually scanned the crowd. Sure enough, Jack was standing slightly apart, leaning against a column.

Jack's five-eight, slightly plump figure, nearly bald head, and unre-markable face would attract no one's attention. His somewhat worn, not-quite-fresh gray suit, and dark reddish tie, helped him to blend in with those around him. One could walk by Jack ten times and not notice his presence. Appearing deceptively old, Jack could be taken as Victor's father.

As Victor made his way through the crowd, Jack smiled only with his sparkling eyes, accentuated by the extensive wrinkles around his brows. Jack extended his hand. "Hello, stranger. How are you doing?"

"Not bad," replied Victor, "for a dead man."

Jack chuckled. "And that's just the way we want to keep you."

That was true. For two years now.

As they walked from the airport building towards Jack's car, Jack lit his beloved Comoy pipe. While fiddling with it, Jack kept his eyes on the nearly empty George Washington Parkway as if it were packed with challenging traffic. He didn't engage in his usual cheerful chitchat, and didn't crack a single joke.

"Anything wrong, Jack?"

"No. Not at all." Jack paused. "Just remember, you got what you asked for. I did not suggest this meeting."

"Remember your promises to me?"

"What do you mean?"

"Come on, you know exactly what I mean. One is U. S. citizen-ship. Another is establishing contact with my parents, to let them know we're all right. Not to mention the money."

Jack was evasive: "Well, in regard to your parents, that's the busi-ness of the SE Division. I asked them again, and the answer was no."

"Jack, I've heard this answer before. Look, the KGB's investigation in Moscow is closed, and I think it's about time to get it done."

"It's not easy—you know that better then I do."

"And citizenship?"

"Well, that's a problem because everything indicates that the KGB bought the idea of you being dead. Nobody wants to risk tipping them off now. This could happen if we try to contact your parents, or intro-duce a special bill in the Senate to give you citizenship."

"Jack, just remember that it was I who arranged the whole deception in Moscow. Your folks laughed when I suggested it might be successful—though that's irrelevant. And I reject the idea there could be a leak in the Senate. Don't tell me that you can't find a senator or two that can be trusted."

"Victor, you don't know the game between the Agency and the Senate."

After driving through the back gate of the CIA Langley compound, Jack took Victor through the main entrance. Upstairs, after walking down a corridor, Victor suddenly found himself in one of the strangest rooms he'd ever seen outside of a museum. Although the room was not impressively large, its grandeur was overwhelming—clearly by design. The rich wooden paneling was of the highest quality, and the furniture, mostly valuable antiques, in no way resembled government-issue. The oil paintings on the walls and in display cases would have been appropriate exhibits in a world-class gallery. Most splendiferous of all was the room's centerpiece, an ancient-looking gold crown that glittered under the display lights of its custom-made showcase. Apparently created to both enthrall and intimidate, the room might have been transported magically from a Hapsburg palace. In any case, it was hardly in keeping with the decor of workplaces normally inhabited by United States civil servants.

Victor looked at Jack, who was smiling. "Jack, what in the world is this?"

"Well, this is one of the Director's reception rooms. Reserved by the Chief of the SE Division specifically for this occasion. Do you like it?"

"Well, considering what I now know about this country, let's say it's very unusual."

At that moment a door at the other end of the room opened, and a gray-haired man in a well-tailored light-gray suit walked in briskly, followed by two aides a pace and a half behind. About five-ten, with fine features, the man walked confidently towards Victor and stopped abruptly, facing him directly, no hand extended. What struck Victor was the unmistakable, almost palpable hostility in the man's eyes, focused intensely on him. *Why? We've had no contact, direct or indirect. Or had we? But no time to think about that now.*

Victor attempted to concentrate, to disregard everything subjective. *Trying to intimidate me? It's pretty crude.* Victor took two steps toward the man. "Hello."

"Hello. I'm David Smith."

Every man and his dog knows you're David Nedrof.

"I'm Victor Sheymov."

Jack evidently felt obliged to jump in. "Victor, this is the Chief of the Soviet Division. At your request he took time out of his busy schedule to meet with you."

Victor needed time to assess the situation. "You have a very interesting room here." Turning towards the showcase, Victor said: "I was wondering about this crown—what is it, exactly?"

"Oh, it's a present." Nedrof apparently didn't know more about it.

"Really? Is it authentic?"

"Everything here is authentic."

"What a collection! I wonder, how you managed to acquire it? Must have taken a great deal of effort."

"Yes," said David Nedrof, somewhat impatiently. "I understand that you're lobbying for us to contact your parents."

"Well, 'lobbying' is probably not the right word. I'm trying to convince you to keep your promise."

"You have to understand that we have a very difficult operating environment in Moscow right now. We have no capacity for a nonessential operation."

"As I have reason to know, the operational environment in Moscow has always been very difficult. Besides, we're not talking about a terribly complicated operation."

They still stood face to face, for Nedrof had made no suggestion that they sit. "And you're going to bang everybody's door with this thing forever?"

"First, I haven't banged any doors—yet. Second, are you implying that you're never going to honor your promises?"

Nedrof's face showed annoyance. He was not too hard to read. Making an effort to smile, Nedrof said: "I tell you what. As a favor to you, considering your previous heroic achievements, I'll have it done." David paused, seemingly to let the full weight of his commitment sink in. "We can arrange a phone call from here, through our channels, and you can tell them in Aesopian language that you're fine."

Victor could hardly believe what he'd heard. This was something out of a bad spy novel. There were two critical points that needed to be considered, and Victor homed in on one. "I didn't realize you have the capability to "smuggle" a phone call from abroad into the Soviet Union, so that it looks like a local phone call."

"I never said that. I'm just saying that we can channel the call so it would look like it's coming to Moscow from, say, Paris or Vienna."

"But that wouldn't solve the problem. The KGB would eavesdrop on it, like any foreign call. So, no matter what's said, they'd put two and two together without much effort, and my existence would be blown."

"Well, that's your interpretation. Others might see it differently."

"That's not just my interpretation, that's the reality, basic OpSec, Operational Security, which I happen to know as well as anybody. But, there's another point here. You should know that because of my father's job his phone is under surveillance by the KGB. So, no matter where I call from, my existence would be known and I'd put my father in a very difficult situation. If he reports the call, he'll be in a lot of hot water, and would probably be accused of helping me in 1980. If he doesn't report it, he'll go to jail for abetting an enemy of the people. I can't put him in that position."

"Well, it's your decision, but I suggest that you think about it. This option is open. Any other form of contact, not." He glanced at his watch. "I have to go now. Thank you for stopping by," he said sarcastically. "And for your expertise."

They parted without shaking hands.

On the drive back to the airport, Victor and Jack hardly spoke. While walking toward the gate, Victor said: "Jack, I want to know only one thing. We've never crossed paths—at least not that I know of—so why does he hate me so much – it's pretty obvious?"

Victor expected that Jack would give him a pep talk, maintaining that Victor had misread the man. Instead, Jack shook his head slowly. "I don't know."

After a few minutes Victor said: "All right. At least he gave me a definitive answer. By the way, the next time the CIA needs me, I'm not available." He paused. "And I won't be—until the CIA fulfills all its promises."

"What's this? A strike?"

"No, just getting on equal footing." Then Victor added: "Of course, this applies only to the CIA. I'm available to anyone else."

Back home in Phoenix, Olga was waiting impatiently. They went to their two-person swing in the backyard, under one of the large oaks.

"I know this stone-faced look of yours—what happened?"

Victor described the meeting in detail.

"So, are you saying there's no hope they'll do it?"

"No. No hope."

"Well, that's hardly news. We've sort of felt they wouldn't for a long time now. What's bothering you? There's something you haven't told me."

Victor was not quick to answer. "There's one thing that I'm not even sure I want to consider. You see, what he suggested the CIA could do, is—in plain language—intelligence sabotage."

"What?"

"That's precisely what it is. A call made the way he pushed for would undoubtedly tell the KGB that we're alive, and in the United States. And this is one of the most cherished intelligence secrets in Washington. It doesn't take James Bond to realize that– he has no excuse for not knowing."

"So?"

"So, why did he try to push me into it?"

"Maybe he's just ignorant."

"He doesn't seem to be very knowledgeable, true. But he's not that stupid. Besides, in his position, he can easily get the advice of an expert who would tell him the same thing I did."

"What if he just wanted to say 'no', and that was his way of doing it. It would anger you more than just a 'no'."

"I've already thought of that. He could have said 'No, because I just don't feel like it', which would piss me off even more." Victor shook his head. "No, he was dead serious about his idea. He would have been all too happy to do it if I had agreed."

"Then, Victor, what are you trying to say?"

"I'm trying to say that I can't see any other reason for doing what he suggested than to tell the KGB that I'm here, and to blame me for it."

"You mean, to have a legitimate excuse for covering up the leak."

"Correct."

"And the guy you suspect of trying to do this just happens to be Chief of the Soviet Division?"

"Unfortunately. But I have to have more information. Hopefully, another explanation exists, something like some internal bureaucratic fight."

Olga glanced at Victor. "Anything else?"

Slowly, Victor said: "Yes. It was in his eyes. Hatred."

"Why, have you ever met before?"

"No. But it was there, I felt it. Strange. It was..." He tried to find word. "Personal. Yes, very personal. Makes no sense at all, but it was there—unmistakably."

7

Victor called Jack and demanded clarification of the citizenship situation. Jack brought a CIA lawyer to Phoenix.

When they met for lunch in a restaurant, Victor was taken aback. The lawyer was obviously drunk: his speech was slurred, and his level of comprehension well sub-par. Consequently, the conversation was hardly substantive. Barely able to speak coherently, Richard told Victor that he had to wait for another ten years for U. S. citizenship because of his former membership in the communist party. After lunch the lawyer departed immediately, allegedly for his hotel.

While walking to Jack's rental car, Victor said, "I want to talk to you."

"That's why I'm here."

"Where do we go? To a hotel lobby?"

Jack's eyes sparkled mischievously. "We can do much better than that. Where would two spies be least suspected of talking shop?"

Victor got the hint. "A strip club?"

"Exactly. I know a good strip dancing place minutes from here."

Fifteen minutes later they sat at a dark corner table, having warded off the hospitable approaches of a few girls.

"Jack, what's going on? Where did you get that drunk?"

Jack looked embarrassed. "Well, he's really not that bad, you know." Seeing that Victor was still annoyed, Jack added: "When he's sober."

Victor chuckled.

"Look," said Jack. "Let's just discuss substance, OK?"

"OK. What the hell was he blabbing about? What ten years?"

"Oh, don't worry. He was just talking about the law in general. The law is that you can get naturalized after five years in this country, unless you've been a member of the communist party. Then, it's ten years."

"What about an act of Congress? He didn't mention that."

"Oh, well, that's a rare exception."

"But all this contradicts everything that we discussed earlier—and everything you promised."

"Well, he didn't know the particulars of your case."

"If that's the case, why the hell did you bring him down here?"

"Because he's a lawyer. Besides, I didn't bring him—my boss sent him, OK?"

"All right, Jack. Let me make sure I understand the situation. You were sent here to tell me that the CIA has broken its promise to give me immediate citizenship, and that I have to wait five years? That is, if I'm a good boy. If not, it'll be ten years. Right?"

Jack looked Victor straight in the eye and said softly, "Yes."

When Victor didn't respond, Jack seemed uneasy. "Look, Victor. I've come to like you." He chuckled. "Even you. And I like Olga, of course. Needless to say, Elena's my soft spot." Everyone knew that Jack adored Elena.

Victor smiled: "So?"

"I want to give you some advice, personal." Victor nodded, and Jack continued: "Lay low. Don't do anything, don't ask anything. Just keep quiet for a few years, and everything will be OK. Right now, you can't win with the forces against you, so don't even try to fight."

"I'm not sure I'm with you, Jack. Who could be against me? I was told, more than once, that I'm the best thing that's happened to the CIA in years."

Jack took his pen and started doodling on a napkin. "Well, Victor, you're a professional. You know that there're a lot of things I can't tell you, and there're a lot of things I don't know myself. But I can tell you—and that is strictly between us—that you have very powerful enemies here."

Victor was incredulous. "In the Resettlement Center?"

Jack shook his head: "No, they treat everyone the same."

"In the SE Division?"

Jack did not answer. When Victor glanced at Jack's napkin, he saw Jack draw a big letter **Y**; then he gave Victor a long look.

Victor nodded. "David Nedrof?"

Jack drew another large **Y**.

Victor looked at Jack with amazement. "Why?"

Jack shrugged his shoulders. "The off-the-book order that came down to us just before you left Washington is: Give him a hard time."

"I don't understand."

"Neither do I. But it doesn't matter. What matters is the fact. So, I'm telling you: lay low, you can't win."

They were silent for a while, watching a new group of girls dancing in the strobe lights.

Victor broke the silence. "I gather you got stuck in the middle of this mess, and my hunch is that you're not very happy about it."

"Your hunch is correct."

"Why don't you get out?"

Jack smiled. "If I do, they'll eat you up. You're dealing with an old fool who's stupid enough to see right from wrong."

"I don't want you to suffer for it, you know."

Jack laughed. "Don't worry, I'm a tough nut. Besides, I never forget my own interests."

Victor shook his head and started watching the girls again.

After a while, Jack said: "Victor, I'd like to see Olga and Elena." He paused. "On my way down here, I decided I shouldn't see them, considering the circumstances. But now I would like to. That is, if you don't mind."

"Of course not. As a matter of fact, I have strict orders to bring you home for dinner. Olga's made borscht especially for you." Olga's Russian borscht was Jack's favorite.

Victor was disturbed, perplexed. The CIA had displayed exemplary competence in arranging his exfiltration and later awarded him its highest medal for his contributions to U. S. intelligence, so why had David Nedrof issued an off-the-book order to make his life miserable? Victor could not imagine any reason why the agency that benefited so much from his defection, and was charged with being his protector, would suddenly become his persecutor. He didn't even want to think about a possibility that something was seriously wrong within the CIA. Was a hostile pattern of some kind emerging? Then, what was the game, and who was playing it?

8

Victor was really running out of patience with the CIA. Talking to Olga about this was not easy, because Olga by nature did not like confrontations. She asked him to be patient a little longer, so he agreed to give the CIA one more chance.

Victor by then had become comfortable with finance, and he grew increasingly irritated that the CIA never provided any accounting for his money. After numerous requests through his CIA-designated lawyer he finally got a statement. What he saw troubled him. Among numerous highly questionable items that would not fly anywhere outside the CIA, one line really stood out. The CIA had paid about four hundred seventy thousand dollars for Victor's annuity. Since there were no survivor benefits and no yearly adjustments, it was very easy to evaluate. Using 1980 interest rates and GAAP, Generally Accepted Accounting Principles, the accounting standard of the United States, Victor calculated that the annuity was worth no more than half of what the CIA paid for it.

When he explained that to Olga she could hardly believe it.

"How can that possibly be? Maybe some incompetent bureaucrat made a bad decision?"

"No, it's much simpler than that. I'll bet you the mysterious insurance company that actually issued the annuity is a hole-in-the-wall operation owned by a former CIA man."

"What are you saying?"

"I am saying that upon the transaction in 1980 somebody immediately pocketed over two hundred thousand of our money. See, to simplify, when you buy an annuity whoever sells it to you takes your money and buys long-term Government bonds, taking a small percentage as a transaction fee. From the coupons of these bonds he'd pay your monthly income. That's all there is to it."

"And you are saying that the guy took almost half a million of our money from the CIA and, with no money of his own, paid less than half of it for the bonds that pay us monthly twenty five hundred?"

"Precisely. And he pocketed the difference, which happened to be over two hundred thousand. Nice deal."

Victor paused and added, "not to mention that their accounting contains such expense items as 'security guards at initial quarters—$10,000' and 'rental cars — $41,912.'"

Olga was shocked. "You mean that they charged us for their officers guarding the safehouse?"

"Yes."

Olga chuckled. "Now I understand why they wanted us to stay longer at that safehouse. I'm glad that we got out of there in just about three weeks. What about the rental cars? They did not rent any cars for us."

"Of course not. That was for the cars rented by the CIA for the officers that were working with us."

Olga just shook her head.

Victor called Jack and requested a meeting with a responsible financial officer. Two weeks later he was in a nondescript McLean office rented by the CIA.

An older man reminiscent of a classic Swiss dwarf came in, carrying a large pile of folders. After a brief introduction he identified himself as an officer responsible for investments in 1980. He gave Victor a long lecture on the difficult investment environment of 1980, saying that what looked like a bad deal now was the best available at the time. Victor understood that getting into a financial investment dogfight was not a good idea. They would just part with their opinions intact. He decided to cut the knot.

"Excuse me, I think that we're getting nowhere with this discussion. Let's make it simple. Find just one legitimate investment in the whole country nearly as bad as this one that was made at that time, and I'll walk away and you'll never hear from me again."

It took the man a few seconds to understand Victor's suggestion. He was obviously stunned. He mumbled something and asked for a coffee break, and vanished.

Jack quipped, "I knew we should never let you go to a business school." Victor chuckled. Jack left to take a phone call, and asked Victor to wait for a few minutes for the man to return.

About half an hour later the door opened and David Nedrof burst in. Victor was sitting in the middle of the long side of the conference table, and without saying a word Nedrof took the opposite chair. Then he stared at Victor and spoke sarcastically.

"So, here you are again, complaining about something else. Do you realize how annoying it is to deal with you?"

Victor's tone was conciliatory. "Well, I am just inquiring about a case of extreme accounting creativity, and wondering who was the real beneficiary of the transaction."

Nedrof blew up. He stood up abruptly, leaned toward Victor across the table and shouted: "You are really the most ungrateful guy I ever met. I don't want to talk to you any more unless you grow up and understand reality."

Victor mimicked Nedrof. He also rose, and with their faces inches apart, he shouted back: "No, it's me who doesn't want to talk to you, unless you acquire some decency."

Victor turned and stalked out of the conference room. In the reception area two CIA guards were staring at him, their jaws dropped.

"I should've charged you guys for tickets to hear somebody shouting at that bastard." Victor went outside, and walked to the village to find a taxi to the airport.

Back in Phoenix Victor wrote a letter to CIA Director Casey, essentially saying that the CIA had broken its promises and, if it did not get its act together, Victor would feel free to take any action he sees fit. He was sure that Casey would never see the letter.

A week later Jack came for a short visit. When Victor met him at the airport Jack asked to go to a quiet place, and Victor drove to a nearby park. They strolled, chatting, but Jack was radiating unease. Victor waited patiently. After a long pause Jack said: "Victor, I really want to plead with you to lay low and stop creating problems. I understand that you have strong reasons to complain, but now is the wrong time. You may be making this game dangerous. Please stop, at least for Elena's and Olga's sake.

That was a stronger suggestion than any Victor had yet received. "Well, this sounds like a bit of a threat."

Jack did not answer. A long, long pause followed. Finally Jack cleared his throat. In a very official voice he said:

"Victor, I was instructed to deliver a message to you." He paused again and Victor did not respond. "Remember, you don't kill the messenger."

Victor again did not respond, and Jack was forced to continue. "The message is that you are a very ungrateful person. You should realize that a window in a certain car could have opened with a silenced submachine gun sticking out of it. Instead of the three of you being picked up and brought to the best country in the world, there could have been three bodies lying in the street of an obscure Russian town."

Victor felt that something was stuck in his throat. A thousand thoughts raced through his mind. Operationally the suggestion was nonsensical, but emotionally it was truly shocking. He was barely able to say a few words. "And one of those bodies would be of a five-year-old girl? Is that what you are saying, Jack?"

"Victor, I told you, don't kill the messenger."

With a little thought following the initial shock, Victor understood clearly that from an intelligence perspective the message was idiotic. But it was sickening and could only have been designed to produce a psychological shock.

Victor went straight to his car and Jack followed. Without a word Victor opened the passenger door to let Jack in, closed the door, and got behind the wheel.

There was silence in the car. The road to the airport was hilly, what they call in Europe "serpentine," with almost no shoulder. Victor drove very fast, intentionally passing some trees on the right shoulder within inches from Jack's head. Jack was obviously scared, but did not say a word. Entering the airport grounds, Victor slowed down and rolled up to the departure door with the smoothness of a stretched limo. He stopped and just quietly said, "Have a nice flight."

Jack got out of the car and went through the terminal door without looking back.

A few days later Victor called Donald and told him about the CIA message.

Donald was furious. Both of them knew that operationally it was ridiculous, but the fact that it had been used at all was inexcusable on any count. Donald was adamant in demanding the name of who delivered the message, and said, "I'll have him fired tomorrow." Victor felt he was serious. Obviously, Victor could not give Jack away, he was just the messenger.

"You know, Donald, if you really feel that way, it shouldn't be difficult for you to find out. But the important thing is to find the one who sent the message, and why, not who delivered it."

Donald didn't answer.

Victor concluded, " I can only tell you that I cannot have any respect for an organization that makes it possible for a bastard to send messages like this." Donald never referred to that topic again.

After a two-week courtesy period with no answer from Director Casey, Victor said to Olga, "That's enough. Time for a trip." Olga just nodded.

A mechanical problem forced Victor's plane to land in Boston, where there was a substantial delay. Instead of arriving at London in early morning as scheduled, Victor landed at Gatwick around 10 AM.

Victor arrived at Victoria station shortly before noon and left his suitcase in a locker. Since MI6, British foreign intelligence, did not officially exist, he wasn't surprised that he could not find a listing for it in the London phonebook. Neither could he find MI5, British counter-intelligence. Victor was left with two options: calling the Metropolitan Police or the Ministry of Defense.

Victor dialed the main number of the Ministry of Defense, aware that he had to be circumspect because the KGB was possibly eavesdropping on unsecured telephone calls to the Ministry. Yet, he had to pique their interest sufficiently with a cold call to prevent their dismissing him as a hoaxer. *Even if the KGB intercepts this call, it is highly likely that it wouldn't be monitored live, but taped. But even if they did intercept it live, they'd need time to get to the meeting place to see what Russian was approaching British intelligence. That's what I need to play for—time.*

A female operator answered.

"I would like to speak to MI6, please."

"There is no such listing in the Ministry of Defense."

"All right. Then, I would like you to switch me to the intelligence branch." *My accent should do the trick, if she's smart.*

"One moment, sir."

Another female voice: "Hello."

"Is this the intelligence branch?"

"Yes. How can I help you?"

"I would like to speak to the MI6 duty officer, please."

"Sir, I am not aware of such an organization."

Sure. OK, let's play it out then. "All right. Then I would like to talk to a military intelligence duty officer." Victor chuckled. "And please, make sure he is close to MI6, even if there is no such thing."

"May I have your name, sir?"

"Not on this phone."

"Very well. May I have your native country please?"

"USSR."

"Very well. Can you tell me your organization?"

Damn it. I don't want to trigger anything in the KGB. Their computers search for key words and then zoom in on the conversation. "KGB" is the number one key word.

"It's bad."

"Is it GRU?"

"No, it's worse than that." *Come on, think. Only the KGB is worse than the GRU.*

"Very well, sir. I'll have to put you on hold for a moment. Please, don't hang up."

Victor had to wait for several minutes, which was understandable. A lady waiting outside the telephone booth, whom Victor had avoided looking at, gave him a scowl and left. At last a man answered in a clear, low voice. "Hello?"

"Yes, I would like to talk to the duty officer."

"Speaking. In case we lose this connection, please tell me the number you're calling from. I presume it's a pay phone."

"Of course." Victor gave him the number.

"Very well. If we lose our connection, I'll call there every fifteen minutes for an hour, then every hour until evening. If that fails, I'm afraid you'll have to call again when you can. Meanwhile, how can I help you?"

Very professional. Good. "I think it could be of considerable interest to MI6 to talk to me, and I would like to do it rather quickly."

A chuckle. "I'm not aware of any such organization. However, we can arrange to talk to you so that you are unlikely to be disappointed." After pausing, he said, "I'd like to ask you a few questions, though."

"All right. But please, don't make them too specific."

"Of course. I was briefed on what you said before. I understand that you work for the really bad guys."

The only way I can get their attention is to pretend I'm a defector from the KGB. Otherwise I'd have to give lots of explanations to a bunch of low-level people, jeopardizing security—it could turn into a mess. Well, one more sin on my soul.

"That is correct."

"Are you under any time constraints right now?"

"Some."

"And you want to help us, correct?"

"Yes. And I would like to meet as soon as possible."

"Right. Where are you now?"

"Victoria station."

"Is an hour sufficient?"

"Yes."

"Do you have any time restrictions for the meeting?"

"No."

"Very well. We'll meet you at the Mayfair Hotel one hour from now. Do you know where it is?"

"No, but I've seen a few taxis around here."

The man laughed. "Then, you should be in good shape. We'll see you at the hotel. How do we recognize you?"

"I'm in my thirties. Five ten, medium build, brown hair, gray suit, burgundy tie, black raincoat on my left arm."

"Very well, see you soon."

Victor first considered going to the hotel right away and snooping around for a while, to see if anything suspicious was going on. Then he recalled that IRA terrorists were active in London. If he hung around the hotel he might draw the attention of security, who were probably on heightened alert now. Hence, he decided that the best course of action would be to avoid making anybody nervous, and to arrive openly in a taxi at the precise time of the meeting.

Having just purchased a map of London, Victor unfolded it and searched for some famous places that he'd read so much about, such as Buckingham Palace and the Tower of London. After studying the map for a few minutes, he took a taxi to Piccadilly Circus because he hadn't enough time for much else. After walking for half an hour he took another taxi.

Victor arrived at the Mayfair Hotel right on time in a standard London taxi. It was crowded in front of the entrance. When the doors to the lobby swung open, Victor saw that it was even more crowded there. *Check-out time.* While exiting the taxi he noticed a slim, strikingly handsome gray-haired man in his forties in a perfectly fitting light-gray suit standing just inside the entrance door. One glance was enough for recognition, which didn't surprise Victor. *It's funny. You never need a description to spot an intelligence officer who's waiting to meet you.* Victor slowly paid the driver, and strolled to the lobby. He was sure that he'd been identified, and that the man knew that he'd been identified as well. *OK, let's play it by the book.*

He purposely passed the man near the door without glancing at him. Moving inside the lobby, Victor navigated slowly among the throngs of people, then stopped at a display. Seconds later he heard a low voice behind him: "Are you meeting someone here?" Definitely the same voice Victor had heard on the phone.

"Yes, someone I spoke with over the phone an hour ago."

"Follow me, please."

The man took the stairs to the mezzanine and Victor followed a few steps behind. At the stairs he suddenly noticed another man, who had been choosing a postcard from a stand, coming towards him. The man, now only a step behind Victor, was meticulously dressed in a dark-blue striped suit with a burgundy tie and matching handkerchief in his breast pocket; he carried a large, heavy-looking umbrella. *Security backup. These guys are really taking that IRA business seriously. Hard to pick them out in this crowd, but I'm sure there are a few other security guys around here.*

When they reached the mezzanine, the first man opened a door, and he and Victor entered a conference room, followed by the other man, who closed the door behind him.

The first man turned, and extended his hand: "Hello. I'm Ian. This is my colleague Alistair."

I'm glad to meet you. I'm Victor." They shook hands.

"Anything to drink?"

"No, thank you."

They sat at the conference table. Ian immediately took out a pack of Silk Cut cigarettes from his pocket. "Do you mind?"

"Not at all," said Victor. "As a matter of fact, I like the idea." Taking out his cigarettes, he glanced at Alistair, who smiled.

"Don't worry. I'm used to putting up with the bloody habit."

Victor felt the ball was in his court. "Please forgive me, but I would like to know who I'm talking to. It's essential that I talk to MI6, not the police or military intelligence."

Ian nodded slowly and said: "We represent Her Majesty's Government on this matter. As you probably know, officially MI6 does not exist. For our part, we would like to know who you are. From our telephone conversation I gather that you're a KGB officer, and wish to defect."

Now the fun starts. The trick is to prevent them quitting before they have the whole picture.

Victor instinctively responded using his resettlement name. "My name is Victor Schwartz, and I live in the United States."

A mixture of disappointment and frustration showed on both faces. Ian moved his arms as if he were about to stand up and cancel the meeting.

Victor waved his hand, stopping him. "Wait—just another two minutes. If we've gone through all this trouble to meet here, it makes sense to spend a little time together and not rush to judgment. I promise you won't be disappointed. You have nothing to lose by listening to me for a few minutes."

Ian settled back into his chair. Both men were plainly skeptical and impatient. Victor continued. "I'm a former KGB officer, a major. I did defect to the United States in 1980, and I do live in the United States now."

Victor saw Ian look quickly at Alistair, and went on. "I know what you're about to tell me. That there is a firm agreement between the two countries regarding the full sharing of intelligence, and you already have the information that I've provided. Not quite. The positive side of the situation here is that all I'm about to tell you is fully verifiable. And, as I said, you won't be disappointed."

Victor took a breath. "Well, my last job in the KGB was coordination of all aspects of security of cipher communications with its stations abroad." He saw a flicker in Ian's eyes. "For ideological reasons,

I decided to defect to the United States. Since for security reasons my family was prohibited from ever leaving the Soviet Union, my wife, my daughter, and myself were exfiltrated from Russia by the CIA in 1980. Considering my knowledge and expertise, I guess this should not come as a surprise to you. All your agreements with American intelligence notwithstanding, I can assure you that you never heard of me or my defection. Needless to say, you never got any of the information I provided. I don't have to tell you about the importance of such information. You can have it now, if we can come to terms."

There was silence in the room for a long while. Both men were apparently too astonished to respond. Finally, Ian said: "Well, suppose what you told us is true. What do you want from us in return for this treasure chest?"

"The Americans promised to establish contact with my parents in Moscow. See, they don't even know that we're alive. Well, the CIA failed to deliver. So, I can consult with you and offer my expertise if you help me to establish that contact."

Now Ian was incredulous. "Is that all?"

"Yes."

Silence again. Victor couldn't restrain himself any longer, and laughed. "Do I look crazy to you?"

Ian laughed too. "For some reason unknown to me, no. But I urgently need a sanity check myself. If you really are an intelligence officer, you can see the situation."

"Yes, and I find it extremely amusing. I also think that an urgent sanity check is in order. Let's start right now. My original name is Victor Sheymov. Have you ever heard it?"

"No."

"All right, ask me any questions you want, except any related to American intelligence."

Ian was coming to his senses. "Very well. Have you traveled abroad?"

"Yes. Czechoslovakia, China, Poland, Yemen."

"Poland? Well, do you know where the British Embassy is located in Warsaw?"

"Yes. A block away from the Soviet Embassy, around the corner."

"What is the name of the main street there?"

"Marshalkovska."

"Do you remember a park nearby?"

"Yes, near the prime minister's palace."

"Whose statue is in that park right near the entrance?"

"Frederick Chopin."

Ian smiled. "All right. Do you know what caused the mass expulsion of Soviet intelligence officers from London a few years back?"

"The defection of Lyalin, a line 'N' KGB officer." Lyalin had been a KGB officer stationed in London who defected to the British in the 1970s.

"Do you know anything about that defection that was not reported in the press?

Victor thought for a few moments, digging in his memory. "He defected with a woman, the wife of the Trade Representative, I believe. He immediately wrote a letter to an enemy in the KGB. The letter was written in a way that it suggested that the addressee was his close friend. Apparently an attempt to discredit him in the KGB. Pretty clumsy, actually."

Ian rubbed his forehead. Victor's answers had been correct. "Do you know if the KGB found anything odd in its embassy here that raised a lot of fuss?"

"Yes. In a column in the main hall used for official receptions. But it wasn't really much of a fuss."

Ian was shaking his head. "It's still incredible."

Victor smiled. "I understand what you're going through."

"And all you want is to contact your parents?"

"Yes."

Ian turned his head. "Alistair?"

Alistair, quiet until that time, also asked some questions about the KGB, which Victor had no problem answering. In a few minutes the Q & A session was over, for it was obvious that Victor had been a genuine and well-informed KGB officer.

Ian took a deep breath. "Well. You did work for KGB intelligence, and in a capacity where your access was virtually unlimited. There's no question about it. If the Americans notified us of anything related to you, I would have known it." Ian paused. "Which leaves us in a very touchy situation."

Sure. You don't want a contretemps with the Americans, but the offer is too good to pass up.

"Absolutely. And I have no idea how you're going to deal with it."

"By the way, I take it you didn't notify the Americans that you were coming here."

"Of course not. I wrote a letter to the CIA Director saying, in essence, 'You broke your promise about contacting my parents, you played games with me for a long time. If you don't get your act together, I feel free to take any action I see fit.' I gave him two weeks to answer. Sure enough, he didn't respond. So, I took off."

"Tell you what. I'll go to the office, and make some reports and inquiries there. We have to notify the Americans, you see."

"I understand. You want to keep your end of the bargain, no matter what they do. A matter of British pride."

"If you will."

"All right. Just keep it to a small circle, please. The security around me there is pretty tight. Very few people even know of my existence."

"Very well. And don't worry. In any case it would go through the very top. Meanwhile, Alistair and you will have lunch. He'll host you, show you around. Where are you staying?"

"Nowhere. My bag is at Victoria Station."

"We'll arrange a hotel and all the details. You came to us, and we'd like to show our hospitality."

"You don't have to worry about it. I'll manage."

"It's a non-issue. Besides, you're on our territory, and we're responsible for your security now. The last thing we want is something happening to you here. The KGB is alive and well in London, remember?"

"All right, thank you."

Ian was on his way, and Victor said to him: "I'm sorry you'll miss your lunch."

Ian laughed. "I need a drink right now, not a lunch. Unfortunately, I really must go straight to the office, but I'll join you in the evening."

At lunch Alistair was as an excellent companion. He displayed an almost encyclopedic knowledge of history while kindly answering questions posed by Victor, who had a keen interest in Britain. After leaving the restaurant, they went sightseeing in London. Alistair suggested that Victor's tour should begin with Westminster Abbey and St. Paul's Cathedral.

Alistair also had an extensive knowledge of architecture. When they passed an interesting building, he immediately provided its history and an architectural digest. Victor was surprised to discover that the statues of knights lying down on their stone tombs in St. Paul's Cathedral had to conform to strict rules. When Victor noted that some knights lay with their ankles resting on a dog, Alistair explained that this was a privilege granted only to those knights who had participated in the Crusades.

Alistair impressed Victor as a man of finely honed tact, for he directed their tour unobtrusively without a hint of impatience. Victor was convinced that he couldn't have found a better guide in England. Alistair's one phone call to the office confirmed a hotel reservation for Victor. After picking up his bag at Victoria Station, they checked Victor into the hotel. For the rest of the afternoon Alistair and Victor took pleasant walks and short rides through London, while Alistair pointed out important landmarks and explained the general layout of London.

In the evening, Alistair took Victor to the piano bar at a restaurant where Ian was waiting. His smile was sincere and slightly apologetic. "Well, Victor, every word you told us proved to be true."

Victor chuckled. "Oh, really? Who could imagine that?"

They all laughed. "Well, you have to realize that we don't deal with this kind of thing every day. I apologize for any mistrust."

"Don't worry. Frankly, the whole thing was a bit unfair of me. I knew the situation, you didn't. I want to ask just one question, a matter of curiosity. Why didn't you stop the meeting at the very beginning, when I told you I was living in America?"

"I don't know. A sixth sense, if you will. I felt that you were credible." That was a very candid answer. Only a top-level pro could afford to have this attitude, and be so frank about it. To Victor's surprise, they were soon joined by a charming young lady who worked in Ian's office, Allison. Somehow, she combined genuine warmth and the social skills of a high-society regular with the acuity of a seasoned professional.

Ian said, "Victor, I need not tell you about the sensitivity of your being here. We will arrange the top level of security. Later on, I will introduce you to two more people, Stella and John. Only five people know exactly who you are, and where you're staying. You can talk freely to us, but nobody else. Needless to say, we'd be happy to help you here any way we can. Obviously, you're free to go anywhere you want whenever you want. If you need anything, let us know."

"Thank you very much. No need to worry."

"We'll discuss that in detail tomorrow. I can only say right now that it will be done."

The group left the piano bar and got a table. In half an hour the atmosphere at the table was exceedingly warm and friendly, and the food was good. Victor caught himself thinking that he hadn't had such pleasant company in a long time. Like many first-time visitors to England, he assumed that the British would be rather cold and formal. But his companions displayed such conviviality that Victor felt ashamed for having accepted the stereotype. Victor instinctively felt that a friendship was developing, one that would last for many years to come.

After dinner they moved back to the piano bar.

Ian said: "I can tell you, Victor, you just stirred up quite a bit of turmoil on both sides of the ocean."

"Why's that?"

Everybody laughed, and Victor asked, "Seriously, how did the CIA react?"

"Forget the CIA. After I briefed him, my own boss told me that I was over the top. He thought it was a hoax. 'Ian, do you want me to become the laughing stock of the Americans?' I barely talked him into sending a cable."

"And then?"

"Well, then all hell broke loose. We got several cables back, each one saying different things. None of them disputed you, though. Good Lord, they did a lot dancing in those cables."

Alistair said: "Of course. They've been caught cheating their closest ally. It's a disgrace, no matter how you look at it."

Victor disagreed. "Don't kid yourself, Alistair. They're just mad at being caught, that's all. They have no sense of disgrace, believe me. I know them well enough. Their idea of intelligence is cheating everybody, allies included, and not being caught. Since they're not good enough to cheat their enemies, they cheat their allies."

"Come, Victor. Give them some credit. They're not that bad."

Victor just shook his head.

Ian said: "By the way, Casey's representative is already on his way here. He wants to meet you tomorrow."

"I have nothing to talk to him about."

"Well, it's your call, of course. But by refusing you'll put us in a touchy position, you know. So, if it doesn't bother you too much, I'd like to ask you to at least meet him. It would not obligate you to anything, and you can walk away any time."

"All right."

"Thanks. By the way, what are your plans for this visit?"

"Nothing in particular. I'd love to see London. I have a few days, but I don't want to take too much time off from my schooling. I imagine the GCHQ people want to talk to me?" The GCHQ, or Government Communications Headquarters, was the British equivalent of the NSA.

Ian chuckled. "The GCHQ, yes, but so do we."

"Sure. Let's work it out tomorrow."

It was very late, and the delightful evening was over.

At the hotel, Victor called home. "Victor! How are you?"

"Very well. Everything's going as planned. At least, I've got everybody's attention."

"You most certainly have. I got a lot of phone calls last night. Everyone was interested in where you were. And then that Mr. Ed, along with some other jerk, literally stormed into the house today, demanding to know where you were."

"What did you tell them?"

"Nothing, as we agreed. Just played it dumb. I said that you just stepped out. They asked when you would be back. I said, in a few days. They were fuming when they left."

"Good."

"When are you coming back?"

"I don't know yet. I'll call you tomorrow.

10

After breakfast the next day Alistair joined Victor for coffee. He suggested a sightseeing tour of London. Victor's pleasure in the tour was enhanced both by Alistair's comprehensive knowledge and his genuine love for his country, which Victor found infectious. At the Tower of London Victor was sure that Alistair could have recited virtually all the names of its former inhabitants. At the display of the Crown Jewels, Alistair explained their sources and the meanings of these priceless symbols of royal power.

After lunch it was back to business. They decided to meet in the conference room of another hotel, where Ian was supposed to join them with the newly arrived CIA representative. In the hotel lobby they were surprised to see Ian, who took them aside to a quiet corner.

"Victor, I've now heard a lot about your case, and by now I'm generally familiar with it. First, let me express my admiration and respect for your courage, determination and professional skills. It's my privilege to meet you, and to work with you, if possible."

"Thank you. You're very kind."

"I also would like to keep things straight between us, and don't want to confront you with an unpleasant surprise. As I told you yesterday, the CIA Director's personal representative has come here to see you. What I didn't know was his name. It's David Nedrof. He's upstairs now, waiting for you."

Ian obviously understood by now that Nedrof was less than neutral. Victor said, "Well, I've had enough of meetings with him already. He made every effort to make our encounters very unpleasant, and he did it in a very arrogant way. I haven't the slightest desire to see that bastard ever again."

"I'm aware that you probably don't have a good rapport with him. But the situation now is quite dissimilar, and you'll probably find him very different. Casey was upset and embarrassed about your trip here. You can easily gauge that by the speed with which he sent someone here, and by whom he sent—as you're aware, Nedrof's high in the CIA. He didn't even have a chance to pack his bag, you know. My understanding is that Casey sent Nedrof to apologize."

Victor understood the awkwardness of the situation. And, on top of everything else, that the British were in a delicate position. They didn't want to appear to be seizing the moment and taking advantage of a situation humiliating to the CIA. After all, the Americans were their number one ally. Of course, Victor could simply refuse to talk to Nedrof, but it be would be wiser professionally, and certainly kinder to his hosts, if he demonstrated his goodwill. He didn't want to appear capricious, nor did he want to explain to the British all the aspects of his tumultuous relationship with the CIA—they probably wouldn't believe him anyway.

"Okay. I don't want to be rude, let's talk to him. I guess that would be better for you."

"Much better. Thank you."

Ian opened the door, and let Victor in first. David Nedrof, who was standing near the window, immediately approached Victor. This was indeed a totally different David Nedrof. All traces of his arrogance were gone. His face was pale, perhaps showing the effects of a sleepless night flight from Washington. His meek demeanor was that of a whipped boy—the arrogant SE Division Chief was nowhere in evidence.

"Hello, Victor."

"Hello."

Ian and Alistair were standing at the door. Ian said: "I think, gentlemen, we'd better let you alone for a while. You may need to have a private chat."

Victor appreciated Ian's tact, yet he couldn't resist needling the CIA chief. "No need to. I'm sure that Mr. Nedrof doesn't have any secrets from you."

Nedrof tried to compose himself, but his voice was feeble. "Well, of course not, but I have a private message to you from Mr. Casey. We may as well discuss it alone."

"Given my experience, I would prefer to have witnesses to our conversation." Seeing that Nedrof was about to press the issue, Victor added: "After all, I don't remember asking you to come here."

The message was received. Nedrof nodded without saying another word. He obviously had enough sense to know when to stop, and did not want to take chances.

Victor moved toward the table and rather conspicuously took a chair with his back to the window. Nedrof had no choice but to sit across from him with light beaming into his face. Ian and Alistair took the side seats.

Now there was silence, which added to the tension in the room. Apparently having lost hope that Victor would speak first, Nedrof cleared his throat.

"Well, I'm sorry about what happened."

Victor did not say a word, and Nedrof continued, "Mr. Casey asked me to come here. He also asked me to say to you that he is very sorry about the misunderstanding, and he would like to convey his sincere apologies to you."

"I don't see any misunderstanding. After my numerous attempts at several different levels to persuade the CIA to live up to its promises, you personally made it quite clear that it's not going to happen."

"As I said, we apologize. I'm sorry."

Victor had always disliked arrogant people. The worst kind are those whose arrogance is replaced by abject begging when they get into a tight spot. They are ruthless to subordinates and obsequious to superiors. Nedrof was a classic of that breed.

Finally Victor asked: "By the way, the message that Jack Decker brought to me a while ago, was that from you?" Decker's statement that the CIA could have killed all three of them, including Victor's five-year-old daughter, instead of exfiltrating them still rang in Victor's head.

"What message?" said Nedrof in a trembling voice, while shrinking in his easy chair.

"You know exactly what message. Do you want me to quote it?"

There was a deafening silence in the room. Though Ian and Alistair couldn't possibly have understood what it was all about, they clearly sensed the intensity of the exchange and did not try to intervene.

Nedrof's voice cracked. "No."

Suddenly, Victor saw Nedrof's eyes watering. Nedrof quickly stood up, walked to the window, and put his handkerchief to his face.

I don't know what else is on his plate, but I bet Casey told him in no uncertain terms that the consequences would be severe if he failed to make peace in London. Nobody likes to be embarrassed, and Casey least of all.

Then, totally unexpectedly, Victor realized that, in addition to disgust, he felt pity for this pathetic figure. On the one hand, he would avoid touching this repellent person just as he would avoid touching something filthy. On the other, he knew that he'd feel guilty about finishing off a man lying face down on the ground. But Victor knew he was on the brink of making a mistake submitting to a sense of pity. It could be costly.

Victor glanced at Ian and Alistair. Though both struggled to conceal their feelings, their faces reflected a mixture of astonishment, puzzlement, and compassion. Victor shrugged his shoulders, and nodded to Ian.

Ian's low resonant voice was calming. "Well, gentlemen. I feel that there are many emotions involved here, apparently related to some issues going back a long time. I have a suggestion. Why don't we try to make a fresh start, and look forward instead of back."

Victor said: "I agree." Then he went on. "However, an intelligent look into the future must make use of knowledge gained in the past." He was sure that everyone got the right translation: *OK, I won't shut the door. Let's see what you have in mind; but make no mistake, I'll take a hard look at everything you do.*

Nedrof hurriedly returned to the table with reddish eyes, entirely submissive.

Ian, ever the diplomat, rose to the occasion. "Well, David, it is our understanding that whatever unfortunate events occurred, your Director, your organization, and you personally regret that, and express your apologies."

Nedrof said softly, "Yes."

Ian turned to Victor. "Well, are the apologies accepted?"

Victor appreciated the skill of Ian's maneuvering. "Yes."

"All right. David, is there anything concrete that you want to suggest?"

Nedrof's face began showing signs of life. "Yes, of course. Victor, we would be happy to contact your parents and to pass on a letter from you."

"This is kind of late in the game. I've already promised Ian and his organization my cooperation in return for contacting my parents. And, frankly, I prefer that they do it."

"That's no problem at all. Obviously, we don't mind if you offer your expertise in consulting with our British friends." He looked as if he were going to expand on the topic of cooperation between the two intelligence services, employing traditional rhetoric; but when Nedrof glanced at Ian and Alistair, and then at Victor, he must have realized the absurdity of it given the circumstances, and shut up.

Ian, with a straight face, said: "We appreciate it very much." Then he turned to Victor. "If you insist, Victor, we'll do it. However—and this is just a friendly suggestion—wouldn't it be nice if you gave them a chance?"

Victor was about to reply that they'd had all the chances in the world and blew every one. But it was, after all, the CIA's responsibility. Let them work for a change. While looking at Ian and Alistair he said, "I think with all the political issues involved this situation is getting awkward. You have enough to resolve without my adding to them." Nedrof and Ian glanced at each other as if asking, *What else does he know?*

"I can agree on the CIA handling the operation, but on one condition."

"What's that?" asked Nedrof.

Victor turned to Ian: "If they start playing games again, you step in and do it without delay."

Nedrof had no choice but to nod his assent, and so did Ian.

Victor pressed on: "Do I have your guarantee, Ian?"

"Yes."

With this major obstacle out of the way, Victor wanted to discuss the particulars of the operation.

Nedrof said: "We can plan whatever you want, but we don't even know if your parents are still living at the same place. First, we should verify that, or locate them." That was a valid point, and everybody understood the underlying question: Are they still alive? After three years, anything could have happened.

"Agreed. How are you going to do that?"

"With the phone, of course."

Victor still remembered Nedrof's previous outrageous suggestion regarding phone use. He wanted to make sure that nothing like that was on his mind again. "I hope you're going to call from a Moscow pay phone?"

"Of course. A case officer will make sure that he's in the black" – meaning that the officer would be free of surveillance— "and make the phone call. Evening, I presume, is the best time."

"Yes, on a workday. Otherwise they could be at their dacha." Then Victor asked, "Does the officer in question speak non-accented Russian?"

"A slight accent."

"Than you have to follow a security procedure to keep the call clean."

"What do you mean?"

"My father's phone, because of his job, is under surveillance. So, any caller with an accent is suspicious in the KGB's eyes. Even a blank call, with nothing said, is perceived as a possible intelligence signal. So, you have to anticipate that."

"Yes. The officer would say nothing, and will tape-record the answer on the line. Hopefully, you will recognize the voice."

"That's not good enough. He has to hang up, and repeat the call in a few seconds from the same pay phone."

"Never heard of that. Why?"

"Because one phone call to a monitored number is suspicious to the KGB. As you well know, a blank phone call can be an intelligence signal. However, a lot of pay phones in Moscow are vandalized or are just simply out of order. When you can't make a connection, you try again. If it still doesn't work, you call later. Maybe in a few hours, if there is no other pay phone nearby. So, a double call is absolutely normal, and the KGB won't suspect it."

While Nedrof scribbled in his notebook, Ian chuckled. "Victor, we have to talk more about this sort of thing."

Victor nodded. "Oh, there's another point here, too. Just in case they decide to check it out, your guy has to find a single pay phone, of course, not a bank of phones. Otherwise, it would be logical to try another one right away. And he has to take the microphone out of the phone after the call. Or, better, before. That's in case the KGB checks out the phone, to see if it was actually out of order."

Nedrof said: "That's very useful. So, we'll give you the tape, and, if a positive ID is made, we'll deliver a letter from you."

"All right. When can I expect the tape?"

"In a few weeks."

With the planning session over, Nedrof was in a positive mood: "Oh, Victor, there's one more point. Mr. Casey asked me to bring you back."

Victor slowly raised his head and looked him in the eyes. "I beg your pardon?"

Nedrof realized his mistake and back-pedaled full speed. "I mean that, uh, if you don't mind, of course. We'll pay for your trip, first class."

Victor's voice became icy. "I already have a ticket, and I'm comfortable in coach."

Nedrof hurriedly said: "Sure, no problem. If you need anything, just let me know, okay?"

"Sure."

Victor rose, and the others followed. The meeting was over.

Nedrof said. "Well, I think I'd better get going."

Ian asked: "David, do you need a car?"

"No, thank you. I'll get a cab to the embassy." He left, and the three men relaxed in their armchairs.

Ian said: "Victor, I have a lot of respect for the way you handled this sticky issue. You obviously understand politics and were kind enough to abstain from making the situation more difficult for everybody."

Victor chuckled. "I think you're the one who is a master diplomat. Look at the result. You get hold of a mother-lode of valuable information, and you don't even have to make a phone call."

Ian and Alistair cracked up. Finally Alistair said: "Well, it's not exactly like that."

"Yes, it is. But that's all right. I'd like to help you if I can. After all, my goal is to damage communism as much as I can. The CIA is deep in well-deserved shit, and they have to finally do what they promised. Let the bastards work. I've got what I wanted. And you'll finally get what you've been cheated out of for a long time. I think that's a reasonable approximation of justice."

Over coffee, Ian said: "Well, since we won't be helping you with your parents, we have to work out a way to reimburse you for your help?"

"No, thank you. First, a deal is a deal. Second, you've already helped me. Without you the CIA would never even talk to me about the issue."

"Well, think about it." After a pause Ian said, "In all honesty, I can't understand them. What are they thinking? To jeopardize the security of a source like you over such a minor issue is insane. Or is there something more to it?"

"Not much. They cheated me out of money, about a million dollars' worth, and on U. S. citizenship. That's basically all."

"Wait. Do you mean to say that they didn't provide you with citizenship, and you travel without a passport, just on a reentry permit, which stands out and raises an alarm at every border?"

"Precisely."

Ian shook his head unbelievingly. "Not to mention that you fully deserved it, they should have given it to you even if you didn't ask, just to keep you from roaming around with that fishy piece of paper."

Victor smiled. "The next thing you want to ask me is how much did they pay me, and don't know how to."

Ian laughed. "I have to watch out when talking to you."

"Well, so far effectively they have paid me about two hundred thousand dollars."

"What? And you say that they cheated you out of a million?"

"Yes."

Ian and Alistair looked at each other as if to ask, *Well, what's the next surprise from this guy?* Finally Ian said: "So, they alienated you and jeopardized the security of the information you provided—worth hundreds of millions of dollars—for just a million dollars, a citizenship, and a contact in Moscow? Forgive me, but that's very difficult for me to believe."

"It's true."

Ian suddenly asked: "Victor, can I ask you why you chose to go to the American Embassy in Warsaw?"

"I knew I would be more vulnerable to the KGB in London, but the decisive factor probably was, ironically, the issue at hand. For my security it was imperative that as few people as possible know about me. If I had chosen one of your embassies, you would have told the Americans about me, but the reverse is not true."

"You mean that you knew that back then?"

"Yes. Also, it's easier to 'disappear' in America than anywhere else."

For the next several days Victor was caught up in a very intense mix of work—involving both MI6 and the GCHQ—and fun. He was hosted on more tours of London, taken to theatres, and invited to dinners with stimulating, gracious companions. On some occasions Victor was joined by a veteran of British intelligence, John Pinto, and Stella Rimington, a rising star of MI5. John, a compassionate man with extensive experience in operations, seemed to have countless contacts around the planet and at all social levels. Stella displayed a winning combination of sisterly warmth and the no-nonsense demeanor of a counterintelligence professional.

On the evening before Victor's departure the gang—comprised of Ian, Alistair, Stella, Allison, and Victor—enjoyed a cozy dinner at a Portuguese restaurant.

Stella asked, "Victor, tell me something honestly. What was the most surprising thing for you here?"

"Let me think. Well, there was only one really surprising thing here. The people. I was expecting pretty much a bunch of snobs in top hats and tails. I was expecting formalities, coldness, and a total lack of humor. Instead, I found a lot of warm, caring people with very human emotions. I found a great sense of humor. I found a remarkable sense of dignity in difficult circumstances, and impeccable tactfulness. All that was a surprise."

Alistair asked: "Were you afraid at all that we'd use you to get the information from the Americans and then give you a cold shoulder?"

"Absolutely not."

Allison broke in: "Why not? You knew nothing about us."

"So what? You know that the CIA double-crossed you, and you know that they'll do it again. After all, you must have your own professional judgment of the CIA. You wouldn't trust their reports, however honestly given. You'd rather hear it from the horse's mouth."

Everybody laughed, and Allison said: "Oh, you cold-blooded bastard. Can't you ever just trust people?"

"Sure, as much as you can." The laughter was general.

Towards the end of dinner, Ian asked: "Obviously, we'd like to get as much as we can of your time. When can we see you again? By the way, needless to say, we'd love to meet your wife."

"Well, I'll be back here pretty soon, with my university class. See, part of the curriculum is a study of the British banking system. It'll take about four weeks, scheduled to begin at the end of June. I can stay a few days after that. But Olga's not coming then. Perhaps later, a month or two after graduation."

"Splendid. Let's plan on that."

11

Victor was busy putting the last touches on his MBA thesis. Basically mathematical, it developed a methodology that companies could use to determine the value of proprietary information, and a formula that would enable them to decide how much was appropriate to spend on providing security measures to protect it. Victor's math professor told him, "I'm the only one here who understands this. Great piece, but you'll have to go well beyond this university to have it used."

Soon after Victor's graduation Nedrof's lieutenant, Tom, a tall quiet man, delivered a tape to Victor. For the first time in three years Victor and Olga would hear the voice of his father or mother. Although it would only be "Hello," Victor longed to listen to it.

Victor turned the tape recorder on, inserted the tape, and pushed the play button.

"Hello." *My father's voice.* Victor felt his heart accelerating.

He was stunned by what he heard next: a male voice with a heavy American accent.

"Hello. Is this Peter?"

"No. You have a wrong number." *Father's voice—without a doubt.*

"Oh, I'm sorry. Is this 126-25-51?"

"No." He hung up.

After several moments, Victor heard an exact repetition of the exchange, except that his father sounded slightly annoyed.

When Victor turned off the tape recorder, silence filled the room.

Victor stood up and said evenly: "Well, Tom, thank you very much. I don't want to tie you up here."

"All right. I'd better get going. Let us know about delivering your letter to them, OK?"

"Sure. I'd like to listen to the tape a couple more times. I'll call you soon."

"I understand."

The minute Tom left, Olga asked: "Something's wrong, isn't it?"

"Yes. Very wrong."

"Why didn't you say something to Tom?"

"I didn't want to mention it to Tom, and I'm not sure if I want to mention it to anyone else in the CIA."

"What are you saying?"

"I'm saying that I'm not sure who's doing what around here."

After Victor told Olga about his instructions to Nedrof on how to place the phone call. She was stunned. "So, they violated every security precaution, right?"

"Right. The key question is why."

"Maybe your instructions got lost somehow in the chain of command?"

"It's not even a question of my instructions. You don't have to be an intelligence officer to realize what's going on here. Look, they know that the phone is monitored by the KGB. So, virtually every call will be checked out to be sure it's legitimate, right?"

"Of course."

"The caller pretended that he was calling someone named Peter at 126-25-51, which differs from my parents' number by only one digit. It doesn't take even a high school education to look it up in the phone-book and see if there's a Peter at that number. Obviously, there isn't. So, the call is a signal of some sort. And when it's made with a strong American accent, that's enough for the KGB to arrest my father."

"What if Peter really exists?"

"In that case the KGB would call him and ask if he had received any calls from someone with an American accent near the time of the call to my father. He would of course say no."

"My God, this is horrible. What's going to happen? Are they going to arrest your father?"

"Probably not. But they'd put him under blanket surveillance, use him as bait, and watch what happens next."

"Do you think it was intentional? Everybody makes mistakes."

"Not this kind of mistake. If the agent had only asked for Peter, he'd just be sloppy operationally. Sloppy enough to fire him on the spot. But he volunteered the number, a dead giveaway. Why? My father didn't ask him what number he was calling. One of the cardinal rules of intelligence is that you never volunteer anything unless you have a very good reason for it."

Olga sighed. "Well, it doesn't look too good then."

"Not to mention that I told Nedrof in detail how to make a safe call under the circumstances. That he didn't know the right way to do it just means he's not too good operationally. The point is he wrote it all down, and agreed that it was a good idea. And now this screw-up happens. Actually, it's not a screw-up, it's sabotage. I now have just two questions: why, and who?"

"So, what are you going to do?"

"I don't know."

"And that's why you didn't mention it to Tom?"

"Right. I need time to think. One thing is clear, though. Any attempt to contact my parents anytime soon would put them in great danger. I can't take that kind of chance with their lives. Now we must wait at least several months, perhaps a year."

It had been a bittersweet day for Victor. Although he had learned that his father was alive and at the same phone number, he had also learned that something was very wrong on his side of the ocean.

Victor's CIA-approved lawyer called.

"I guess congratulations are in order for getting your MBA."

"Thank you."

"Really, it's quite an achievement—for anybody. But for someone with a language disadvantage, it's doubly so. By the way, what're you going to do now?"

"Look for a job. It's not too easy, you know."

"Come on, with an Executive MBA I'm sure you'll get plenty of offers."

"True, but I have another disadvantage. I don't have a track record and references in this country, and that means a likely background check. For someone with a cover background that's a problem. The usual story is that the house you were brought up in burned down, your village was abandoned, no relatives are alive, and so on. But any decent background check will raise more questions than I care to answer. So, getting a job at a major company right off the bat is going to be difficult."

"I think you've met my law partner's brother Fred—a good friend of mine."

"Yes, a few times. The last time was at your birthday party."

"Right. So, Fred's looking for a sharp guy for his company."

"Is he in some sort of investment business?"

"Yes. And I mentioned your graduation to Fred the other night at the club, and he's interested in talking to you. What do you say?"

"I'd be happy to talk to him."

Victor made a few inquiries about the firm, and all the responses were very positive. In a few days Victor met Fred, a quiet, friendly man, in his office downtown.

"Well, Victor, I've heard a lot of good things about you from Rusty."

"He's very kind."

Fred got straight to business. "We work a lot with sophisticated, major investors. Some are corporations, some are individuals. So, there's plenty of room for romance, so to speak. But I must tell you that this is a cutthroat business. Only the strong survive. If you're not afraid of this jungle, we can talk."

"I'm not."

"What's your strength?"

"Well, I like finance, and I have a pretty good math background. I can analyze businesses, and I can be pretty creative in financially structuring a deal."

"That's precisely what we need. But I have to warn you again—this is a cutthroat business. Much of your income will come from your portion of our fees. In other words, you pretty much get to eat what you kill. Does that scare you?"

"No."

"Perfect. We'll make you a vice president. When can you start?"

Victor was the only student to have just one family member attending the graduation ceremony. Others had whole families; many had a dozen relatives to cheer them. Olga and Victor were content with that, but it was a little sad for both of them. The ceremony was formal but very joyful.

Both Olga and Victor were looking forward to the new phase in their lives.

12

A couple of months later Victor received a call from Jack that altered the flow of events. "Victor, you should come up here tomorrow, if at all possible."

"Anything wrong?"

"Yes. But don't worry about your family. So far." Victor got the message: the KGB was on his trail, and he'd find out the details in Washington.

"The reservation's already been made—your flight leaves at eight thirty. Pick up your ticket at the airport in the morning. I'll meet you here at the gate."

Victor anticipated he'd be shown top-secret documents in Washington; otherwise, Jack would have come to Phoenix. Victor briefed Olga on the conversation, and she was understandably worried.

"It must be very serious. What do you think, Victor?"

"Jack made clear that it is. But don't worry too much. If it was really serious, all of us would have left here by now, and somebody would pack our bags later. Jack didn't suggest that."

Jack met Victor at National Airport and drove him straight to the office. An attendant handed Jack a briefcase. Without saying a word, Jack took a piece of paper out of a briefcase and put it on the table in front of Victor. It was a photograph of a KGB cipher telegram informing KGB stations around the world that information had surfaced that Victor and his family had defected to the West and were alive. When Victor finished reading the cable he noticed that Jack was watching him intently, probably to observe Victor absorbing its implications and gauge his reaction to it. Making sure to conceal his emotions, Victor carefully read the cable again. Then he stood up, walked over to the window, and looked out.

What the hell is going on? Why are they doing this to me? Somebody went to great lengths to pull this trick. Who?

The cable was made out in the KGB Center format with the Center letterhead. Incredibly, it was in the format for incoming cables, while the cable itself was clearly outgoing. *Maybe they tried to disguise the cable to conceal their source from me? No way, the reference number confirms that.* Because the reference numbers on KGB cables started with "1" at the beginning of each year, the reference number on the cable he read didn't make sense to Victor—it wasn't at all in keeping with the traffic volume that would have been reached by this time of year the cable was sent. *Maybe they changed the ref number too, to conceal something else from me? No chance. There's nothing to conceal with the ref number. So, this is a fake—beyond any doubt. Besides, the photo was taken with a regular camera, not a miniature one. No one could've gotten away with using a regular camera inside the KGB.*

When Victor returned to the table, Jack had a sympathetic expression on his face. "Want some water, Victor?"

"No, thanks. But I'd like some coffee, though." Victor went to the utility room and poured himself a cup of coffee.

When Victor got back Jack asked: "So, what do you think?"

"Well, there's really not much to say. Tell me, what do you think, Jack."

"Well, I think it's very serious business. Luckily, they don't seem to know where you are."

"Sure. What else?"

"Well, look at the date. It's just after your trip to London. To me, it's a sign of where the leak is."

"Yeah. But it could be a coincidence, you know."

"Not likely. You know as well as I do—in this profession we don't believe in coincidences."

"That's true."

"All in all, it means that you have to be extra careful now."

"You're absolutely right."

After lunch together, Jack drove Victor to the airport; by dinnertime he was home. After Elena had gone to bed, Victor took Olga to their swing in the backyard, where he told her about the cable.

"It's really strange," said Olga.

"Strange beyond belief. Not to say that the damn thing was written by somebody who'd never written a KGB cable before. By the way, grammatically it was perfectly correct, but the KGB cable lingo is all off. Even if it was given to me as an intercept, I wouldn't have bought it."

"Are you sure the cable is a fake?"

"Of course, all of it. Look, I've seen thousands of these things. I know the KGB's procedures exactly. I'm one of those least likely to be fooled by something like this." Victor paused. "So, I still have the same two questions: Who? And why?"

"I can tell you why. To discourage you from working with the British."

"Yeah, Jack even hinted about that right away. But that's a rather obvious answer. Is there another one, that's not so obvious?"

Olga sighed. "Do you have an idea who?"

"Not precisely. For them to produce a thing like a forged cipher telegram isn't easy. They'd have to know the format of KGB cables and the correct letterhead—even the fact that it is known would be kept behind seven locks in the CIA. So, whoever gave the order must be very, very high up."

After a short silence, Olga asked: "What are you thinking about?"

"About the whole situation. Trying to make sense of what's been happening to us here."

Olga chuckled. "Any success?"

"No. But I can see a trend or two now."

"What do you mean?"

"Well, I've been cheated on everything that was promised to me. And, overall, we've been treated very badly."

"Victor, you're important to the national security of this county—everybody agrees with that."

"You're right. But the point I'm making is not just the fact of bad treatment—it's also the *way* it was done. Very bluntly, very flagrantly, as if someone was provoking me to revolt—to either go public, or defect back. In fact, I was told on several occasions by CIA people that all defectors quickly become alcoholics and die or, go public and then become alcoholics and die, or they go back to the Soviet Union."

"You're right. I've noticed that the idea of going public or going back has been carefully introduced to both of us. Occasionally somebody from the CIA mentions to us that a lot of defectors do that. You know, Victor, they really do seem to be provoking you, pushing you toward the edge."

Victor chuckled. "I'm glad you noticed. But why?"

"Beats me. It's definitely against the interests of this country."

"Go one step further. It is, however, in the best interests of the KGB."

Olga looked sharply at Victor. "What are you suggesting?"

Victor looked her straight in the eye. "My point is that somebody who acts in the best interests of the KGB—someone inside the CIA, a mole—is doing all these bad things to us. This guy keeps pounding, hoping for a fumble."

Olga was visibly alarmed by the suggestion. "If there were such a person here, I'm sure that we—or at least you—would be dead by now."

"Not necessarily. If anything happens to me, it would trigger one hell of an investigation. Because few people know about me here, and fewer still know where I am, the circle of investigation would be so small that any bad guy would shiver at the prospect of being thoroughly investigated. In intelligence, once you have attracted the attention—that's the end of the game. Besides, even if he can do whatever he wants in the CIA, he can't control the NSA, who would investigate as well. So, it would be much too dangerous for him. He needs to vastly increase the circle of people who know my whereabouts so he can be just one of many potential suspects."

"And the KGB wouldn't touch you, to keep him alive?"

"Yes, that's one explanation. Not too likely, but possible."

"What's the other?"

"If he has a brain, he'd know that if the KGB learned about me they'd most likely act. So, to keep himself from being investigated and found out, he simply wouldn't report my existence to the KGB. Moles not reporting certain things is quite common. The instinct of self-preservation is pretty strong, you know."

"So what would this guy do?"

"He'd put pressure on us, try to force us to do something that would allow a lot of people to know about us—and then strike."

"But how could he pressure us with so many others watching?"

"Well, from what I've observed, it's not too difficult for a mole to manipulate the CIA. He can play them like a violin, and get them to do what he can't do himself. See, the easiest people to manipulate are the manipulators. But it's dangerous to speculate any further, at this point, anyway, until I have much more information."

After several moments Olga asked: "There's another thing. Does that messed-up phone call to your father fit in?"

"Actually, it fits in perfectly. If the bad guy gave specific enough orders to make the call in a particular way, it would be done without question. He could have designed the thing specifically to blow it, and then blame it on me."

"How he can blame it on you? You described a totally different procedure."

"Sure. But who knows about that? Only Nedrof and the British. Nedrof might not have reported that I asked for a specific procedure, or might not have specified the details. The British are far away, and nobody would bother to ask them. So, strictly speaking I don't know who ordered that procedure, but it could easily be attributed to me. How do I know what was reported—or by whom?"

Olga shook her head. "If there's a mole in the CIA, he should either just leave you alone, or, if he's bold enough, try to develop good relations with you. Wouldn't that be a safer scenario for him? That'd mean we have to look carefully at our friends."

"Not necessarily. When we disappeared, the KGB immediately examined all the documents I ever read. Standard procedure."

"How would they know what you had read?"

"Every time you read a top-secret document, like a cable, you're supposed to put your signature on it. Once in a while it doesn't happen, but most of the time it does."

"So?"

"So, if one of those cables with my signature concerns a particular mole, he would be notified of a possible danger. That would happen

right after my disappearance, while the search for me was underway—
a standard precautionary measure." Victor continued. "I could well
have forgotten about that cable long ago. When you read thousands
of cables, as I did when I was a shift chief, that could easily happen."

"But if you've forgotten, that's the end of it."

"Not necessarily. What if I suddenly recall it? That could happen if
the mole got too close to me, tried to become friends. He could trigger
my memory."

"So, are you saying that under this scenario you're a constant threat
to him? He can't afford to identify you and get the KGB to kidnap you
or kill you because he fears being investigated, but he's also afraid to
have you around. Is that it?"

"Exactly."

"Boy, this would really make him dislike you."

"Of course. He'd see two solutions: either push me into going back
to Moscow, or doing something stupid that would reveal my identity,
and where I am, to a lot of people. Then, he'd move in for the kill."

"Why don't you go to the FBI and tell them all this?"

"With the evidence I have so far, they'd just laugh. They'd dismiss
it as a fantasy."

"You want to wait and do nothing?"

"Do I have a reasonable alternative?"

Olga thought for a moment. "Not that I can see, but I still want to
know the truth about a possible CIA mole."

"It should be apparent pretty soon. If my mole theory is correct,
the CIA has effectively lost all its network in Russia, but doesn't know
about it. In fact, their network in Russia is probably working under
KGB control. At some point, the KGB will roll it up."

"Why haven't they done it before now?"

"It'd be unprofessional. They must protect their valuable sources
in the CIA. Andropov, an old intelligence hand, understood that. But
now he's dead. A typical political decision at the top is to 'roll 'em' up'.
To do this, the KGB must prepare a diversionary operation that the
CIA will assume is the reason for the loss of their assets, to prevent the
actual source from being suspected. And that's not easy at all."

"Are you sure that we'd know about the roll-up?"

"In this country we'd probably hear about it. After some delay."

Earlier in the year the intelligence community had been excited over the defection of Vitaly Yurchenko, a colonel who worked in the security directorate of KGB intelligence, whose duties included maintaining security at Soviet embassies. Victor remembered communicating with him from Moscow in 1976-77, when Yurchenko was the security officer at the Soviet Embassy in Washington. Victor was responsible for supervising the installation of the cipher communications center there, a project that required the utmost security.

In the fall of 1985, Yurchenko caused great turmoil in the West when he decided to re-defect to the Soviet Union, and announced his intentions at a nationally televised press conference at the Soviet Embassy in Washington. Everyone wondered why.

While watching Yurchenko's press conference with Victor, Olga said: "Victor, I think I know why he re-defected. They mistreated him. I just feel this is true based on bits and pieces I've picked up."

"I'm pretty sure you're right."

At that moment television commentators appeared on programs covering the press conference. Victor flipped through the channels, navigating past commercial breaks. In a few minutes it became clear that their opinions leaned toward Yurchenko being a false defector from the very beginning, who'd been planted to embarrass the CIA.

"What do you think about that, Victor?"

"I think it's the biggest load of baloney I've heard all week. I can understand that reporters knowing little or nothing about intelligence came up with that idea after reading too many bad spy novels. But coming from all these experts—it's unbelievable. It's nothing more than CIA-staged damage control—to put a political spin on the situation."

"You don't believe in false defections?"

"It's only possible in military intelligence during a war, when information is highly perishable—often valid for just a few hours. You have to make up your mind almost immediately whether or not to believe a defector, based on having little or no information about his background. In peacetime it's a different story. If someone defects, investigators already know about the defector's background, the position he held. They know what information he's supposed to have, and not have. A good investigator can figure out very quickly whether the guy's for real or not. If a guy comes to you and gives you twenty pieces of easily verifiable, worthless information, and then gives you an unverifiable 'crown jewel,' that leads you in a particular way in a very important decision that you have to make, you've got your answer. In fact, you have two answers: one, that the guy is a fake, and the other that your enemy wants you to go in a particular direction."

"It's that simple?"

"Nothing is simple in intelligence, but a real professional would know it right away."

Around this time a new face showed up on television—Alex Costa.

Victor and Olga knew about her. A courageous woman, Alex had been stationed at the Soviet embassy in Washington when she defected in 1978 with her two small children, as part of a complex FBI operation. She left behind her husband, a promising career in sociology, and all her possessions. Given her credentials, she was hoping to find a professionally satisfying job in the United States. She was deeply dismayed when the CIA offered her a secretary's job, and humiliated her in a variety of other ways.

Hence, she chose to break ties with the CIA. Displaying enormous energy and optimism, she won her MBA from the University of Pennsylvania's Wharton School of Business and launched a successful independent career.

To Victor's gratification, Alex took a firm and correct line in her televised comments on Yurchenko's re-defection. Putting blame squarely where it belonged—on the CIA—she described their blunders point by point. Her frank, informed commentary was a gust of fresh air.

Olga observed: "She knows what she's talking about and obviously has lots of guts. I hope we'll get to meet her one day."

Later they did, and became good friends.

Years later Victor learned an interesting fact about Yurchenko: one of his CIA debriefers was a KGB mole in the CIA—Aldrich Ames. It wasn't too difficult to conclude that Ames was subversively and quietly encouraging Yurchenko's bad treatment, and that encouragement obviously fell on a fertile ground.

13

1985 promised to be a great year for the Sheymovs, with U.S. citizenship for all of them, Victor's new job, Olga's graduation coming, and Elena doing very well in school. They were happy. The future looked bright.

When Victor made his first deal shortly after joining the firm, his colleagues were startled. They said he'd been successful because he hadn't considered the possibility that the deal was unmakeable. By the time Victor had been with Roberts & Dobbs a year, he'd enjoyed more deal-making successes and had acquired all the accoutrements of a successful executive: a Mont Blanc pen, a Rolex watch, Savile Row suits, an assigned parking space in the basement garage. In short order Victor was a member of the most prestigious tennis club in town and, more important, the exclusive Phoenix Business Club. Getting in was extremely difficult, and being a member gave him significant status. Even as one of the youngest members, Victor rubbed shoulders easily with the most powerful business people in town. Exactly one year after joining the firm, he was promoted to senior vice-president.

When Olga teased Victor about his power business trappings, Victor chuckled. "I'll get rid of these toys, don't worry. Remember, I'm just a rookie. When you begin the game you follow all the conventions, whether you like them or not. When you're well established, you can follow those you choose."

Olga laughed. "Oh, don't worry. I enjoy being a member of a great country club, and things like that. I don't even mind going to the charity balls. What I find funny is seeing how you, of all people, manage to put up with these conventions."

Over Christmas the Sheymovs spent two weeks skiing in Vail. Towards the end of the vacation, Olga and Victor were sitting by the fireplace in their room, and Olga began a serious conversation.

"Victor, needless to say, your career is going beyond anyone's expectations. Of course, I'm very happy for you. I'm also very happy with my painting and I'm looking forward to graduating from art school soon. We also manage to keep abreast of what's going on in Russia. All this is good and well. But I still can't forget our conversation after the CIA showed you that faked cable. Since then, we've had very little contact with the CIA. Do you expect this to go on?"

"I'm not sure I'm with you."

"Well, I have a feeling that something's going to happen in that area sooner or later."

Victor smiled. "I'm sure something will happen, and soon." He noticed Olga's expectant expression, and continued: "It's been more than a year since they made that stupid call to my father. It was too dangerous to try to deliver a letter after that flop. I've been wondering how to establish contact with my parents without setting them up. You know, I may have found the answer."

"What's that?"

"This year will be the thirtieth anniversary of the victory over Nazi Germany. Obviously, there will be huge celebrations. Both my mother and father ended the war in Vienna and were stationed in Austria for a few months before returning to Moscow. So, I'm thinking there's a chance that the KGB would let them go to Vienna in May for the festivities. That could be a perfect opportunity to contact them."

"How would you find them there?"

"There is one "must" place they would surely be, the memorial to the Soviet soldiers who died there. So I need to go there in advance, to check the place out, to formulate a plan."

"How're you going to go– you don't have a passport?"

"The CIA will provide one."

"Are you insane? What about the possible bad guy there?"

"If only a few people know about my trip, he wouldn't dare try anything—on the same theory I suggested before. Besides, to conduct any operation, you need time to prepare for it. That's exactly what I'm not going to give them: time to prepare."

"When do you want to go?"

"The sooner the better. But I'll need to wait for an opening before bringing it up."

Victor's opportunity came just a few weeks later, when Jack flew down to Phoenix to talk about citizenship.

"Victor, I know the five-year anniversary of your arrival here is coming up pretty soon. But I'm afraid there are a few difficulties. As I told you before, you've been a member of the Communist party, and the law is that you need to wait ten years instead of five. That's what our lawyer told me."

"Is that the same drunkard you brought here a couple of years ago?"

"Come on, Victor. He's an alcoholic. It's an illness, you know. Anyway, this is the Agency position."

"Jack, you know as well as I do that the rule stipulates that the ten-year requirement doesn't apply if there was an 'effective break of affiliation.' The CIA has to step in and testify to that effect. So, I don't see any problem."

"The problem is that our organization is not willing to step forward and acknowledge your contributions to this country's security. For *your* security's sake. They don't want you to attract undesirable attention."

Victor said in a low voice: "You keep throwing this crap at me...and now you're saying that you're doing it for my sake?"

"Yes."

Victor lowered his voice even further, almost to a whisper. "All right, then. Let me tell you something. If the court hearing on my citizenship does not occur before June 15th this year, I'll go to Congress and inquire whether the CIA's position on my citizenship is justified."

Jack's demeanor changed from friendly-sympathetic to very serious. "I hope you're only having fun at my expense, Victor."

"Not yet. But I will, when the CIA is faced with a Congressional investigation."

"Okay. I think this is the wrong move. But all I can do is report it to the top."

"Do that, Jack." Victor took a deep breath. "By the way, I'm going to Austria in two days. For your information, I'll be going through passport control in Vienna with the frickin' re-entry permit. That's the only document I have for international travel."

"You can't do that, Victor. You know that."

"Yes, I can. And I will. Do you want me to show you my ticket?" The ticket had been bought the same morning that Victor learned that Jack was coming to Phoenix.

"You know damn well that this is dangerous. You know that the KGB does pretty much whatever it wants in Vienna. You know they're looking for you now, you saw that cable. So, why?"

Victor's voice became reminiscent of Morris the Cat. "Businiss. When you've got to go, you've got to go." In a normal voice Victor said, "As for the risk, yes—I'm aware of it as well as you are. Remember, you created this danger, and you'll have a lot of explaining to do if anything happens to me there."

"Victor, I think you're going nuts. There's no reason for such hostility, you know."

"That's a very odd statement, coming from the CIA."

"When's your flight?"

Victor went upstairs, brought down his ticket, and gave it to Jack. He wrote down the particulars in his notebook, which Victor regarded as significant.

The next evening Jack called and said: "Victor, I have your passport for the trip. I'll accompany you."

"What? I don't need a chaperone."

"It's not that. Regulations, you know. I'll carry your passport. You are not a US citizen, so we cannot give you a US passport. There's no other way. I'm booked on the same flight. See you at the gate."

On the flight, Jack had managed to get a seat next to Victor's. After landing at London Gatwick, they'd take an Austrian Airlines flight to Vienna.

"Victor, seriously, what're you going to do in Vienna?"

"Some business, some sightseeing. Nothing spectacular."

"As you wish. If you don't want to talk about it, you don't have to talk about it."

Victor laughed. "This is the first reasonable statement I've heard from you in a long while." Jack smiled, and Victor continued: "Jack, I'd like to get some things straight right now—to avoid any misunderstandings later."

Jack nodded.

"This is a private trip. If you can't trust me with a passport, okay—that's ridiculous—but I'll go along with it. You can carry it as long as you want. What I don't want to see is you poking into my business—where I'm going, when I'm going, and so on. Is that clear?"

"But Victor, I have to know where you are at any given moment."

"Why's that?"

"Oh, just in case." After several moments, Jack continued. "Well, what if I drop dead, or something? Your passport is with me."

"Oh, Jack, don't worry. If you drop dead, I'd go to the police, say that you stole my passport, and they'd get it back for me. No problem." They both laughed, and then Jack mumbled: "It's a pleasure working with you."

At Gatwick Victor bought a good tour guide to Vienna, which he studied during his flight. Arriving in Vienna around lunchtime, they checked into the Europa a small but comfortable hotel located on a side street in the middle of the tourist district. Because the hotel was not well known to travel agents, it was uncrowded and quiet, which suited Victor's purposes perfectly.

After lunch Victor went outside. He planned to go to the Russian War memorial at the far end of Schwarzenberg Platz . First he strolled around the tourist district, feeling at ease with his environment. Operationally, Vienna was his kind of turf. Similar to a Russian city in layout and very different from any American one, Vienna was a maze to anyone unfamiliar with it. Not surprisingly, the KGB trained its foreign intelligence cadets here.

Within ten minutes Victor spotted Jack trailing him. Victor led him away from his target area for a half-hour, making sure that Jack fell into a comfortable surveillance routine and suspected nothing unusual. Then Victor ducked into a crowded store, quickly exited through a side entrance, doubled back, and began tailing Jack.

Victor smiled because Jack, having lost him, didn't panic. Instead, Jack showed no sign that he'd lost his target as he began methodically searching the area. After allowing Jack to search for five minutes, Victor closed in and tapped Jack on the shoulder from behind. "Hey, handsome, looking for someone?"

Jack jerked sharply around and looked at Victor with his mouth agape.

"Look, Jack, I don't care what's in your report, okay? I told you, leave me alone. That means leave me alone." Victor grinned at Jack, who was clearly embarrassed. "If you get on my tail again, I'll lead you deep into the forest, and then lose you there. You'll be lost, and the wolves will eat you up. Do we have a deal?"

"Do I have a choice?"

"No."

"All right, it's a deal. But promise me that if you get into any sort of trouble, don't be a hero. Just leave a message for me at the hotel."

"Okay. Deal."

Victor took a taxi, and went back to his hotel, but didn't go in. He walked to Karlsplatz Square, only ten minutes away, and began assessing it. On the left side of the large square were government buildings; on the right stood the prestigious Imperial Hotel. At the far end of the square he saw what he came to examine: a typical Stalinist-era memorial to the Soviet soldiers who had liberated Austria.

As Victor neared the memorial, he imagined the anniversary-day celebration scene. *The crowd will be standing here, facing the memorial during the gathering and placement of wreaths.*

Victor scanned the area, trying to find a suitable vantage point that would allow him to study the faces of the crowd without being seen himself. Nothing. He strolled behind the memorial, where he saw a palace behind a row of trees. A perfect location, except that the spring foliage of the trees would block his view. After Victor entered the grounds and walked up to the palace, he stopped in his tracks as he read with sudden relief the brass plaque next to the entrance: "Hotel Im Palais Scharzenberg Platz."

Obviously exclusive, the building clearly had not been conceived as a hotel. *Must be twenty to thirty rooms, no more.* Victor looked at the windows facing the square; the only rooms high enough to give him an unrestricted view of the square were those on the top floor, probably quarters for servants of the previous owner. In a top-floor room of the hotel, which was situated behind the memorial, Victor could inspect every face. *Perfect.* He had achieved his primary goal.

The next morning Victor set off for the local tour bureau, where he picked out an old man in the uniform of a tour guide to show him around Vienna, figuring he would know the city much better than anyone young. Victor's guide arranged for a car and driver, and they spent the whole afternoon cruising the streets of the city.

Victor casually turned their discussion to the war, and learned who had been where during wartime Vienna and shortly thereafter. Thus, he found out where the Soviet Army had fought—those would be the places his mother and father would likely visit.

In his hotel room Victor marked every location on his map while his memory was still fresh. Now his mission was done and it was time to get out. He called Jack.

"Jack, I've finished up here. We can catch the last flight to London if you wish, or we can go in the morning."

Jack hesitated just enough for Victor to take notice. Victor asked: "Any problem, Jack?"

My son's stationed in Germany. He's coming here tonight to see me."

"Fine. You want to stay longer?"

"I'd prefer to leave tomorrow, if you don't mind."

"Sure. Make our reservations for any flight you want."

Victor hadn't expected Jack to invite him to meet his son. Victor tried to bail out, but Jack insisted. At dinner Jack seemed pleased to introduce Victor to Michael, an electronics engineer who was a personable, intelligent young man.

On the way back, Jack and Victor stopped off in London because Victor needed to spend a few days consulting with British Intelligence. When he told them about Jack carrying his passport, the British intelligence officers reacted with disbelief, which turned into a general uproar. When the laughter subsided, somebody asked: "Come now, Victor, are you really saying that our American cousins sent a man with you just to carry your passport?"

"I'm serious. Ask them, if you want."

"A miserable passport, the loss of which would do no harm to anybody! How do you feel about it as a taxpayer?"

"As a taxpayer, or as anybody else, I'm pissed off."

"I don't blame you. I've heard a lot of stories about the Company, but this one is certainly one of the most bizarre."

While Victor worked in London, Jack was free to roam around and shop. During their flight to the US, Jack seemed elated. "You know, Victor, I haven't been to Britain for a long time. My grandfather came from Scotland, so I was delighted to spend a couple of days there. By the way, I bought a few things in London."

Victor was familiar with Jack's parsimonious ways. "What did you buy, Jack?"

I got a genuine bobby whistle for Elena, and an overcoat for myself."

Victor smiled. "I'm sure Elena will be delighted." Jack knew her tastes well.

"I decided, what the heck. I've had my old coat for fifteen years now. It's pure cashmere, but kind of worn. So, I bought a new one, also pure cashmere. It'll be good enough for another fifteen, you know." Jack was clearly pleased with his purchase.

When Victor returned to Vienna in the spring, Victor stayed first in the Europa hotel. The day before the anniversary celebration, he checked into the Im Palais Scharzenberg. With keen anticipation Victor prepared to make contact with his parents. When he failed to spot them among the crowd at the memorial, disappointment flooded through him. Victor's gamble had failed. Victor remained determined that he would succeed someday in making contact.

14

The CIA was forced to give in. In June, a Phoenix judge presided over the Sheymovs' citizenship hearing in a room closed to the public. The three Sheymovs were in attendance. Jack was accompanied by Richard, the CIA alcoholic lawyer. But this time Richard appeared sober, though he reeked of cologne that Victor smelled ten feet away. Richard's argument before the judge was an elaborate one that cited, in overblown generalities, Victor's important achievements and valuable contributions to the national security of the United States. Richard said nothing concrete or substantive; he couldn't because he didn't even know who Victor was. Victor frowned in consternation when Richard implied that he was somehow responsible for his client's heroics.

Yet Richard's presentation impressed the judge, who was a kind man. "So I understand, sir, that you were his case officer during all these dangerous events?"

Victor glanced at Jack, and both fought to keep from smiling. Victor wondered how Richard would get out of this one.

Richard responded, "Not exactly, you honor. I could not do that because I was on a different assignment at the time. I wish I could say more."

"That's perfectly all right. I understand."

The friendly judge ruled to grant the Sheymovs US citizenship. Richard hurriedly offered his congratulations and vanished— presumably to go straight to the airport. At home, the Sheymovs celebrated their long-fought victory with Jack, who offered a toast: "Victor and Olga, I've seen a lot of people come to this country, and I don't know anyone who deserves more to be United States citizens than you. I propose this toast to you both, and Elena. I wish you all happiness in this country."

Victor was touched when he noticed that Jack's eyes were a little wet. His voice had also cracked slightly during his toast. Unusual for flinty Jack Decker.

During the remainder of the evening Jack was still uncharacteristically emotional. As often happened, Olga noticed something that Victor didn't. In a sly voice she asked: "Jack, I observe something on your hand which was not there before. May I ask a personal question?"

Jack blushed. "All right, all right. I should've told you before. I just got married."

All the Sheymovs congratulated him and gave him their best wishes. Victor saw that Jack was genuinely happy, and that he looked younger. He'd been married once before, but had divorced before the Sheymovs first met him. When Olga started teasing the newlywed, he said: "Olga, I'm not as old as you think. Sure, I have to take a few pills a day which my good doctor prescribed, but so what? Nobody's perfect. My health's fine, believe me."

Two weeks later Jack flew to Phoenix again to present the Sheymovs with their official certificates of citizenship. Victor felt that something was bothering him, but didn't dwell on it. Just before Jack was ready to leave, he mentioned that he had bought a boat. "Not too big, but it's comfortable. Next time you're in Washington, bring Elena with you. I'll take her out on the Bay, fishing. She'll have lots of fun."

"I didn't know you were into boating and fishing, Jack."

"I wasn't. But now's as good a time as any to start. So, will you bring her?"

"Sure."

The conversation turned to other things, and soon Jack was ready to go. "By the way, don't forget to send me your passport photos in a couple weeks, okay?"

"Of course, it's in our best interest, you know."

Suddenly something altered Jack's demeanor, as if a shadow had passed quickly over his face. "So, you trust me enough to let me take your daughter out on the Bay in my boat?"

Victor chuckled. "Sure. If I trust myself to sail with her, why not with you?"

Jack spoke rapidly: "Oh, I'm running really late. Good by, Victor."

Jack shook Victor's hand, and rushed out the door.

Two days later, Victor had just come home early from work when the phone rang. It was Jack. His voice was all business—a man in a hurry.

"Do you remember the photos we discussed last time I saw you?"

"Yes."

"Do you actually have them now?"

Victor was puzzled by Jack's curtness and the urgency in his voice. "Yes."

"Send them to me immediately by Fedex."

"Okay. Will send within an hour." What was wrong? "Jack, can you talk?"

" No. No time."

"All right."

"All the best to the three of you."

"Same back. Thanks, Jack."

"Yeah." Jack hung up.

Victor grabbed the photos and took off for the downtown Fedex office to get there before it closed.

When he came back Olga was curious. " I'd say that was a little unexpected."

"I know. Jack asked to me send the photos as soon as possible. He had no time to talk and explain anything. So, I just did as he asked."

Seeing that Olga was worried, Victor said: "Look, there are a hundred different possibilities. He could be going somewhere in a rush, needed the photos so the processing of our passports wouldn't stall."

"I see."

"There's another thing I can think of. Maybe he's retiring, and wants to clear his desk. But that's highly unlikely. First, he's never talked about retiring, and second, people just don't retire in such a hurry."

Victor and Olga forgot about the incident. But not for long. Three days later the phone rang at home. It was the Chief of Resettlement.

"Victor, I have very sad news for you. Jack Decker passed away."

Victor paused, absorbing the devastating news.

"It's a great loss for all of us. Everyone liked him so much."

After several moments, Victor spoke. "What happened?"

"A heart attack."

"When's the funeral? I'm flying up."

"I'm sorry to say this, but I just returned from the funeral."

Bastards. The way Victor was brought up, to miss a friend's funeral, to not pay last respects was considered disgraceful. He said nothing.

"Look, I'm sorry. It happened so unexpectedly, we couldn't notify a lot of people. He had a great many friends. You're one of the first I'm calling."

"I appreciate it. Thank you. When did he die?"

"On Tuesday, in the evening."

That was right after he called Victor. Instinctively, he felt that something was wrong. "I see."

In another minute the conversation was over.

Olga was sitting nearby. "Who?"

"Jack."

"My God!"

Both fell silent.

With tears welling in her eyes, Olga finally spoke: "What do you think?"

"What can I think, if I don't even know what happened? It's easy to become paranoid, but highly inadvisable."

By placing a few calls to Washington, Victor learned nothing more of any significance. Every person he talked to said Jack died of a heart attack, and not much beyond that.

Victor came to Olga. "Nothing."

"Are you going to find out if he really had a heart attack?"

"Of course. But I have to wait for a few days."

"Why?"

"They know I'll be curious, and will try to make sure that I'm not snooping around. I bet I get a couple of calls about Jack in the next two or three days just to check that I'm here. I'll put them to sleep, and then go to Washington."

Just as Victor expected, he received several calls from people who discussed Jack's death and asked what Victor thought about it, to feel him out. He put on a good show by talking about the deviousness of heart attacks; they always come when you least expect. After the calls dried up, Victor flew to Washington.

Victor found it both odd and sad that Jack was not waiting for him at the gate at National. Victor rented a car, and drove to the hotel. That evening he called one of his old friends from CIA Security. "Hello, Don."

"Victor! Many moons, no see."

"Yeah. How're you doing?"

"Have you heard about Jack?"

"I have. By the way, I'm in Washington for the night. Care for a drink?"

"Sure. Just stop by. Or, I can pick you up."

"I'm already in a bar. I'd rather stay here."

"Sure. Are you all right?"

"Couldn't be better. Do you know that joint at Seven Corners, right near route fifty?"

"Yeah. See you there in about half an hour."

Victor got into his car and drove from his hotel to Seven Corners. He had deliberately chosen that bar because he had had drinks there several years earlier with Don and Jack.

The corner table where they had sat together, in what seemed like another lifetime, was vacant. Victor took it and waited for Don, who arrived shortly.

After greetings and small talk, Don suddenly remembered something. "Hey—something was bothering me, and I just realized what it is. This is the same place where you and I were sitting with Jack in 1981, isn't it?"

"It is."

"And you, you bastard, dragged me out here."

"I did."

Don grinned. "Now I get it. You smelled something strange about Jack's death, and you're snooping around, trying to get more out of me."

"That's right. Any objections?"

"Damn right, and strong ones, too. Why didn't you just tell me on the phone what you're after?"

"If I did, you'd given me a bunch of bull. And then it would be difficult to talk to you because you'd already been committed to a position."

"You old fox. Still operating, huh?"

"Not in the least. But when I'm forced to, I still can pull a thing or two."

"All right. What do you want to know?"

"What really happened?"

Don smiled. "A heart attack. Don't you know?"

"I do. Even more than that. Don't tell me all my effort was wasted." Victor hoped his bluff would work.

"All right. Then by now you probably know that it was a suicide."

That's what it was! Victor nodded as casually as he could, and said, "I also know that it was illogical."

"Oh, my God. You too are falling for those rumors. He was sick, Victor. That's all there is to it. He was taking tons of strong medications. Some could even cause hallucinations. He was very, very sick. We talked to his doctor. Apparently, he was getting very depressed because he was worried that soon he wouldn't be able to take care of himself. That would've been too much for his pride. So, instead of dying in slow agony, he chose a quick way out. That's all."

"How long was he that sick?"

"For a couple of years, I guess. But he never complained to anybody, you know him."

"Yeah. How about his family?"

"Well, they don't even believe it was a suicide. But that's normal. Usually the families don't believe that."

"Don, are you sure it was a suicide? Was it that clean?"

"Look. We got a call from his wife at night, saying that he hadn't come home. So, we went to the office to look around. A key from one of our rented offices was missing. Well, we went to that office with a spare key. I don't even want to tell you what we saw."

Dan waved to the waitress for another round, and continued: "It was a mess. A real mess. He took his big gun, I think it was a .45, and blew his brains out. Literally. It was all over the room."

"Any chance of a power play?"

"Not a chance. On the conference table there were several envelopes, sealed and addressed to different people. And a note, saying he 'can't take it anymore.' The headaches and the nightmares were apparently too much for him. His handwriting, no doubt about it. That's it."

"Must've been a real mess, with all those envelopes covered in blood and brain tissue."

"Not really. He was apparently sitting in a chair in the corner of the room when he shot himself."

"In the corner?"

"Yes, there was a small side chair in the corner, and he was apparently facing the room with his back to the corner when he fired. He body was lying like he fell from that chair."

Well, people do not sit in the corner of an empty conference room. They can be put there when interrogated, though.

"I see. What about his boat?"

"What boat?"

"I heard that he just bought a boat. Didn't he?"

"No. In one of the envelopes there was a complete list of his possessions, down to some pretty small things. You know how meticulous he was. By the way, I was surprised by how well off he really was. But no boat."

"Well, I must've been mistaken. By the way, since when do you guys jump into action when a wife calls to say her husband's late coming home?"

Don laughed. "True. Happens all the time, and nobody pays much attention. But this time, luckily, somebody decided to go and take a look. Can you imagine what a mess it'd be in the press if the police got there first?"

Victor said softly: "Yeah. That was real luck."

At home, Victor told Olga what he had learned, without the gruesome details.

"You know, Victor, it doesn't make sense to me."

" I agree. It may have been a suicide all right. All the letters, a suicide note. It's pretty hard to fake things like that." He paused. "However, I must say that the letters could've been in his safe for a while. People often have stuff like that in their safes. And the note could be forged."

"And all that you've been told, it's hearsay."

"True. But I'm relying more on his last call. It was just hours before his death. According to Don, Jack didn't talk to anyone after that. He was obviously cleaning his desk. I didn't get it at the time, but it was clearly a 'good-bye' call. Nobody can fake that. So it's likely either a suicide or he'd known that somebody was closing in on him and his chance of survival was low. What bothers me, even if it really was a suicide, is why?"

"What do you mean?"

"Well, you know Jack, meticulous, always in control, tight with money, not prone to making emotional decisions. Consider this: he buys a new house; he takes me there, tells me his plans to buy a grandfather clock and a rug for his study; he gets married; he tells me that he's going to write a book. He buys an expensive new coat, the first one in fifteen years. He looks younger, more energetic. And then, in a couple of days, he changes his mind about writing a book. He shoots himself."

"Besides, he wasn't really the kind of a man who'd be ashamed if somebody had to take care of him. He knew that he'd done a lot for others and wouldn't hesitate to ask for help in return. Once he even hinted that he was pretty well off and would be very comfortable after his retirement."

"What really bothers me is the boat. He buys a boat, doesn't tell anyone about it except us. He calls me to ask for some stupid photos just before shooting himself. What's it all about? When he called me, his mind was made up. But he was anything but emotional."

"Yes. It looks really strange."

"That phone call just doesn't make sense. He knew that he'd never get the pictures. So why did he ask for them? Was it some kind of message? If so, what was it?"

"It sure looks like it. Try to recall what he said, verbatim."

"I already have. Nothing that I can see there."

At that moment the phone rang. It was Don.

After talking briefly, Victor hung up and told Olga: "There was no call to me charged either to his office or home phone. Nor was the call charged to either of his phone cards. Another puzzle."

"How do you know?"

"I asked Don to check it out for me. He did. So, Jack either called me from somebody else's phone, which is inconceivable for him for security reasons, or used a pay phone, which would've been really unusual. But why?"

"I can see only one reason. He thought it was very important that nobody knew about that phone call."

"That's precisely the point. What's the difference to a dead man if the call is known or not?"

"Then, he saw a difference for the living. For you, perhaps."

"That's exactly what bothers me. He saw that difference, and I don't."

15

Victor was as busy as ever in his job, and found it very difficult to travel. The British Intelligence people understood that. Whenever an urgent matter came up, they sent an officer to Phoenix to talk to Victor. To address security and to accommodate Victor's distaste for the CIA "security," they introduced Victor to the FBI. Only the head of local office and a very experienced Special Agent, Wayne Jackson, were informed of Victor's true identity. Victor was given the FBI codename Tiebreaker.

One visit from the British took place in March 1987, when Victor's old friend John Pinto showed up. Victor picked John up at the airport in mid-afternoon, and they worked in his suite at the Doubletree Hotel until they broke early for dinner at a downtown restaurant, where Olga joined them. After dinner, John and Victor headed back to the hotel to finish up their work because John needed to go back to London the next day.

Sitting on a large piece of property, the brand new hotel was the only occupied structure in a complex that included office buildings and retail stores still under construction. After Victor and John turned onto the four-lane divided road that ran through the sprawling complex, they passed a construction fence on the right and a man-made lake on the left that bordered a quarter-mile of their drive.

John admired the lake that reflected the waning light of the day. "Beautiful. I like the scale of American developments, but this one is especially attractive. The lake makes all the difference—imagine how magnificent it'll be when they install the streetlights along here."

"You'll have to wait a few months, John. They don't start with the lights."

After parking the car in the hotel garage, they went to John's room and worked until one in the morning. Victor was tired, but John, having just flown from London, must have been exhausted.

"I really appreciate that you could make it on such short notice, Victor."

"No problem. Working with you is always a pleasure."

"I can now catch a morning flight to New York, and make an afternoon flight to London."

"Good. But right now you'd better get a good night's sleep."

Victor took an elevator to the garage and got into his car. He was anxious to get home because he had an appointment early the next day. He drove out of the garage, and accelerated briskly along the drive. Only then did he think about putting on his seat belt because of a security routine deeply embedded in his subconscious: Don't fasten your seatbelt when your car is at rest or when maneuvering in a tight space. If you do, you're a strapped-in sitting duck.

With the lights of the hotel receding behind, Victor faced total blackness. Just as Victor reached across his left shoulder to grab his seatbelt, he noticed a large dark car without lights parked on the opposite side of the drive, parallel to the construction fence. *What a place to break down.* The rear door window of the car, illuminated by the beams of Victor's headlights, was down. Victor watched the car closely, trying to see if there was anybody inside.

Suddenly a painfully brilliant flash of white light struck Victor's eyes. *I'm blinded! Ambush! Where's the turn?* Victor knew there was a curve ahead. *Where is it?* He almost stomped on the brake pedal. *No! I'll flip over.* He took his foot off the brake and clutched the wheel. *Keep the car going straight. My only chance.*

Victor felt a violent jolt as his car ran over the curb and careened down the steep embankment next to the lake. *Hang on. Keep the wheel steady.* The car impacted the shallow lake water nose down with a dull sound. Another bright light—his head smashing against the wheel.

Then, silence. Victor heard the sound of water flowing into his car, which was slowly sliding into the lake, sinking. *Concentrate! You can't pass out.* He turned off the ignition and lights. When he tried to open the door, his left arm didn't respond. With great effort Victor managed to push open the door with his right hand. Then he quickly opened the glove compartment and grabbed his 357 Magnum. *Notes in the attaché! Hurry.* With his right hand he lifted the attaché case and handed it to his left. He forced his fingers around the handle. His aching hand barely held. *Thank God it's not heavy.*

As Victor struggled out of the car, he felt sharp pains in his neck and right thigh. He glanced at the top of the embankment—no silhouettes. Waist deep in water, he closed the door with barely a sound, and slogged to the bottom of the embankment. *Get the hell out of here!* He wanted to run, but his legs refused. Badly limping, with gun in hand, he trudged toward the hotel with the embankment on his right. After covering some fifty feet, he stopped.

Who are they? How many? Why don't they leave their car and pursue me, finish me off? If the bastards do try to get me they'll have a fight on their hands.

Time to assess the damage. He carefully tried to turn his head, and was instantly sorry. His neck was obviously injured. *Careful. You can't pass out.* He poked at his left arm—pretty numb, but no broken bones. But when he touched his right thigh he clenched his teeth from the searing pain. Because of the total darkness he couldn't see blood, but he knew his leg was covered with it. Victor took his belt off and cinched it tightly above the wound on his outside thigh. He felt his leg below the wound. *No broken bones, and I can move. This is the first piece of good news since I left John. But I can't walk home in this shape. That's the bad news. Pity, it's just four miles.*

With difficulty Victor moved on a little more than a hundred feet and climbed slowly up the embankment, which was less steep here than at the crash site. He looked around, his gun at the ready. What he saw puzzled him. The black car was still there with nobody in sight. Then another car turned onto the road, a taxi. Now he clearly saw the rear door window of the black car had been raised, but no one was visible inside. He lowered his head to prevent his face from being illuminated by the taxi's headlights. After it passed by, Victor again searched for signs of life in the black car. There was something evil about that car—in its stillness, and absolute silence. *Well, whoever you are, if you're sure that waiting's in your favor—it's certainly not in mine. I'd better get going.*

Victor slid gingerly down the embankment to the shallows of the lakeshore and began walking slowly toward the hotel, limping heavily. After finally reaching a point directly opposite the Doubletree, he saw the taxi waiting at the main entrance with its "for hire" sign turned on. It's sight was so inviting. *No way. It could be a trap.* He moved further in the same direction, beyond and around the service entrance to get out of the black car's line of sight—Victor couldn't be positive that no one was inside. *What the hell's going on? Why didn't they follow through? It's not the KGB's style. They're not in the habit of getting shy in the middle of a hit.* Victor thought several seconds. *No, it's highly unlikely this is a KGB operation. But who else? Criminals? Not likely. Enemies? I don't have any around here. Was I mistaken for somebody else? Could be, but it's still weird.*

When he was in the clear, he crossed the driveway and limped to the service entrance. That it was brightly lit was a mixed blessing. On one hand, a greeting party would find it hard to hide nearby. On the other, he'd prefer more intimate lighting with his somewhat conspicuous appearance.

Victor opened the door decisively, still holding his gun. Luckily, nobody was around. He put his gun in the pocket, but it was bulky and heavy. He wedged it inside the waist of his trousers, behind, where it would be concealed by his jacket. With no belt, the revolver sagged heavily, but Victor had no other option. As he followed the corridor to the lobby, he remembered seeing a restroom sign there. *Where there are restrooms, there are pay phones.* He found three, none in use.

Calling John was out of the question; it would be utterly unprofessional to lead anyone to him. Besides, Victor had neglected to ask John about his official status here. Victor couldn't possibly attract attention to John and get him involved in an imbroglio. Victor dialed his home number.

"Hello," Olga said sleepily.

"Hi. Are you all right?" Victor suddenly realized he could only talk with considerable difficulty. He could hardly move his tongue.

"Sure. What's wrong?"

"I had a car accident."

"Are you all okay?"

"Yes. Can you pick me up?"

"Of course, but you sound like you need an ambulance."

"Not really. But something strange is going on—can't figure out what. You remember John's hotel?"

"Yes."

"Pick me up, uh, at the intersection of the street which leads to our village, and another street—the one you usually take to school. Do you know it—know exactly where it is?"

"Yes," said Olga, with deep concern in her voice. Olga knew Victor's predicament was serious; Victor hadn't given the street names.

"Be there twenty minutes from now. If you see anything unusual— *anything*—like a parked car, don't stop. Go home and call the FBI."

16

Victor was unaware that he'd just made a very bad mistake. After hanging up, he went into the restroom. What he saw in the mirror exceeded his expectations. His face was swollen, his nose was bleeding and obviously broken. Large hematomas under both eyes had begun turning burgundy-blue. His lip was torn and still bled. His trousers were blood-soaked and ripped open at his right thigh, which was numb and still oozing blood. Completing his grotesque appearance was his water-stained, heavily wrinkled Savile Row suit. With an elegant black leather attaché in his hand, Victor knew he looked truly ridiculous.

He tried to improve his appearance, but to little effect. He couldn't get the blood out of his white shirt, nor could he wash off much from his jacket. *The only thing not ruined is my tie. I've got to get moving.* By now Victor had spent four minutes in the hotel. That was already too long.

Coming out of the restroom, Victor's hand slid to his gun when he almost bumped into a man. But the old man in a tuxedo, a hotel employee, was clearly harmless.

Victor automatically mumbled: "Hi."

Not a muscle moved on the old man's face. "Good evening, Sir. I hope you have a good night." Like an old-school servant. Victor almost laughed as he limped off, as proudly as he could manage.

He slipped out of the hotel through the same service entrance, and walked to his right, away from the crash site. His eyes became used to the darkness again. When a car drove away from the hotel Victor saw by its headlights that the black car had vanished. *A mixed blessing. If they're still cruising around they can get me before Olga picks me up.* He kept moving toward the pick-up point, hiding behind trees and shrubbery to make sure he wasn't visible to passing cars.

As he approached the intersection Victor counted three police cruisers slowly passing by. *That's odd. In this neighborhood you rarely see one cruiser. Crime is almost unheard-of around here. Something must be going on.* Flagging down a police cruiser appealed to him, but Victor decided against it because he couldn't tell the police what really happened. If he did, he'd provoke questions that nobody in the intelligence community wanted. Besides, if he talked to a policeman outside of his cruiser with flashing lights, he'd be a sitting duck for the bad guys, who were probably still in the vicinity. Victor glanced at his watch, and kept limping along.

He didn't have long to wait in the bushes near the pick-up point. He spotted Olga's white car coming far down the road. No other cars or people were in sight. Victor stepped out of the bushes only soon enough to give Olga time to see him and stop. When he opened the right front door to get in, he saw car headlights behind less than a quarter of a mile away. Either it was a coincidence, or the car was following Olga.

Victor asked: "Have you been followed?" Instantly he realized that Olga would find the question offensive. He knew all too well that if she were being followed, she wouldn't have stopped.

But Olga didn't take it as an offense. "Don't worry, that's a police car. It picked me up right in our neighborhood. I guess he's just bored."

Victor was disturbed by what Olga had just said, but couldn't put his finger on why. "All right."

While Olga accelerated, Victor took the gun from his waist and put it in his attaché case, which he shoved on the back seat.

Olga tried not to show that she was worried. "The way you look, I'd rather take you straight to the hospital."

"No. I need to make a couple of calls from home right away. Anyway, it's not as bad as it looks."

"Are you sure?"

"Yeah. My neck is the only question mark. The rest isn't that serious."

Olga smiled. "There's a mirror in your sun visor. Take a look."

"Oh, you mean the nose. Don't worry, I've broken it before."

At that moment blue lights went off behind them. Victor sighed: "Oh, brother. Precisely what I need right now."

Olga stopped the car and took her driver's license out of her purse. While the officer walked toward them from his cruiser behind, she opened her window and held out her hand with her license. The stocky officer came up to the window and completely ignored Olga: instead, he pointed the beam of his flashlight directly on Victor's face. "Have you had a car accident?"

"I didn't collide with anybody." Victor had chosen his words carefully.

Finally the officer acknowledged Olga's presence. "Follow me, Ma'am." The officer walked back to his cruiser.

Olga looked at Victor. "Strange. The police are always so polite, particularly in this area. This guy didn't bother to say a word to me."

The police cruiser passed by and Olga followed. When the officer drove directly to the crash site instead of the police station, Victor was alarmed. *How could he possibly know? Nobody witnessed the crash— there was no activity whatsoever around at the time. While walking I was sensitive to any lights—only two cars passed by, but no one in them could've seen my car because of the steep bank around the lake. What's going on? The notion that the KGB can recruit local police officers at will is something you see only in the movies.*

Olga interrupted Victor's thoughts. "What happened?"

"Well, somebody made me run off the road—quite deliberately."

"With a car?"

"No, with a light."

"What?"

"Some kind of light gun, tremendously bright. Blinded me completely, just before a curve. I ended up in the lake near John's hotel."

"And then?"

"I got away, and so did they. This doesn't look much like the KGB. Those guys never stop halfway through a hit." Victor sighed. "The question is, how could this officer possibly know where my car is, and even that there was a crash in the first place. Nobody was around at the time, or afterward. I was watching pretty carefully."

The officer turned onto the four-lane road to the hotel and stopped exactly opposite the crash site—no more that twenty feet from the spot where the black car had been parked. The darkness was broken only by two pairs of headlights and the flashing blue lights of the cruiser.

Straining, Victor climbed out of Olga's car. When he limped across the drive and stood at the top of the embankment, he couldn't see his car. The policeman walked to the top of the embankment as well and turned on his flashlight. Only when Victor moved to the very edge could he see the very top of the roof of his car, which had slid further into the lake.

"Is that your car?"

"Yes."

"Let's go." The officer walked toward his cruiser and Victor followed, wondering how to keep the situation as low-profile as possible. Suddenly a new thought crossed his mind. *Wait. He never even asked me if anybody was riding with me. How does he know there isn't somebody in my car right now? How can he possibly know so much? Is he a real police officer? He certainly seems to be. What the hell's going on?*

While standing with the officer near his cruiser, something suddenly dawned on Victor. *That's what's wrong with what Olga said. Our neighborhood is two miles inside another county. How come this cop is roaming out of his jurisdiction at will?* Victor glanced at the side of the cruiser. It bore the insignia of the county in which he crashed, the county where all the Federal offices were located.

Now Victor thought he was ready for the unexpected. He was wrong. The officer turned to Victor. "You're under arrest."

Unbelievable. "I beg your pardon?"

Instead of answering, the policeman twisted Victor's disabled left arm and threw him on the hood of the cruiser, slamming his head against it. The sharp pains in his injured neck generated sparks in Victor's eyes.

"My God, what're you doing?" Olga's voice sounded as if she was far away.

And then, a thought exploded in his mind with burning clarity. *Idiot! How could you miss it? I should never have called Olga, I should have called the FBI.* He shouted to Olga: "Go home! Call the lawyer."

Olga ran to her car. Suddenly the officer released the pressure on Victor's left arm. He couldn't feel handcuffs, but was pretty certain they were there. Victor stood up, and turned around. He saw Olga in her car, apparently trying to start the engine. The officer rushed over, swung open the passenger door, and wrestled the keys out of her hand. He had only needed to say "Don't leave" to stop her.

Olga cried out in pain.

Trying to divert the officer's attention, Victor shouted: "You cowardly son of a bitch! Proud that you can beat up on a woman?" The officer's fat ass stuck out right in front of Victor and he wanted to give it a hard kick, but couldn't; his right leg was numb. The officer ceased harassing Olga, and got out of her car holding her keys. Victor looked him straight in the eye to challenge him, but the policeman walked to his cruiser and reached in for his mike. With a smirk on his face, he said: "Assault on officer! Assault on officer!" He gave no location, just his call sign.

Within one minute two police cruisers pulled up with two officers in each. Conveniently, one was a female officer. She and her partner arrested Olga; the other two concentrated on Victor.

Victor demanded to contact his lawyer. They ignored him, and told him to take a breathalyzer test. *This is a pretty cheap shot. I had two glasses of wine at dinner around 7:00 p.m. But with this setup I'd show something like fifty percent.* "Sure. In the presence of my lawyer."

"You can call your lawyer as soon as you take the test."

"No way. I'll have my lawyer present. Besides, I want a blood test—this is my right, I believe."

"Be reasonable—take the test. Then we'll let you call your lawyer."

Victor refused. Then he heard Olga say, "I have a daughter sleeping at home."

Olga had no idea what was really going on.

A sarcastic voice responded: "Don't worry, ma'am. We'll take her into custody, for as long as you're in jail."

"There's a dog in the house—he won't let you in." Victor had heard desperation in Olga's voice.

The same sarcastic voice answered: "Don't you worry, Ma'am. We'll shoot the dog."

There was silence. Then Olga said: "Who are you people? Are you sure you're Americans?"

In response Olga was thrown into the back seat of the cruiser, and driven away. One of the remaining officers said: "Okay. We'll go to the house, and you, Joe, take him to jail."

They never even bothered to ask for my driver's license or my name.

One cruiser carried Victor to jail, and another went straight to the Sheymovs' house—in another county. Victor was flooded with guilt, more than at any other time in his life. He had dragged Olga and now Elena into this ugly mess. By asking Olga to come get him he'd been totally unprofessional—downright stupid. How could he help them now?

Instead of being taken to the local precinct, or a county jail, Victor was driven to one in yet a third jurisdiction, three times as far away. Victor realized that by crossing the boundaries of jurisdictions the police hoped to conceal their tracks in the unlikely event of an investigation.

By now it was around three in the morning. Finally, Victor had time to think. *The whole thing was a setup. Someone just wanted me in jail. They knew I had a gun in the car. Not long ago one of the CIA guys asked what kind it was. So, using an armored car, they knocked me off the road by blinding me with a light gun, counting on my taking it as a KGB assault. All they wanted was for me to start shooting. That's why they didn't get out of the black car. If I started shooting, they'd claim that I assaulted them, and put me in jail. Who would believe a story about a blinding light? And then, after I was stuck in jail, they'd have me for lunch. Idiot! How could you not think of it earlier? Looks like a CIA setup. Who else could do a thing like that?*

During Victor's booking the police took everything from him, including his wallet. When they allowed him to post bond, as obligated by law, they agreed to take a credit card.

"Okay. My credit card's in my wallet."

"We can't give you your wallet before you're released."

Well, this fits the picture. "I think I'm entitled to a phone call."

"Yeah. The phone's right there, we can walk you to it."

"Can I have my change to make a call?"

"Nope."

"All right. I'll make a collect call then."

"This phone doesn't handle collect calls."

Victor was deeply worried about Olga and Elena. But he could do nothing now but wait.

All right. These CIA bastards have to show themselves one way or the other now because things didn't go exactly as planned—they have no choice. Besides, what can they charge me with? Losing control of my car?

17

Because Victor's holding cell was just around the corner from the front desk, he was able to hear a most welcome sound: John Pinto's clearly enunciated speech.

"Officer, I'm a senior diplomat on Her Majesty's service. I know that Mr. and Mrs. Schwartz were arrested and brought here. I'm a close friend of the family and I demand to know what's going on here."

"Sir, you're not a relative, are you?"

"To my knowledge, Mr. and Mrs. Schwartz were arrested immediately following a meeting with me. That puts me right into the situation. And my Government would like to know if the arrests are related to that meeting. Do you want to be the subject of an official note to the State Department from my Embassy in Washington?"

The desk officer frowned. "Well, Sir. I think we can probably work things out without making it into an international incident."

"That depends on you, young man. You can have it either way."

"Okay. I can tell you they've been arrested, and are being held here."

"Where is their daughter?"

"As far as I know, she's at home. Our officers couldn't get in."

"What do you mean by that?"

"I don't know, Sir. That's what I was told."

"Very well. What is the bond?"

"Two thousand for Mr. Schwartz, and five thousand for Mrs. Schwartz."

"Here—this is my credit card. Put it on that."

Victor heard nothing for several minutes. Apparently, a clerk was putting the charges on John's card.

"What are the charges?"

"Driving under the influence for Mr. Schwartz, and assaulting a police officer with the intent to kill, for Mrs. Schwartz."

"What? Are you out of your bloody mind?"

"That's what they are, sir."

"All right. We'll sort it out later. Just get them out of here. By the way, do they have a car here?"

"No. Both their cars were towed away."

Within half an hour all three walked out of the jail. Victor's briefcase was returned to him, no questions asked. In the taxi they barely spoke. Arriving at the Sheymov home they encountered Bernie, an FBI Special Agent who lived across the street, armed and camped-out in Sheymovs' backyard. For security reasons, he'd been told about Victor and Olga, and though he knew they were Russian, he didn't know their real names or who they really were. Bernie had been asked to provide assistance, if needed, using any appropriate force. Only the chief of the local FBI field office and another special agent, Wayne Jackson, were informed.

Victor asked, "What happened here, Bernie?"

"Oh, about three in the morning a police cruiser pulled up. They started their high-profile routine, you know. Were getting ready to break into the house." He paused. "So, I walked over, asked what's going on. At first, they tried to be rude. Then I showed them my FBI ID, and demanded explanations."

"What did they say?"

"Nothing, really. Started mumbling. Then I noticed that the cruisers were from another county. When I mentioned that they just backpedaled like hell and got out of here fast. That's all. But just in case, I camped out here, you know. Was gonna wait 'till morning to find out what happened. I didn't want to get the whole FBI field office involved."

"Yeah. Thanks, Bernie."

"What happened to you guys?"

"Not sure yet. Some sort of setup. I got forced off the road, and Olga was given a rough time for nothing. I'll tell you about it later. Right now I think we need a shower. But it's not the KGB—don't worry. Thanks again, Bernie."

Bernie smiled. "Any time."

When they entered the house, Elena was still sleeping.

John was agitated. "Victor, what in the world's going on?"

"I'll tell you in a minute. First, tell me how you got wind of what happened?"

"Olga called me."

Victor looked at Olga, who said: "Victor, I knew that something was seriously wrong. But I just didn't want to call our lawyer. I felt that John was our best bet."

John jumped in: "And she was right, Victor. Why didn't *you* call, for Christ's sake?"

"I didn't know your status."

"To hell with my status when somebody knocks you off the road." Looking intently at Victor, John continued. "Look. I know exactly what you mean, but we're not operating in a hostile country. I don't know what I would have done, all right? But Olga called, and she was right to do that. Let's just leave it at that. Okay, you'd better tell me what happened. It's important."

While Olga made breakfast, Victor briefed John thoroughly on what happened.

"That's really odd. Doesn't fall into any category, does it? Any ideas?"

"Yeah. Probably the CIA."

VICTOR SHEYMOV

"Victor, you really do need some rest. Why on earth would they do something like that?"

"For the same reason they've been going after me again and again. This time, they got me in jail, because that's where they really want me—ideally. Then they could do pretty much whatever they want with me. But their other objective was to deliver a psychological blow."

"I can't believe that."

"All right. Any better ideas?"

"Well, it's certainly not the KGB. Too grandiose, too clumsy not finishing the hit."

"Who else could be after me, John?"

"Nobody I'm aware of."

"That's the point. Things like that just don't happen on their own."

"Well, whatever it was, something went wrong, it didn't go as planned."

"Sure. They miscalculated. I picked up speed faster than they calculated—a turbocharged Audi is pretty fast. They thought that I'd just hit the curb, maybe bend the front suspension, and stop."

"Suppose so. What then?"

"Then, I'd think it was an ambush, and start shooting at that car. It was just sitting there, inviting me to do that."

"All right. So?"

"So, the car was armored, I'm sure. I wouldn't hurt anyone, just make a lot of noise. That's why the police cruisers, which you don't generally see in that location, were roaming around, waiting. So, they'd arrest me and charge me with an assault with a deadly weapon. Nobody would believe a story about a bright white light. I could claim I saw a flying saucer with the same chance of success." Victor inhaled deeply. "Well, the rest of it fits the picture doesn't it? A typical off-the-books operation."

"If that's the case, what if the whole thing blows up?"

"It won't, and they know it."

"Because of your cover?"

"Precisely. I'm the only one who could start bitching about it. If I do, my resettlement name and all the rest will go to hell. I'd have to start all over again."

"Well, I still have trouble visualizing the CIA doing this kind of thing. They're far from perfect, but this would make them incredible bastards."

"Okay, John. Just think about it. If you come up with a better idea—or any idea, for that matter—please let me know."

After breakfast the pain in Olga's inflamed hand, twisted roughly by the policeman, worsened. John refused to listen to Victor and Olga's objections to his canceling his flight. He called the British Embassy and asked them to send a courier to pick up his materials and take them to London.

They called a taxi, dropped Elena off at school, and recovered Olga's car. When Victor peered inside his own car, which was totaled, he saw that the gear shifter was broken. Observing that its sharp metal edges were stained with blood, Victor knew that the shifter was what had torn into his thigh.

John went with Victor and Olga to the hospital in her car. Olga's arm was put into a cast. Victor got a cervical collar for his neck, and rows of stitches in his leg and mouth.

By the time they left the hospital, Elena's school day was over, and they went to pick her up. John, the designated driver for the occasion, mumbled: "Christ! I might as well put a red cross on this car. Never drove an ambulance before."

Victor avoided his CIA-appointed lawyer, and contacted a sharp young lawyer in a large local firm and retained him to deal with the "accident" and its aftermath. John, who stayed on for several days, kindly executed an affidavit attesting to the facts as he knew them, and promised to return to testify at the trial if necessary.

18

Victor tried to obtain more information on Jack's death. When Olga asked him about it, Victor replied: "I couldn't come up with anything definitive. Drew all blanks."

Olga sighed. "He loved life so much. What could possibly have been the reason?"

"Certainly not his health, according to Jack. Anything but."

"All right, let's just think…what could be the reason for someone committing suicide, particularly a man like Jack? Blackmail?"

"Come on, show me someone who can blackmail Jack. Blackmail in intelligence, in my estimation, is grossly exaggerated."

"Why is that? We read about it all the time, someone being blackmailed by a spy."

Victor laughed. "Let me tell you a story. Some time ago a young and pretty French secretary at the NATO headquarters was targeted by the KGB. Very promising operation. They directed one of their local agents, I think he was a Spaniard, to seduce the woman. A very attractive and charming man, he succeeded. Of course, all the sex was clandestinely photographed. Then the big day arrived. A hotshot from Moscow flew to meet her. So, instead of her lover she faced a KGB officer at the apartment. The officer showed her the photos. A recruitment pitch would follow immediately. But the woman kept going though the photos with clear interest. She picked a few and asked "These are pretty good. Can I have them? I'd like to show them to my husband. See, he's cooling off for me lately. This can warm him up." Needless to say , the KGB guy was stunned, and had no choice but to vanish."

Olga laughed. "Is this a true story?"

"Yes. See, the point here is that most of the time if the blackmailee says 'no', what realistically can a spy do? Complain to his or her superior? They never do, except in very rare cases when they want to get someone out of his job and replaced by a more favorable figure."

He took a breath and continued. "The point here is that it rarely works, and only on some very weak people; it's damn near impossible to blackmail any intelligence officer worth his salt." Victor thought about it. "Wait. There may be a way to blackmail an intelligence officer from the inside—probably the only way."

"What's that?"

"If someone sets him up, leads him to do certain things, seemingly harmless at the time, and then suddenly puts those things in a different light—by lining them up in a certain way—the guy looks like he's committed treason."

"I don't understand."

"The key word here is 'do.' Suppose a guy asks his target to get some information which is, officially, inaccessible to the guy. But he's got a good reason for asking, of course—he's beyond suspicion. This sort of thing happens all the time in any intelligence organization. So the target complies. Then, the guy asks the target to do another thing, then something else. Again the target complies, believing he's doing these things for a legitimate cause, for somebody who's beyond suspicion. But, technically, the target has violated the official rules—repeatedly. We've all done it at one time or another. Does this makes sense to you?"

"Sure. Sort of going around the bureaucracy for a good reason, to get things done."

"Right. But then, all of a sudden, the man takes the target for walk, and tells the target he's actually working for—say, the KGB. The target's shocked, in disbelief. Then the guy tells the target, 'Look at what you've done. You've provided me—the KGB, that is—with lots of information they wouldn't have known otherwise. You've done things at my request that the KGB wanted. Who cares that you didn't know who the information was going to? The result's still the same. Now you're in deep doodoo. I can report you. But if you report me, nobody would believe you—you'd just be laughed at."

"That's horrible. But you've said yourself that Jack was a tough man—he knew all the tricks of the game."

"True. But it doesn't matter how tough you are. Every request made of you can be explained by at least two reasons. And one of them usually sounds legitimate. So, you comply. Especially if the guy who makes the requests is a superior—not necessarily a direct boss, but someone senior who's beyond suspicion.

"OK. And then what?"

"And then you're trapped, even though you haven't actually done anything wrong. You're already framed for the things you've done, and probably for other things you haven't. Of course, you could—and should—report the whole thing. They might go easy on you, or they might not. But, in any case, you can't escape your own conscience. Your professional pride is badly wounded, if not extinguished. You know you've damaged your own organization—nothing can change that. So, to your colleagues, you're a pariah. A tempting solution is to blow your brains out."

"If that's the case, why wouldn't Jack turn the man in, since he was going to commit suicide?"

"Knowing Jack, I'd say he did. But he would've done it indirectly, so that nobody could trace the man to him. Jack was proud of his professional reputation, and wouldn't have wanted his name dragged through the mud, even after his death."

"But nothing's happened since. If the scenario you've described is true, his message got lost."

"Well, this may be way-over-the-top speculation in the first place. All this stuff about a possible blackmail is a really wild stretch. Theoretically it's possible, but I personally don't think it was the case. If it is his message got lost…or got stopped. I don't know the answer. But I do feel that something big is behind Jack's death. It wasn't the suicide of a man whose health was rapidly failing."

"What about Jack's boat?"

"I couldn't find evidence that he registered one in his name, or his alias. But, he could've easily done so using one of a dozen aliases I don't know about."

Despite the fact that much of the CIA's contemptible treatment of Victor had been channeled through Jack Decker, Victor soon realized that Jack had been, in fact, the CIA's version of a guardian angel. For, after his death, troubles visited the Sheymovs in rapid succession.

Soon after joining Roberts & Dobbs, Victor had opened a money-market account at a bank other than the one "recommended" by the CIA. Pressed by Victor, Jack admitted to that, saying that it was just for Victor's own protection. They didn't close the account, to avoid triggering the CIA's suspicion, which could lead to wider scrutiny. The Sheymovs took care to pay their routine expenses using the CIA-recommended account, to which they made periodic deposits from their money-market funds. When the British intelligence service asked Victor to come to London for a consultation, he wrote a money-market check and deposited it into checking; it was enough to cover family expenses for two months—though he expected to be gone only a week. The day before he left Olga wrote checks covering most of the current month's expenses.

Having developed business connections in London, Victor had legitimate work to take care of there on behalf of Roberts & Dobbs. To account for the time he'd spend consulting with the British, he told colleagues that he planned to sightsee for several days after completing his work.

Victor's business took longer than expected, and ten days later he was still in London. When he called Olga one morning, she said everything was normal at home, except one thing.

"Darling, you sound upset. What happened?"

"Well, I just didn't want to distract you, that's why I didn't tell you earlier. There's a problem at the bank—with our checking account."

"What problem? I put more than enough money in the account right before I left."

"I know. That's why I can't understand why I'm getting an awful lot of phone calls saying my checks bounced. It's very annoying, and so embarrassing. Some people are very rude about it."

"I don't understand how it could've happened. Did you talk to the bank?"

"Yes. But I can't get hold of anybody who knows anything. They gave me the run-around, and keep bouncing our checks!"

"All right—don't get upset. Just go to the branch manager and demand an explanation."

"I've already done that. No use."

"Okay. Just hang on. I'll be home tomorrow and sort it all out."

Victor returned to Phoenix in the evening. The next morning, even before going to his office, he went to the bank. The branch manager was polite, but useless.

"Ma'am, I'd like to know what's going on with my account. Why are you bouncing my checks?"

"Mr. Schwartz, they bounced because you have insufficient funds in your account to cover them."

"That's not true." Victor put the deposit receipt in front of the manager. "This amount was deposited less than two weeks ago—it's much more than what's been drawn on my account."

The manager glanced at the receipt. "Your wife showed it to me a few days back. Unfortunately, we can't find the funds—the money's not in the computer. We're trying to trace the money. But, meanwhile, we have no choice but to decline honoring your checks."

"Did you contact the bank on which the check was drawn?"

"I understand we're in the process of doing that. I'm not involved personally."

"That bank confirmed to me that you received the funds the day after my deposit."

"Mr. Schwartz, I've told you everything I know. When and if I know anything else, I'll update you."

Victor heard nothing from the bank for three days; meanwhile, more checks bounced. When he called the bank's vice-president for customer relations, he elicited only a polite promise to "look into it."

Upset, Victor went to see Rusty, who said: "Banks around here usually don't treat people like that, you know. Maybe your CIA chums are playing games with you?"

"You know, I was thinking the same thing. Whoever it is, I'm mad enough to sue the bastards. They bounced a lot of checks without even bothering to notify us!"

"Cool off, Victor. You don't really want a lawsuit, do you?"

"No."

"All right. Let me make a few phone calls and straighten things out."

Rusty indeed sorted things out. He even extracted a letter from the money-market bank saying that a computer error had been made, and that the bounced checks were not the fault of Mr. or Mrs. Schwartz. There had of course been no error, but the bank was kind enough to admit the error they never made to help the reputation of a good customer.

While Victor was glad that the affair was over, Olga was still quite upset.

"Victor, do you believe that the whole thing with the bounced checks was accidental?"

"Very unlikely. It's probably the CIA. They matched us up with this bank, remember?"

"Yes, I was thinking about that. But why would they do a low thing like this?"

"To destabilize us. Why are we now getting phone calls every two or three days in the middle of the night—calls with nothing but silence at the other end? Same thing."

"What are we going to do about it?"

"What can we do? Go to local police saying that the CIA is harassing us with phone calls and messing up our bank account? They'd laugh, and put me under psychiatric care."

"Victor, this is a small town. People know us. Now the word's out that we write bad checks. You can't show this letter to everybody."

"I know. But—as I said—there's nothing we can do about it. At least for the moment."

A few days later Olga went shopping at the supermarket in their village. As always, she paid by check. She had just stepped into the parking lot with her cart full of groceries when she was pursued by a supermarket employee, who shouted: "Mrs. Schwartz, Mrs. Schwartz! We can't accept your check! You wrote bad checks here before!" While those in the village square within earshot stared, he wrested the cart from Olga, grabbed her arm, and forced her back into the store.

Having been humiliated in a place where many knew her, Olga came home in tears. She'd had enough. She demanded that Rusty file a lawsuit against the supermarket and the bank.

Olga's deposition was entirely convincing, and soon lawyers for the bank and supermarket offered sixty-thousand dollars to open settlement negotiations. Before Rusty could respond to their offer, the unexpected happened once again. The judge abruptly dismissed the case. The government had intervened, claiming that classified information of the utmost importance to the national security of the United States could be disclosed at trial. Moreover, he dismissed it with prejudice, meaning that the lawsuit could never be filed again.

Victor was livid. "Rusty, this means that anybody can do anything to me or my wife, and there's not a damn thing we can do about it!"

"You're right."

"But this is a double violation of my civil rights."

"You're right again."

"So?"

"So, you can try to sue the CIA for violating your civil rights. But I don't think that you'd get anywhere. They'd just kill another lawsuit as they did this one—because of the overriding interests of national security." He shook his head. "I'm sorry, Victor. But I can't help you here."

One day John came on very short notice. At the airport, with little prelude, John asked to go so some quiet place–he did not want to talk in either Victor's car nor at home. They went to a city square, found a bench, and John said, "Victor, we have a problem. The KGB is looking for you. They are sending someone to Phoenix. Soon."

Victor nodded. He knew he could not ask for details. John realized that and said, "We don't know the particulars."

"Well, we're lucky you know the fact."

"Yes. You have to get out of here, fast. We are prepared to host you in the UK for a while with full security provided."

Victor paused, thinking. Then he said: "Thank you. I really appreciate your help and hospitality. I think Olga and Elena should go, but I'll stay here."

"Why? This is wrong. It's not the time to be a hero."

"John, it's not that. This is a threat, but it's also an opportunity. If I'm gone, the next time we may not be that lucky. So I should stay here as bait. Did you notify the Bureau?"

"Yes, of course."

"Well, than they can cover me to see who's coming and take it from there."

"Victor, I understand your logic, but I really don't like it. Please get out of here and then we can discuss other security arrangements."

"No, John. I have to stay. Don't worry, I'll be careful."

John shrugged. "The hell you will." He paused. "But I know better than trying to persuade you. Just give me your word that if you feel uncomfortable, you'll get out of here."

"All right, I promise."

John just shook his head.

Olga, Elena, and John left for London the next day. They had a delightful summer in the UK, and enjoyed tremendous British hospitality.

Victor stayed back with the FBI cover, maintaining his usual routine. Nothing happened that Victor could himself detect. After some time the FBI told him that that the KGB visitor could not find Victor and had left Phoenix empty-handed with nothing to report. But the message was loud and clear—Victor, Olga and Elena had lost their cloak of invisibility. The KGB definitely knew they were alive, and they knew Phoenix was one of their possible locations. Victor never heard of any investigation by the CIA of how the information of Victor's existence had reached the KGB.

At the end of the summer Olga and Elena returned. Soon after their arrival Elena's school started, and the family more or less went back to their routine.

One Saturday, with absolutely no warning, Olga received a curt note in the mail from the principal of Elena's school stating that Elena had been expelled for "inappropriate behavior." No explanation, no teacher conference, no phone call. Just a short note.

Bewildered, Olga and Victor rushed to school on Monday. Apparently the staff there had been instructed to keep the Sheymovs at bay because at first they couldn't get past the receptionist. Only after stubbornly demanding to see the principal were they allowed to enter her office. Sitting stiffly in her chair, the principal—who had always been warm and gracious to the Sheymovs—was coldly official and visibly uncomfortable.

Victor got straight to the point: "Expulsion is a very serious punishment. Needless to say, we're very surprised by your decision. But what really puzzles us is that you gave us no explanation—and no warning—whatsoever. We weren't invited to discuss the matter with you or her teacher, or even given the courtesy of a phone call. I'm sure, madam, that you have an explanation, and we hope that we can hear it now."

"Mr. Schwartz, the explanation was given in our official note: inappropriate behavior."

"Can you be a little more specific?"

"During the computer introduction course, Elena keyed in a bad word that her teacher saw on the monitor."

"What word exactly?"

"Well, if you insist…'shit.' "

Victor and Olga looked at each other. Victor cleared his throat. "Well, I'm very sorry that it happened. As a parent, I'm obviously embarrassed, and I must apologize for my daughter's behavior." He took a deep breath. "However, I'd like to make two points. One is that—while not trying to excuse the act—I can assure you Elena didn't learn that word in our family. Since she hardly has an independent social life, she must have learned it at school. And the second point is that, in my humble opinion, this punishment seems a bit harsh for the offense. After all, this is her first serious infraction, and her grades certainly warrant praise—not to mention her numerous academic awards."

"Mr. Schwartz, I'm well aware of your daughter's academic standing. I know that all her grades are above ninety, and that her SAT tests come within the top five percent. But this isn't the point. She was expelled for unacceptable behavior, not poor grades."

Olga stepped in. "Excuse me, but I'm much more aware than my husband about what's going on in Elena's class. As you well know, I participate in all parents' activities here. I regularly talk to other mothers, as well as with Elena's classmates. It's my understanding that things similar to what Elena did have happened before in class—on quite a few occasions, unfortunately. Yet, I'm not aware of a single expulsion. As a matter of fact, a boy in Elena's class severely cursed his teacher in front of all the students just last week. Elena's offense pales in comparison with the language that boy used repeatedly. I understand that the boy's parents were called in for a conference with the teacher, but he wasn't dismissed—not even officially reprimanded. I'd like to know why Elena was singled out."

The principal showed irritation. "Mrs. Schwartz, it's the school's prerogative to determine punishment for student offenses, and we've done so. I prefer not to go any further into it."

Olga was undeterred. "I want you to understand that I'm very concerned about my daughter's psychological well-being, among other things. This expulsion is going to be a severe blow to her, a heavy burden she'll have to carry for a long time. Frankly, I fail to see the appropriateness of the punishment. So, I'd like to propose a compromise for the sake of Elena's psychological health. Why don't you let her finish this school year—or at least this semester—and then we'll transfer her to another school."

"Mrs. Schwartz, the decision has already been made. I'm afraid there's nothing I can do."

Victor understood. "Are you saying that this discussion is pointless, and we're just wasting our time?"

"Precisely, Mr. Schwartz."

"Well, then I must thank you for your kindness—and integrity, all directed to the well-being of the children entrusted to you."

In the car, Olga said: "I just can't believe it! I don't understand. She was always so forthcoming and friendly before. She was so disarmingly nice that I couldn't imagine her doing something like that."

"I can."

"What do you mean?"

"It's very simple. 'Give him a hard time'—remember?"

"Come on," said Olga, shaking her head. Then she suddenly turned toward Victor. "Oh my God. It was the CIA who got Elena enrolled in this school, wasn't it?"

"Right. In fact, they insisted on this school because they didn't want her in a public one. They said they could get her in easily. Obviously, they do whatever they want at that school. See, they've decided to take another shot at me. This isn't about Elena, but me."

"But Victor, this is so…so cruel. Hurting children to get at their parents is below anybody's standards."

"Except for the CIA's—it's in their culture. They really must be hiring a rare breed—people capable of doing inhumane things. Nobody could persuade a decent human being to do things like that. Almost any American I know, except those in the CIA, would say: 'I'm sorry, sir, but I don't do this kind of thing.' "

"You know, Victor, I really feel sorry for that principal. She's the one who actually had to do it."

The expulsion was indeed a traumatic event in Elena's life, with adverse effects that persisted into her adult years. It also put Olga and Victor, as parents, in a difficult position. They couldn't destroy Elena's respect for the educational system and her trust in the integrity of teachers—important role models—by telling her that both her teacher and principal were bad people. Neither could they explain to a child that CIA bastards had played dirty games with her life.

19

After the lawyer hired by Victor and Olga completed his investigation, a date for trial was set, nearly a year after the accident.

While waiting for trial Victor refused to have any contact with the CIA. Then, just before the trial began, the head of Resettlement showed up in Phoenix. When he pressed Victor for a meeting on "an extremely important security matter," Victor had no choice but to agree.

"Victor, this is so important to your personal security. You must understand that with a jury something sensitive could pop up at any time. So, my superiors told me to ask you to decline a jury trial. Just let the judge handle it."

"Let me get this straight. You set up a so-called 'accident,' you set up the police to rough me up and—what's worse—to rough up my wife, and now you're trying to tell me what to do?"

"Victor, Victor. You can't understand how upset we all are about this accident. I give you my word that we didn't set you up. That would be criminal."

"It is."

"From what I gather, there's a possibility that it was an ambush. We're investigating it. Quietly, of course. We want to know who did it to you."

"If that's the case, why didn't you go to the police and have them drop the charges?"

"Security. You know better than that. You can't rely on the police to keep secrets. But, we're certainly going to intervene on your behalf with the judge, who we'll ask to dismiss the charges. That is, if there's no jury trial. Only you can decline that."

"You know what? After being attacked and victimized, my wife and I had to spend ten thousand dollars for lawyers. Can you guess why?"

"Beats me. They offered you to let you plead guilty to greatly reduced charges—that would've been the end of it. Instead you stubbornly chose to fight, and now, almost a year later, it's still a ticking bomb."

"I can tell you why. Crimes were committed against my wife and me—but we're the ones on trial. That's totally wrong. And I hope that'll come out at the trial."

"I know, I know. It's your choice. I just want to make sure there's no jury trial, that's all. I guarantee you that the charges will be dismissed."

They parted without Victor making any promises.

The question of a jury trial came up again when Victor and Olga met with their lawyer.

"Considering the evidence we have, all the charges stink. If the prosecutor maintains that a five-four, one-twenty-pound, unarmed Olga tried to kill a six-foot, two-hundred-pound armed policeman, the jury would laugh. The charges against you, Victor, are more serious. Technically, you refused to take a breathalyzer test. By law, you're automatically charged with drunk driving. Not much we can do here."

"But I didn't refuse. I just wanted it done in the presence of my lawyer."

"That's what you're saying. I guarantee you that the policeman will say quite the opposite—and that'd be it. He'd be believed, and you wouldn't."

"So, what's your recommendation?"

"Jury trial."

"We have problems with that. When under oath, I'd have to tell the truth about some routine stuff—like past addresses, employment, and so on. Some sensitive things could come out inadvertently. To avoid this, the CIA would have to intervene. If they do, the jury would think that something's fishy. So, I see that as a Catch-22."

The lawyer thought for a few moments. "Well, you've got a point there. The impression will have been made. How many sticky questions could come up?"

"Nobody knows. Our whole cover background is a lie. Sure, it's a white lie necessary for our security protection. But it's still a lie."

"Well, you're the client. It's your call."

"I hate to do it, but we have no choice except to decline a jury trial. And the CIA said they'd talk to the judge—they promised that the charges would be dismissed."

"Do you believe them?"

"In this case, maybe fifty-fifty."

The trial for both of them was conducted in the judge's chamber. The judge' first comment was, "Oh, this is the case where I can't even ask the original names or national origin of the defendants?"

As the trial got underway, the Sheymovs' lawyer tried to play the improper-arrest card. Cross-examining the arresting policeman, he asked: "And so—you stopped Mrs. Schwartz' car, and then ordered her to follow you?"

Though he was under oath, the policeman testified: "No, sir. She followed me of her own free will."

"With her injured husband in her car, who needed medical help and her daughter alone at home she chose to follow you nobody knows where?

"Yes, sir."

"All right, officer. But how did you know where to go? You've testified that you hadn't seen the crashed car before"

"I got directions from the dispatcher over the radio."

"And how did the dispatcher get that information?"

"I understand that somebody called him."

After the arresting officer completed his testimony, the prosecution called a surprise witness—a night guard at an office complex across the lake, about a third of a mile away.

"What is your previous employment, sir?"

"I was a police officer."

"So, it was you who called the police about the crashed car?"

"Yes."

"Tell us how you came do that."

"Well, I looked out of the window and saw a car in the lake. So, I called the police."

"All right. What floor is your station on, sir?"

"Ground floor."

"And you can see the lake from the first floor of your building?"

"No."

"So, how could you see the car?"

"I was making my rounds of the building, and looked out of the seventh-floor window."

"I see. What was the color of the car that you saw in the lake?"

"I don't remember."

"Was the lake lighted?"

"No, it was very dark."

"Oh, it was very dark. And at one in the morning you happened to go to the seventh floor of your building, looked out, and just happened to see the dark blue roof of a car sitting in the middle of the lake a third of a mile away?"

"Yes, sir."

The judge suddenly jumped in: "I think everything's already quite clear to me. Further testimony would be a waste of time. The defendants are found guilty as charged. However, considering that these are their first offenses, I'm prepared to consider leniency for Mrs. Schwartz. Her sentence is suspended. Do you understand?"

Olga said: "What does that mean?"

"It means that you'll have no conviction—no criminal record— unless you break the law again. That's it."

All that transpired within a few minutes. Victor's trial never opened, and he was not asked a single question.

After the trial, Olga said: "This whole thing stinks so much—all I want is to just forget about it. Besides, I'd already lost hope of getting any justice."

John Pinto, who had insisted on coming from England for the trial, observed: "I've been around quite a few years, and I've never seen police officers lying through their teeth like they did here. And the judge knew it, but she didn't give a damn." He sighed. "Frankly, I've never seen a kangaroo court like this before in my life."

Victor responded: "It was that, for sure. But I'm aware of others that were like it—sponsored by the KGB."

20

Wayne Jackson, Victor's contact at the Phoenix FBI office, called and arranged a meeting that they routinely held once in a while.

Wayne was an FBI Special Agent. He embodied the best of the FBI: intelligent, laid-back, earnest and tough-minded. Always friendly, calm, and composed, he possessed considerable analytical ability combined with street smartness and, despite a teddy-bear demeanor, was always ready to spring into action. Victor was surprised to learn that Wayne had declined numerous promotions to management. He preferred to stay 'in the street'. Unusual for the FBI, he also stayed in Phoenix, taking care of his elderly mother.

They settled down at a table in a favorite small Southern BBQ restaurant in a less than glamorous part of Phoenix, and ordered without even glancing at the menu.

"What's up, Wayne?"

"Nothing much, just checking up on you. Is everything OK?"

"Yeah," Victor paused slightly, "I guess."

Wayne just looked at him quizzically.

"I have a funny feeling that something is brewing, but can't put my finger on it. Anything new on your side?"

Wayne became serious. "No. All quiet."

Victor nodded.

They attended to their perfect Southern pork ribs, the best in town. After some small talk Wayne said, "By the way, I talked to a couple of our guys during my last trip to Washington, the few that know about you at the Bureau, and they told me that the NSA is wondering why you're refusing to talk to them." Wayne glanced at Victor and added: "Frankly, I was wondering too. I understand that you have a bunch of reasons to send the CIA to hell, but why the rest of the US Intel community? They did nothing bad to you, and you're still working with the British."

"I didn't."

"What?"

"I did not refuse to talk to anybody except the CIA, and I explicitly said that to them."

"I can't believe it. The CIA told the NSA that you refuse to talk to any US organization."

"That's a lie. I can raise my right hand and state that anywhere."

"Incredible. Are you saying that if the NSA and the Bureau would like to talk to you, you're available?"

"Of course."

Wayne was clearly shocked. "OK, let me talk to our guys at the headquarters. I'm sure they'd want to get to the bottom of it."

Victor chuckled. "Good luck."

"Oh, and Victor, call me right away if you notice any slight thing, don't wait."

Victor nodded. Lunch was over.

The phone rang in the evening. It was Wayne. "Victor, what you told me last week caused quite a stir in Washington. Long story short, one of our senior guys from the Headquarters and one from the NSA are planning to come here to meet with you, they want to spend the whole day. Are you free next Tuesday?"

"That's fine. Thanks."

Victor told Olga what happened. She wasn't surprised: "By now not much from the CIA would surprise me. But still, why would they cut off everyone else if you refused only them?"

"The most benign explanation I can think of is just institutional "pride" – trying to hide their embarrassment. Other possibilities are more sinister."

Olga was silent for a while, and then brought up a sensitive subject. "Any ideas about what happened in your job, when a bunch of your deals died at the same time?"

"Not yet, but I'll find out. I still have a few friends around." Victor paused. "But one way or another, I think that we are better off moving somewhere else."

"A year ago I would've been very reluctant, but after all that's happened here lately I think it's a good idea. Somewhere where we'd be left alone by the KGB, CIA, and all the other 'nice guys'." Then she added, "If there is such a place."

Victor laughed. "There must be, but the Chinese would definitely be there."

"Victor, I'm serious."

"All right. There are two places where the CIA is not popular: California and New York."

"Well, we don't know anybody in California. Also, there are a lot of bad stories about both New York and LA. Where can you find a good job?"

"I guess, I can find a good job in LA, San Francisco, or Manhattan. New York is easier, I dealt with those guys, and a couple of firms hinted that if I want to move to give them a call. I've only had a few contacts with California companies, but I think that's still possible since I have a pretty marketable Executive MBA. All in all, New York would be a little easier, and with less uncertainty."

"Why don't we go to both places and drive around a little?"

"All right, let's start planning."

The Washington team arrived. Victor drove to a downtown hotel where Wayne introduced him to Robert Holderman and Bob Hanssen. Robert was head of Counterintelligence in the NSA. Bob was a Special Agent at the FBI Headquarters in Washington, managing an analytical unit within their counterintelligence division, working against Soviet intelligence. This combination told Victor that there were serious counterintelligence concerns in Washington.

Wayne made the introductions and kept a low profile. Robert took the lead. After the introductions he thanked Victor for agreeing to meet with them. Both men were very professional and clearly knew their business. Victor was glad to see from their good questions that they both understood the nature of the Soviet intelligence services. Bob Hanssen stayed a little back. He sported a laptop computer, a novelty at the time, and he was obviously comfortable using it. He was taking meticulous notes, and only sometimes posed some minor but very pointed questions. Wayne was very quiet, but his occasional remarks went straight to the point and really helped the discussion.

During their working lunch Robert casually asked, "By the way, we were really disappointed that we couldn't talk to you for a long while. We were told that you refused to work with anyone in the American intelligence community." He glanced at Wayne, and continued. "We were really surprised when Wayne conveyed that you indicated that that was a misunderstanding."

"I don't see any misunderstanding here. The CIA broke their promises to me, and very flagrantly. So I refused to work with them, but I explicitly stated that I'd be available for anyone else if needed."

"Are you sure—when was that?"

"Absolutely, right after my meeting with David Nedrof in 1982. I hope you can look into that."

"Well, it's not that easy to poke into a sister Agency's affairs." The other men chuckled. "But we'll try."

After they had dealt with the most urgent matters, Robert suggested they go out to dinner. As a good host Wayne offered his considerable local expertise in selecting a place for the evening. Victor agreed, but Bob Hanssen bailed out: "You guys go ahead, but after all we discussed today, I have plenty of work cut out for me to get my report done."

Victor smiled. "Come on, reporting can wait."

"Not this one. Don't worry, just go ahead."

At the restaurant the three felt at ease. Robert referred to himself and Wayne as the 'two street cops', and Victor was very comfortable with both of them. When he remarked that it was odd that Bob refused to join them, Robert replied, "Don't worry, he's just dull." Wayne added "Yeah, he has that reputation in the Bureau, but he's really very bright."

Robert carefully inquired: "Victor, our technical people asked me to tell you that they miss you. Do you remember James Dwyer? He especially asked to say hello."

"Of course, he's one of the smartest people I've ever met. Give him my regards."

"Well, I think you've guessed that they want to work with you."

"I understand – there were a lot of questions that weren't covered, at least not covered well enough."

"Yes, and we have some projects where your expertise would be especially valuable."

Robert paused. Victor noticed Wayne looking elsewhere, trying not to smile at the developing recruiting pitch. Victor occupied himself with his food and did not respond.

After a while Robert continued: "Are you open to working with us again?"

"Sure, they can come once in a while for a few hours of discussions. No problem."

"I mean full-time."

Victor laughed. "For ten bucks an hour, like it was back then?"

Bob was shocked. "Was that what the CIA was paying you?"

"Yes."

"Bastards. We didn't know."

Victor smiled. "Right."

Robert just shook his head. "Look Victor, we can pay you good money."

"Robert, I don't want to be rude, but let me just say that with my education and experience I can easily make a few hundred thousand a year. Besides, every time I get involved with Intelligence I come to regret it later. Even more importantly, I just want to be left alone. We'll move the hell out of here to someplace where the CIA is not popular like LA or New York so they will avoid me, knowing that I can arrange a pack of reporters to hunt them down."

Wayne chimed in. "Robert, Victor and his family have had some bad experiences here and, it looks like our friends from Langley had a hand in that. So I can understand why he's gun-shy."

Robert went on: "OK. Let's just leave it for now. But I can tell you that we all know you've done a lot for this country, and this country needs you now. You can contribute so much. It can't be about money, and nor about your treatment by some bad people in the CIA, and you know it. I'd like you to think about it. We would relocate you to Washington, provide your security there, rent a house for you and pay you as much as we can pay anybody. You work for a few years for the NSA, and then you can do whatever you want. This is a standing offer, just think about it. No rush."

After an uncomfortable pause Wayne asked: "Victor what are your plans now anyway?"

"We don't have any concrete plans yet, but I have a very good job offer in New York. Olga and I are going to go there to look around, check out the housing situation. Looks like it's a buyer's market now."

Robert just asked: "Are you comfortable with the idea of living in Manhattan?"

"No, we'll be looking in Connecticut and New Jersey.

Just before they parted, Robert asked: "Victor, can you visit our technical people just for a day, say next week? They really need you urgently on a couple of things."

"Sure."

21

It was time to go, but Victor still hesitated, sipping his breakfast tea in the kitchen. He heard the garage door open, and a minute later Olga entered the kitchen after driving Elena to school. She knew why Victor was not on the road.

"Well, just wanted to make sure that you are OK with what we discussed. You still want us to go public?" He sounded slightly apologetic.

Olga sat down. "Yes, enough is enough. Almost a decade under cover is enough under any circumstances, but what we've gone through is really too much."

"All right. I totally agree." Victor stood up and took his jacket and his attaché case. "But let's make sure we do it well, not in a rush." He kissed Olga and left for the garage.

In twenty minutes he was in the lobby of the biggest hotel in downtown Phoenix.

With a good supply of quarters, Victor chose a single payphone near the restroom – much less chance to have somebody next to you than in a large bank of payphones in the main lobby. He called his secretary to say he'd be late. After that he prepared a notebook and a pen, and dialed the *Washington Post* number. After encountering several assistants, he got through to a relevant editor.

"Hello. My name is Victor Orlov. May I have your name?"

"David Ignatius."

"I read an article in yesterday's *Post* that touched on the situation with the Soviet Orthodox Church. It's interesting, but it missed several important points."

"OK. What points?"

"The article implies that the KGB is monitoring the Soviet Orthodox Church. That's not deep enough. There were several phases of this penetration, starting with the 1917 Revolution, and the article does not address any of that. Furthermore, the Church is fully penetrated by the KGB. In fact, KGB officers were routinely trained at the Church's Spiritual Academy, were installed as priests, and had very successful careers in the Church."

"You seem to know the subject. Who are you?"

"I'm a former KGB officer. And I'd like to publish an article making these points, and a few others."

"Sounds interesting. But are you sure the KGB installs its officers in the church under the cover of priests? Do you have any direct knowledge of this?"

"Yes. I was personally tasked with recruiting young KGB officers for this purpose."

Now Ignatius seemed excited. But he was a professional. "We'd be very much interested in publishing your article but, of course, we'd have to verify your bona fides. Is Victor Orlov your real name?"

"Of course not. Unfortunately, I can't give you my real name."

"Well, this makes things difficult. We always must know who the real author is. We can keep your identity in confidence."

Nice try. "My defection was never made public. I appreciate your level of confidentiality, but it's out of the question. However, you can easily verify my bona fides through the CIA."

"Would they verify Victor Orlov?"

"No, I just made it up. You can tell them that I'm the first recipient of the highest grade of their intelligence medal. They'd know who you mean."

"And what if they don't?"

"Tell them that I'm prepared to provide more detailed information for verification, if necessary. Then they will."

"OK. When can I expect to get your article?"

"In a few days. I'll Fedex it to your attention."

"Splendid." He gave Victor his direct number.

Victor wasn't surprised when Olga received a call from the CIA the next day. She said very politely that Victor 'was not available'. No, she didn't know what he's doing now and what his plans are. Of course she'd take the message asking him to call back. And, by the way, she really had to run.

In two days Victor sent the article, and in two more days followed up with a phone call. This time Ignatius was available right away. "Victor, hello. I read your article, it's very good. But we need to edit it a bit. Do you mind?"

"Not at all, but I'd like to see the editing before it's published."

"Sure. By the way, as you predicted, the CIA verified your credentials."

Victor chuckled. "How did it go?"

"Oh, they didn't pay much attention to the inquiry, and said they'd call me back. They did. Two hours later, and they were in a panic. They asked two hundred questions—how did I know about you, what're you up to, and so on. While sounding indignant, they seemed to find some consolation in the fact that you are publishing under a pseudonym, and that it was the only name you gave me."

The article *"Putting the KGB in a Cassock"* was published in the *Washington Post,* and Victor was happy to receive some very good letters from readers.

22

Robert called and asked Victor to come to Washington for a week. Victor was reluctant because he wanted to spend more time with Olga and Elena.

Robert was insistent: "I'll tell you what. Why don't you come here, I mean all three of you. We'll take care of your wife and daughter, we'll show them around with a good guide. We'll entertain you in the evening. How about that?"

The invitation was tempting. He talked to Olga. Olga said: "You know, it may be a good idea, we need a change of pace. It could also be good for Elena to see the Washington Zoo and the Baltimore aquarium. We can go to some museums."

Robert was happy. In a week the Sheymovs were met at the National airport and driven to a hotel close to the NSA in Fort Meade, Maryland.

Next morning Robert took Victor to NSA Headquarters. Several people were waiting in a conference room. During the course of the day Victor saw some familiar faces, and some new ones. The atmosphere was friendly and professional. Victor was happy to see his old friend James Dwyer. Victor felt that he had been genuinely missed here. Also, he quickly recognized that these guys faced extremely challenging technological tasks.

At the outset Victor's disclaimer that he was technologically obsolete was met by James's quip: "Angling for a compliment? Stop it, Victor. You won't get one. I can only say that we'll get you back in shape pretty quickly." Everybody laughed. However, Victor did find he had to ask a lot of questions to get up to speed.

During the breaks the guys teased him: "We heard that you've become a capitalist. Bought yourself a yacht yet?" He sensed their resentment of his 'selling out' and tried to parry the criticism. He realized that it was not really resentment, but rather the slight arrogance of the intellectual elite. Basically, they were saying to him: "Look, you played that game for a bit, entertained yourself, and now it's time to get back to work, to do what the real men do."

The week went by very quickly. During the day Victor worked; Olga and Elena roamed all the tourist spots in Washington and Baltimore. On a couple of occasions they had delightful parties with the NSA people. One evening they were invited to Jim Dwyers' home and enjoyed a dinner with his wonderful family.

One evening, after dinner Olga said: "I really like it here. These are good people, the area is beautiful and quiet." Then it suddenly dawned on Victor that Robert was plotting to get Victor to Washington, and had decided to do it through Olga and Elena.

He looked at Olga suspiciously. "What are you trying to say?"

"Nothing, just that both Elena and I like it here."

"I see." Now Victor had another problem to handle.

Back in Phoenix Victor realized that it was time for them to move on. The question was where. Olga agreed.

"So you still can't decide which is better, Connecticut or New Jersey. I personally prefer Connecticut.

"But Victor, I am not sure I want to go to New York."

"Why?"

"I don't know, I just won't be comfortable there."

"All right, let's go to California."

"We don't know anybody there. How about Washington?"

Victor chuckled. "That's what Robert and his ladies were working on, isn't it?"

Olga just laughed.

"Look, in New York people don't give a damn about the CIA, and the CIA would think three times before attempting something that they've easily done here. They know that if they try that they risk getting into the media and ending up in a big Congressional inquiry. I can't work in business in Washington; the CIA is too powerful in that city on the swamp."

"Well, you don't have to work in business for a while. We can easily live on the money you can make with the NSA."

"Yeah, and forget all I learned in business school, and all my business experience? I'm too old for the technology, you know."

"It's not what they say."

Olga and Victor had several similar discussions. Victor never admitted that he also missed the technology with its distinctly different environment, but the feeling was there, and he was tempted by the idea. Finally, with a lot of misgivings, he agreed.

Fred wasn't surprised when Victor told him that he was finally leaving the firm.

"Well, I can only say that I am very, very sorry to lose you. However, I understand that under the circumstances it's better for everybody. Where are you going?"

"New York, but I may take a few months' break before going there."

"You know a few folks there. Do you want me to make a few calls too?"

"Thanks, Fred. I think I can handle it."

"Needless to say, I can give you the highest references."

"Thank you.

Victor made several visits to Fort Meade. On the way back to the airport one time Robert said: "Victor, thank you again for coming up here, I hope you're enjoying it."

"Yes, I am." Victor caught himself thinking that he missed that atmosphere of purposeful camaraderie and intellectual challenge. He quickly pushed the thought away.

"By the way, Bob Hanssen, the FBI guy who came with me to Phoenix, asked to talk to you at the airport for a few minutes. He has a few follow-up questions. I hope you don't mind."

"No problem, we have plenty of time before the flight."

Bob met them at the airport, and they went to a restaurant. After a short discussion about their business back in Phoenix, Bob changed the subject. "Victor. I heard that you and your wife are going to New York on a reconnaissance trip." He glanced at Robert. Obviously, they had discussed Victor's plans.

"Yes, next week."

"I was stationed in New York for a while, and know the area pretty well, and can be of help there." He paused. "I have a proposition for you. Our counterintelligence guys in New York would love to talk to you. How about spending a day with them. I'll show you around for two-three days, and we'll pay for the whole trip?"

Victor did not need to think. The FBI guys knew their areas better than anybody. That would be invaluable. "Sounds great, thank you." He had a couple of very attractive offers from Wall Street, so this would be ideal.

"Great, I'll call you tomorrow to coordinate."

The following week Olga and Victor were met by Bob Hanssen with an FBI car driven by a local FBI agent. With the light late morning traffic they were in the FBI NY office in no time. Olga went on a tour of Manhattan and Bob took Victor upstairs. He was introduced to the head of counterintelligence in the New York office and several other senior officers.

Pleasantries were disposed of very quickly, and they went straight to the issues of current FBI concern, mainly related to the activities of the KGB *residency* (station) in the UN.

In the evening they went to Connecticut and checked into a small but very comfortable hotel—the FBI definitely knew the best places around.

Now Bob Hanssen turned out to be a strikingly different man, nothing like the one Victor met in Phoenix. He was bright and sociable. He had a very dry sense of humor and had a knack for seeing hidden irony in many situations. All in all he was a good companion.

The next morning Olga and Victor were handed over to a local real estate agent, an acquaintance of the local FBI agent. She drove the couple around, showing them different small towns and neighborhoods, more than enough for a first reconnaissance trip. Olga and Victor liked the area very much. Olga remarked that everything was so expensive, even with the real estate market down. The realtor replied , "Well, this is New York's best bedroom community. You can't compare it with the South." That much was obvious.

The next day they went to New Jersey, and took a similar tour.

Waiting for the plane at La Guardia, Bob said: "Victor, I think your idea of moving here is a good one. You'll like it here, it's your kind of place—vibrant, fast pace, serious business, big stakes." He hesitated slightly. "Don't quote me on this one, but I know that the Fort Meade boys are trying to lure you there. They wanted me to persuade you too. I didn't try. You're better off here."

"Thanks Bob, I appreciate it."

On the plane back to Phoenix Victor asked, "Well, what do you think?"

"I am not sure I'd like to live in Manhattan. It's probably the numbers and diversity of people, combined with the size of the buildings with no space between them. The whole thing is so impersonal."

"I agree, but this is just a workplace, and most of the time is spent inside those buildings. So it probably doesn't matter except for coming into the city and getting out."

"You may be right, but Phoenix is so much friendlier." She paused. "I liked Connecticut more than New Jersey. I think we can be comfortable there, but the prices are unbelievable. Who can afford those houses?"

Victor chuckled. "I guess those folks who work in Manhattan. That's where people make more money than anywhere else. If I work on Wall Street, we can probably afford to live in Connecticut."

Olga shook her head. "It's so different from our environment. I have to digest all this."

23

The cumulative effect of the NSA's persuasiveness, Olga's leaning toward Washington, and the fact that Victor missed the noncommercial, cutting edge technical environment, was the Sheymovs' decision to move to Washington. Victor would work at the NSA as an independent contractor, which would improve his NSA income.

Even before the Sheymovs had finished unpacking, Victor was working full speed with the NSA. He found himself totally immersed in his old profession as he participated in consultations on counterintelligence matters and discussions on highly specialized and complex technical subjects. Victor's work was of two distinctly different kinds: technical issues, and security and counterintelligence problems. The

KGB was the first of the world intelligence services to realize that computer and communication security required close coordination of all technical, procedural, and personnel aspects. In fact, Victor had been the first in the KGB assigned to implement that concept. He was convinced of the viability of that strategy, and was advocating its adoption in the NSA. An obvious difficulty was that this approach required a lot of training in different areas. A decade later, during a trip to Japan, Victor was surprised and impressed by Japanese personnel policy. He was told that Japan now hired only people with an engineering degree for its police force, and only then trained them in traditional police disciplines. The NSA was receptive to the idea, and there were many discussions about how to incorporate this approach.

As before, Victor found the NSA crowd most pleasant and professional to deal with. Together they managed to find solutions to some sticky problems. Most people on the team were on very friendly terms, particularly when not involved in heated technical debates.

On one occasion their discussion centered around the NOB, the new office building of the American Embassy in Moscow. Built in the early 1980s, the Americans had allowed the Russians to handle its construction, even though it was known to the Americans beforehand that the KGB would stuff it full of eavesdropping devices. The Americans had assumed that they'd be able to find and neutralize all the KGB's gadgets.

One of the participants said, "The big question now is: What can we possibly do with that monster. What do you think, Victor?"

"Well, at this point, there's not much you can do. You should've listened to me when I urged you to stop construction, and do it yourselves using your own materials."

"Yeah. Unfortunately, that was a political impossibility. And it still is—we can't tear that building down. We've got to find another solution, even if it costs a fortune."

"Look. As I told you back in 1980, the eavesdropping system installed by the KGB in that building is a new generation of offensive technology. The interior can't be defended against it by any known means."

"Hell, if they installed it, we can either isolate ourselves against it, or disrupt it by selective disassembly."

"But look, that's precisely my point. You can't do that, it's not just a set of sensors planted here and there. It's a complete fully integrated system built into the structure itself —the first of its kind in the world."

"But you yourself found the same kind of approach used in China. You put it out of business, didn't you?"

"Yeah, but that one was purely acoustic. We shut it down by simply filling in the chimneys. The KGB's system uses acoustic, electromagnetic, X-ray, and radioactive-isotope components. It's much, much larger, and way more sophisticated. And, strictly speaking, it's not really an installed system—it's an integral part of the building's structure. The only way to disassemble it is to disassemble the building itself."

"Well, we're more optimistic than you are. We just have to find a viable solution."

"I'm sorry to be blunt, but you know damn well that there's been no meaningful advance in defensive technology in the last ten years— only a few minor improvements. Not nearly enough for the task."

"Well we have strong political pressure to do something. Look, Victor, we're getting off the subject."

"I don't think so—we're right on it. Why did you come to me? Because you have no technical solution and you're scared to tell that to Congress. Now, with me you have two options. One, I might provide you with a miracle. Two, if I don't, I'd concur in prolonging the agony."

One of the guys chuckled. "You have a nasty way of putting things."

"So, the answer is: I don't do miracles. And I'm not going to play this game. Again—a technical solution to protect the information in the building does not exist at the present level of technology—it's not even on the horizon. So, the only feasible solution is to tear the building down, and build a new one—properly."

"Suppose everyone starts playing it straight, which I personally doubt. Even then, we might not get the money to do what you suggest."

"I can tell you this: It'd be much cheaper to relocate all the handling of confidential information, including conversations, to Helsinki."

"That's crazy."

"Not as crazy as giving everything to the KGB."

"But how's the embassy going to function?"

"Very simple. You fly a shuttle from Helsinki to Moscow a couple of times a day. It's just a two-hour flight."

"Well. I must admit that, financially, it's a viable solution. But it's way too radical for anybody to swallow."

"I'm sorry, but I don't have any other ideas."

That issue was the only one, out of many discussed, on which Victor disagreed with the NSA experts.

Months later, at an NSA counterintelligence meeting, the topic of conversation was the aftermath of the scandal at the American Embassy in Moscow involving two US marines who were accused of having sex with KGB "swallows" and allowing access to sensitive parts of the old US Embassy building in Moscow.

One of the participants said: "Well, we're all under pressure after that affair with the marines in the embassy. Nobody's sure what's going on, and everybody wants to move to the new building. I guess it's partly psychological. What do you think, Victor?"

"I think there are loose ends dangling, even after the investigation. I hinted at that before."

"I know, but what's your basis for that?"

"I read Kessler's *Moscow Station,* and I think that he did one hell of an investigative job. Especially considering that he didn't have access to classified information."

"So, you agree with his conclusions?"

"No."

Laughter. "How come?"

"I really meant it when I said that he's done a great job. But he doesn't know the KGB—how it works, its style. So, he missed a lot of those almost imperceptible things, and came to the wrong conclusion."

"Well, what's your conclusion?"

"I think that the marines were set up by the KGB and then given away—to create a diversion." Feeling silent disagreement, Victor paused. "I'm serious. Something's wrong with the picture that's been presented."

"What do you mean?"

"Remember how one of the marines, Bracy, got caught by another American? Having sex with the girl who was the KGB informant in an American diplomat's apartment in Moscow?"

"Yes. So what?"

"Well, the KGB just doesn't operate like that. Period. When their person has a meeting in Moscow, they cover it. And they cover it well. First of all, they have enough secure places to accommodate the whole American embassy having sex at the same time, not just one marine. And they have enough manpower to guard them. You're telling me they couldn't guard a meeting with just one marine? If someone, by accident or otherwise, tries to interfere with a meeting, the KGB just won't let it happen—they'd stall anybody who tried. After all, they have all the tools at their disposal in Moscow. As a last resort, they'd fake a drunken brawl or a robbery just outside the apartment, and they'd kill or die before they let anybody interfere with a meeting in progress. Do you think they'd let an American and his wife in that apartment? Absolutely not."

"Well, that's interesting. So, you're saying that Bracy was blown deliberately?"

"I'd vote for that."

Another participant asked: "Are you also saying that they've deliberately blown their penetration of our secure areas in the embassy?"

"Yes."

"But that's insane. Why would they do that?"

"There can only be one reason. To protect something—or somebody—much more significant."

The faces at the table showed disbelief. "To give up access to everything? No way."

"It's not that far-fetched, if you recall the circumstances at the time. All the CIA's network in Russia had been lost." Referring to a young CIA officer who became a spy for the KGB, Victor said, "Howard couldn't be blamed for everything, we all know that. So, the CIA's search for another reason was underway. The KGB got scared and decided to take a loss—but a small one."

"That's too big to be considered a small loss, you know."

"Not really. At that time, everyone thought that moving to the new American embassy building was imminent. So, the KGB's estimated loss only amounted to a couple months' access. And this was when the CIA had just lost all its assets. Doesn't look like too big a loss to me."

"But what can be so valuable to justify this kind of loss?"

"I see only one possibility—a mole. A highly placed mole in a position to know a lot, if not everything."

There was silence at the table. Then Robert said: "But what about Lonetree? He came to us himself, and confessed. Surely the KGB can't stage that."

"The KGB probably figured that blowing Bracy would be enough—Lonetree's confession would be a bonus. However, the KGB could have induced Lonetree to confess. They've got some very good psychologists, and they're extremely effective at manipulating people."

"We had lots of chances to find that out during our investigations. It still sounds like a stretch to me. How would you make your asset confess to his government?"

"Suppose you tell the guy that something went wrong—somebody defected—and he's about to be caught. Surely they knew that Lonetree would dread the idea of moving to Moscow. So they tell him: 'We're sorry, but the best choice for you now is to confess. If you do, the Americans will give you a break—you'd probably end up with just a year or two in jail. After you get out, we'll take good care of you.' With an unsophisticated guy like Lonetree it could work. Lonetree would have no other choice in that scenario."

"But why blow two people when one is enough?"

Victor chuckled. "I can only speculate. Suppose they blew Bracy—or thought they did, but the CIA didn't take notice. They'd counted on the CIA being competent professionals, and were wrong. So, the KGB's stunned that the CIA didn't catch on. But the KGB still wanted to give the CIA an explanation for their losses, and wanted it quick. See, all sorts of investigations were going on at the time. So, when the KGB realized what happened, they laughed, then they cursed, and then fed Lonetree down the CIA's throat."

There was a long silence at the table. Then one of the participants said: "So, you're saying that it's possible that the KGB gave up a few months of technical penetration to save the skin of their supermole at the CIA?"

Victor nodded. "It's one possibility. Another is that the losses were overstated in the first place. Maybe the KGB didn't really penetrate communications to the extent that enabled them to read your cable traffic at will."

"You know, Victor, this sounds so wild that we need the time to comprehend it. But the funny thing is, it seems to make sense." He paused. "Well, any ideas about that supermole?"

"Well, if this theory's correct, the mole must be highly placed in the right part of the CIA—where he'd know all the details of their network in Russia. He can't be so high that he wouldn't be familiar with the details, or so low that he wouldn't have access."

"Well, that boils down to very few people in the SE Division, and counterintelligence."

"Correct."

The man shook his head. "So, if your hunch is correct, comparing what passed through the communications channels to what was lost should show a clear difference."

"That's right.

In a few weeks, when the hustle and bustle of moving had subsided, the Sheymovs turned to some unfinished business.

Olga asked: "Victor, what are you going to do about the CIA? Do you think they'll leave us alone now?"

"I can't count on that. You know, I could've just written them off if they'd persecuted only me. But now I can't—certainly not after what they've done to you and Elena."

"What can you do?"

"Remember what we were talking about before? Going public and raising our profile?"

"Sure."

"Well, now I'm almost finished with the preliminaries. I've published a few articles in well-known publications, such as the National Review, Christian Science Monitor, Forbes, and I'm close to finishing my book. So, I'm now in a position to speak out—and they'll have a hell of a time trying to shut me up. What would you say if we go public now?"

Olga was not prepared for that. "Darling, I'm scared. Everybody would figure us out very soon. The KGB would know where we are. I understand your logic, but there's a lot of danger in it—for all of us."

"But we discussed that before."

"Yes, but that was hypothetical. Now it's real. Too real for me. I have to think about it."

In a few days Olga returned to the same subject. "What about our security?"

"As we discussed before, our existence is either already known to the KGB, or will be very soon. So, why don't we make a preemptive strike and go public? See, the political cost to hit me immediately after that would be pretty high—it could be sufficient deterrence."

"Well, it's a little scary, but it makes a lot of sense. How are you going to do it?"

"First things first. I'm no longer that defenseless guy who couldn't speak English and had to accept all that CIA bullshit as truth. Now I know what this country is really about. It sure as hell doesn't have anything to do with the CIA. It's about ordinary citizens protecting their rights, and these people are represented by Congress. That's where I'm going to go first. After that I'll hold a press conference."

Still skeptical, Olga agreed.

24

Victor called the Senate Select Committee on Intelligence for an appointment. The next morning he met with a staffer and briefly laid out his predicament. This elicited a mixed reaction, but while much of what he said probably sounded fantastic, Victor demonstrated that he obviously knew and understood quite a bit about intelligence and the CIA. The staffer promised to get back to him.

The next day Victor was invited to come in for a talk with Jay Montgomery, a senior staff member of the committee. At first Jay was cautious. Victor wanted to smile as he imagined all the nonsense that the CIA must have fed to the Intelligence Committee in the rush of several hours the previous day. Realizing that Jay had to take into account that "information," Victor stuck to clear-cut issues that could be easily verified.

After a long discussion, Jay said: "Well, you have quite a few grievances here. Why don't we concentrate on those which are tangible."

"Like what?"

"Like the money. You claim that they cheated you. Money is always verifiable. Let's check that out first." Jay was an accountant and the Director of Finance for the Committee.

"All right." Victor gave a short summary of his financial relationship with the CIA, and put a copy of their fraudulent accounting sheet on the table.

As Jay looked it over, his expression turned incredulous. "Are you sure that this is what they gave you?"

"Absolutely."

Jay looked at the paper again and shook his head.

Victor added: "As a matter of fact, this paper was given officially by a CIA lawyer to my attorney. That should be easy enough to verify."

"It certainly should be. Let me get this straight: You're not only saying that this paper originated in the CIA, but that it was seen by a CIA lawyer?"

"Yes. And it was not just seen—it was officially presented as the CIA accounting of the money paid to me."

Although Jay appeared to be an easygoing, cordial man, his voice became icy-polite. "All right. We'll definitely check it out."

The atmosphere of the meeting had turned tense. In a few minutes Victor left.

Several days later Victor was called in. Jay took Victor to a secure room where they could speak freely. Now Jay's demeanor was markedly relaxed.

"Victor, I have to apologize. Frankly, I didn't believe you."

Victor smiled, nodding. "I understand."

"Not only me. I showed it to the Chairman, and he was convinced that you forged the paper. He said, 'It just can't be true.'"

"So?"

"So, it turned out to be true. The paper is genuine—the CIA had to admit it. They even had the nerve to express their indignation over the fact that you had a copy of this paper in your possession. They said that you've flagrantly violated the rules. That really infuriated us."

"So where are we now?"

"Well, we'll ask the CIA Inspector General to conduct an investigation. And we hope that you'll be a great help."

"The CIA IG? That's like asking a fox to inspect a chicken farm."

Jay laughed. "We can't really do it on our own. But don't worry, we'll be watching."

"Yeah. I'm sure that the CIA will buy a couple more paper shredders in a hurry."

"Oh, come on. They wouldn't dare destroy anything."

Victor responded with a sardonic grin.

The CIA Inspector General investigated Victor's complaint. As a result, the CIA was ordered to correct their "mistakes." This led to Victor meeting with Bill Camp, the deputy to Clair George, Chief of Operations. Bill was so outraged by what Resettlement was doing that he decided to spend his last year at the Agency heading Resettlement. Victor felt he was sincere, and respected that.

The CIA proposed to compensate Victor for the past shortchanging with a lump sum payment and a pension. Victor would have preferred a clean break with the CIA, but Bill got him to agree because of CIA budgetary restrictions, saying, "A big lump sum is difficult, a budgeted amount of pension is easy." Victor did not want to negotiate with them and agreed. All in all, the Sheymovs' financial situation improved. Most important was that Victor could now finance an operation to get his parents out of the Soviet Union.

Bill and Victor liked each other and became friends. They never discussed professional matters, so their friendship was only social. Victor had similar contacts with a few other people from the CIA, NSA, and the FBI. These men and their wives became part of the Sheymovs' social circle in the Intel Community. This group got together at the Sheymovs' house from time to time. The gatherings were strictly informal, definitely "off the record." Everybody enjoyed himself in a relaxed atmosphere.

Victor poured a drink for Olga. "Well, phase one is taken care of. Now, let's concentrate on preparations for phase two."

"The press conference?"

"Right. I'm thinking of getting it announced in an article in a major publication—*The Washington Post.*"

"Well, that should do the trick"

"It's not only important to select a well-known, respected publication, but the right reporter. There's always the danger of being used by someone to further his political agenda—with the result that my information would be twisted and misrepresented."

"So, you want to talk to the same editor at the *Post*?"

"Yes."

The next day Victor called David Ignatius, who was stunned to hear that Victor wanted a face-to-face meeting, and readily agreed to it. To prevent others from observing them, they met at David's townhouse in Foggy Bottom. Victor told him his real name.

"Sheymov? I've never heard that name."

"Well, very few people have. Let's just say that I enjoy a wide popularity in a narrow circle."

"So, are you prepared to tell me what this is all about—to tell me your story?"

"Yes—with some restrictions, though."

"Okay. Lay out the ground rules."

"You don't try to find out my resettlement name. No following me, no taking pictures, no recordings of any kind without my explicit permission. If by chance my resettlement identity becomes known to you, you'll treat it as classified information, which it is."

"Agreed."

"Also, I won't discuss any classified or sensitive information, the public disclosure of which could hurt the national security interests of this country. In other words, you can ask whatever you want, but don't press me if I don't answer."

"No problem."

"All right. Finally, I'll talk only about issues relevant to my activities prior to my arrival in this country in 1980. What happened afterwards is off limits—at least for the time being."

"Okay. As I said, it's your call."

More meetings followed because the editor needed to ask numerous questions about a variety of matters, some of them quite complicated, such as those that related to the KGB. Victor appreciated that the editor was careful to adhere to the restrictions they had agreed upon.

25

Victor needed help, and he asked Olga to do some research for him, which meant that she had to have security clearance. He

asked Robert to take care of it. When Olga was filling out the paperwork, she promptly listed the bogus conviction for the felony offence
of an assault on a two-hundred-fifty-pound police officer. Robert was
obviously familiar with the case, and he just chuckled "Don't worry
about it."

The surprise came a couple of weeks later, when the investigators
who had promptly followed the security clearance procedure discovered that there was no such conviction. Even Hanssen who had seen
more intelligence wonders than most counterintelligence people, was
incredulous. "Olga, we couldn't find any evidence of your conviction,
nor in fact any evidence of you being charged with anything."

"How about being injured by a police thug, being arrested and put
in jail?"

"None. Neither the police nor the jail have any record of you." So, I
can advise you that you have never been convicted, charged or arrested.
Make sure you remember it when you fill out future applications."

Victor quipped: "I wish the CIA was that efficient in their job
abroad."

The next day Victor called the lawyer who had handled their case
and asked for a copy of their case files. The lawyer, now a senior partner at that firm replied that it would not be a problem at all, but the
case was stored in the firm's archives, in some very secure place, and it
would take a week or so to get it.

Two weeks later he called. "Victor, I'm dumfounded. There's nothing there. I handled the case, and I remember it very well. However,
there's not a single piece of paper related to that trial in the entire firm."

"Well, Herb, what do you think?"

He paused. "Victor we all know the CIA was behind that trial. I
was uncomfortable then because they're not supposed to operate in
this country. Stealing records from a law firm representing a client is
unheard of. This is really outrageous. The bad news is that I can't see
what anybody can do about it."

Victor's routine became more congested. His main work was still
with the NSA. FBI contacts were infrequent and usually very focused, so

the FBI was not taking much of his time. All the contacts were through the FBI's designated liaison, Bob Hanssen. On a couple of occasions he traveled to New York, but mainly his work with them required a visit to the FBI Headquarters building on Constitution Avenue. After one such visit, at lunchtime Bob said: "Want to go to a place where there are real people?"

"Sure."

To Victor's surprise they walked to the Fraternal Order of Police Lodge 1. It was not open to the public.

People there obviously knew Bob. The staff greeted him, and he also said hello to a couple of patrons.

"I never knew about this place. Are you a regular here?"

"Not really, but I come here once in a while. I like touching base, going to the roots."

Victor liked the place. It was very different from all the downtown restaurants attended mainly by people who work for the Government or live off the Government, with lobbying everywhere. During lunch Bob told Victor that his father was a retired police captain from Chicago, and he added that that was the police department where his own law enforcement career started. "Yeah, I was in the internal investigations unit, keeping the cops honest. That's when the FBI made me an offer, and I accepted."

Victor asked about Bob's dad. "A police captain in Chicago! That's one tough job."

"Sure, but he was a tough cookie. But his utmost expertise was in the horses."

"Did he own horses?"

"No, he gambled on horse races. He knew horse racing better than anyone I ever knew. He made quite a few bucks at it."

It was a very pleasant lunch. On their way back Victor walked Bob back to the FBI building. Bob suddenly said: "I want to ask you something." That was a little unusual since their business discussion ended before lunch.

"Do you want me to go back in?"

"No. It's very sensitive."

So sensitive that it is not to be discussed in the FBI Headquarters? Hmmm.

They went to the internal courtyard of the building and sat down on one of the benches.

After some small talk Bob looked at Victor with that dark sparkle in his eyes and said: "Are you afraid to travel far?"

What kind of question is that? Victor laughed. "Bob, you know I am not. Why?"

"Can you go to Afghanistan with me?"

Victor laughed. "What are you going to do in Afghanistan?"

Bob did not answer.

"Will you go or not?" Then he added, "with full personal protection, of course, and me with you all the time."

"Conceivably, yes. But frankly I can't see what I can possibly do there."

"Well, this is really sensitive." He paused again. "We are going to ransack the Soviet Embassy in Kabul, and you can guide us to what is valuable there and where it might be hidden."

Victor could not believe his own ears. "You are going to do *what?*"

Bob backpedalled. "Well, it's not really we. It's one of the many Afghan mujahidin factions that is very friendly to us. We'll just stand by. After they storm and seize the Embassy, we'll move in, and quickly out. Kabul is going to fall soon anyway, the situation is very unstable there now. Nobody knows what's going to happen there next."

Victor was speechless. After a while he said: "Bob, whoever concocted that really should go to a good drug rehab."

Bob did not reply, and Victor went on. "Bob, I think that's highly immoral and unusually stupid. It's truly barbaric. Storming a foreign Embassy? To my knowledge it happened in history only twice, both times in Teheran. Once with the Russian Embassy in the mid-nineteenth century, and once with the American Embassy in 1979. I hate communism as much as anybody, certifiably. But it's wrong to do this to anybody."

Victor felt angry. He took a deep breath. "Apart from the moral side of it, can you imagine the fallout when it comes to light? Can you imagine the precedent it would set, and the retaliation that will follow, and fully justified?"

Bob's tone became conciliatory. "Well, it can be done cleanly."

"Bullshit. Everything comes to light sooner or later. So, make sure you act accordingly."

Bob did not answer again. Now he regretted raising the subject, and was looking for a way out. Victor was still upset. "Bob, I can't imagine that the FBI could concoct something like this, it's so bad."

"I never said it's FBI."

"Bob, let's just stop right here. The answer is that this is unbelievable lunacy, and I absolutely refuse to take part in it or discuss it any further."

The situation was still very tense, and Victor left in a couple of minutes.

About two weeks later Victor met Bob at a party. Bob took Victor aside, and said: "By the way, remember that Afghanistan trip I mentioned a while ago? Well, it's off the table. That Afghan mujahidin faction that was friendly to us was literally wiped out by a competing faction, entirely. Can you imagine that? So, forget the whole thing."

Victor looked Bob straight in the eye and quipped: "I'm glad it's been settled amicably." Bob just chuckled.

PART II

26

Victor's announcement to the NSA that he was going to go public stirred the Intel Community. His colleagues did their best to dissuade him. He listened patiently to everyone and politely disagreed. Victor did not want to engage in prolonged discussions about his decision, and just stayed his course. They were all frustrated, but there was nothing they could do. The CIA was particularly mad—Victor simply refused to talk to them altogether. However, a couple personal friends met with Victor and vividly described the horrors of dealing with the media, and warned him of the dangers of inadvertent disclosure of classified information, reminding him that he would be held responsible if that occurred. So the whole Intel Community was bracing for the fallout.

The one bright moment was when Bob Hanssen privately told him "Good, go ahead, do it." Victor was grateful for this sole voice of support.

After extensive interviews for his Washington Post article, David Ignatius helped Victor arrange a press conference at the National Press Club on the day the story was to be published. This was particularly important to Victor. He knew the KGB would make his parents disappear as soon as the story broke. Victor was sure the KGB would still be watching them, allowing all calls to go through so they could catch them taking a call. So, Victor's plan was to call his parents and establish their presence before the KGB could intervene. He figured that way the KGB could not make them disappear—that would be too much of a public challenge, and Victor reckoned that Gorbachev, their PR man, was not up for that at the moment.

March 1, 1990. *Olga should call anytime now. Will it be a go?* Victor glanced at the clock: ten minutes before 11:00 PM. Olga was standing near *The Washington Post* building, waiting for next day's edition to be put on the nearby stand. There was usually a small crowd there at this time of night—mainly professional people who wanted to be the first to read tomorrow's *Post*. Those who waited anxiously included media gofers, and foreign embassy folks collecting copies for their intelligence chiefs, who could dash out reports before morning deliveries of the *Post,* thereby implying that their information was the result of relentless intelligence efforts.

Not a good crowd for Olga to be in, but she knew how to handle the situation and would make sure not to bring a KGB tail home—an unlikely scenario since the Soviet Embassy gofer, even if he recognized her, would need authorization to follow and that would require getting back to the Embassy.

The phone rang. "Hello."

"It's out. I'm coming back."

"Thanks. Calling now. See you here."

Victor went to the garage and settled comfortably in his car. He knew it would be a long time before he got through. The phone lines to Moscow were perpetually busy. He plugged a friend's mobile phone into the cigarette lighter receptacle and dialed. He hadn't dialed that number since May 1980, almost ten years earlier. Each time he tried he got a recording: "Your call did not go through to the country you are calling." After thirty minutes of dialing in vain, the garage door opened and Olga drove in.

"Any luck?"

"Nope. As expected."

"Let me try. You read this stuff."

Leaving Olga in the garage, Victor went to the kitchen and began reading the lead story on Page One.

'Major' KGB Defector to U. S. Breaks 10 years of Silence; Specialist Knew Entire Code System

Just as Victor had expected. He read on:

…Major named Victor Ivanovich Sheymov disappeared from Moscow with his wife and child.… "He was a major defector who made a highly valuable contribution to our country and national security," said an Administration spokesman.… Press conference in the National Press Club today at 11 A. M..

Victor considered his calculated gamble. *How much time do we have? The Soviet Embassy gofer got the paper when Olga did. Because of the good weather he probably chose to take a walk before going back to the embassy—normally only five minutes from the* Post *building. Would've arrived about the same time Olga got here. The embassy duty officer's getting the paper about now. Another five minutes to call the Resident to come to the Residentura. A total of fifteen minutes—with luck, half an hour. Writing a flash cable, another ten minutes. Transmitting and delivering it in Moscow, another thirty. Initial turmoil—another hour. So, we have maybe two hours before they block my parents' phone. And then, perhaps, whisk them away.*

But if the call went through in time, that wouldn't happen. The line would remain open, and nobody would touch his parents. Even the KGB was shy of wide publicity. They'd assume that the call was monitored by the CIA—or worse, by the media. They'd back off.

If he didn't get through, who could prove that his parents were alive?

Victor went to the garage and relieved Olga on the phone. Fifteen more minutes, and finally the call went through. Eight in the morning in Moscow.

"Hello." Mother's voice. Victor has not heard it for ten years.

Emotions constricted his throat. "Mama? This is me, Victor."

There was a pause on the other end of the line. Then a shaky voice: "Victor? My darling, I knew that you're alive! Ivan! Come, come, Victor's calling!"

"Yes Mama, we're all alive and well. How are you?"

Mother seemed overcome, and talked almost unintelligibly. Then, Father came to the phone. "Hello."

"Papa, dear, hello."

"Who are you, and what do you want?"

"This is Victor. What's wrong?"

"Whoever you are, this is not the first provocation. The KGB, I presume. Have you ever heard of such a thing as decency?"

"This is not a provocation, Papa. This is me."

Father's stern voice suddenly stumbled. "Your voice...certainly sounds like my son's." He regained his composure. "If you are who you say you are, it shouldn't be difficult to answer a few questions. And make sure that you answer quickly."

Father: In control, as always; tough, as always.

"Ask anything."

"What was the last name of the old lady who helped bring you up?"

"Gegero. And her companion's name was Maria."

Father asked for some personal details about distant relatives— which no intelligence service in the world would know. After Victor correctly answered, his father's voice trembled. "Victor, my son. I thought you were dead."

Father and mother took turns on the line. Their conversation was both poignant and joyous.

At the end Victor said: "It's going to be a big deal in the press tomorrow. I mean today, here in Washington. A major press conference, and all that. They won't dare touch you now—not after this call."

"Don't worry about us. We're so happy that all of you are alive and well that nothing else matters. Nobody can take this away from us now."

"I hope to see you soon. And now Olga's going to call her mother."

"Victor...you mean that...you don't know?"

"What?"

"She died last September. A heart attack."

The line suddenly went dead.

Victor knew that the conversation had gone through KGB channels, and that the order had been given to cut it off—too late. Victor had won this round. Olga had been sitting in the car next to Victor for the first few minutes of his call, and then had gone into the house.

Victor found her in the living room and conveyed the sad news. He tried to comfort her for a while, but then she said that she wanted to be alone.

Victor went outside. In a few minutes he managed to regain his concentration. The press conference. Another gamble.

Everyone would presume that the article in the *Post* and the press conference was of the CIA's making, and wonder why the CIA chose this particular time to reveal Victor's existence. In fact, the CIA had been adamantly against the whole thing, and had done everything possible to prevent it from happening. Victor recalled his last conversation with the CIA Resettlement man, a day before the press conference, who almost literally forced Victor into a short meeting.

"Victor, you're about to make a huge mistake. You're jeopardizing your own and your family's security. Why don't you just keep quiet? You've achieved a lot—we'll help you achieve more."

"Whatever I achieved, it's been in spite of your 'help.' May God save everyone from your help."

"Well, let's not argue about it. We're a big organization, you know. Things can go wrong sometimes."

"With you, it's more like all the time. But that isn't the point. I made my decision and, as an undeserved courtesy, I notified you. I did not ask for your advice."

The CIA man lowered his voice. "Victor, how to say it? If you don't go public, we can, uh, perhaps compensate you financially."

Victor only looked at him in disgust.

"Well, you're being unreasonable. In this case, I have to convey to you that it's our organization's position that you can't go public. And I'm authorized by our leadership to notify you that if you go public, you're on your own."

Smiling, Victor said: "That's precisely what I want. Just make sure that you do leave me alone."

27

V ictor sighed. *So be it. Go ahead, face the press.* It was almost four in the morning. Olga was in bed, but not sleeping. He too wouldn't sleep, not for another hour.

Victor needed an effective disguise, not to look better, but very different. He had to protect his resettlement identity. The last thing he needed was to enable paparazzi to camp out in front of his home or to follow him, not to mention harassing Olga and Elena. Also, it needed to be convenient, so he could put it on and take it off quickly. Victor had bought a wig, with sandy-blond hair that was not only quite different in color from his own, but had two more important features: first, its sharply different hairstyle, and second, the slightly oversized, thickly coiffed wig gave the impression that his face was narrower than it actually was. In effect, the wig changed the shape of his skull. Victor had also visited an optician, where he chose glasses with a frame whose upper line cut across his upper eyelids. By altering the appearance of his eyes, he changed his face. To complete his disguise, Victor modified the way he walked. The acid test would come when his next-door neighbor saw his photo in the newspaper or saw him on television.

At nine-thirty in the morning Victor drove off. Donning the disguise at home was out of the question. He'd have to find the right moment to put it on later.

Victor drove to Union Station and parked in a slot in the station garage, between two cars. This way, nobody could interrupt his make-up ceremony, for which the rear-view mirror was adequate. Five minutes later he rode down the escalator and took a taxi to Fourteenth Street. Victor carefully monitored the expressions on people's faces. Nobody gave him a surprised or strange look. In fact, nobody paid him any attention at all. *So far, so good. At least my disguise isn't conspicuous.*

He entered the National Press Club building five minutes before eleven. After stepping out of the elevator on the 13th floor, he found himself in the middle of a crowd that sounded like a beehive. Working his way to the entrance of the press-conference room was difficult. He knew the throng of reporters were on the lookout for him. But, of course, no one paid attention to him, except to express mild annoyance at the man determinedly navigating through the crowd.

When Victor entered the room, it was two minutes after eleven. The place was brimming. People sat on chairs, on the floor, and stood along the walls. *So, the crowd outside are those wanting to get in.* Victor had never seen so many cameras in one place. *Virtually every picture taken of me as an adult was in a controlled environment. Well, I'll have to get used to a different modus operandi.* Even now, as he neared the stage, nobody knew who he was. *Everything's instantly going to change.*

Victor heard a loud noise. Flashes—all the cameras whirred and clicked. More flashes as he took a seat at the table—the picture-taking commotion didn't subside.

Herb Romerstein, a well-known writer on Soviet affairs, was at the podium and briefly introduced Victor by reiterating some points that had appeared in that morning's article in the *Post*.

Victor stood up and came to the microphone. He had no reason to place much trust in the media. He knew that, as in any large group, he could expect some reporters to be honest and objective, and others to welcome his making a mistake: saying something he shouldn't. And there was a great deal he could not say. To Victor, the national security interests of the United States far outweighed those of any journalist. He knew that a favorite trick of reporters was to increase the pace of the questioning, to force an error and then jump all over it. He planned to deal with that by deliberately slowing down the pace, to buy time to think over his answers. Suddenly, at the last moment, he decided to up the ante by drastically modifying his approach.

He answered quickly, immediately switching to the next question. Further, he scrambled the rhythm, mixing relatively long answers with one-liners. In fifteen minutes the pace became dizzying, and he kept it up for almost two hours.

In the early part of the conference Victor received numerous questions relating to the KGB's assassination attempt on the Pope. In responding, Victor had to stick to what he knew and avoid speculation. "The task was to find out how to get physically close to the Pope. In KGB slang it was clearly understood that when you say 'get physically close to' somebody, it means only one thing."

"What was what?"

"To assassinate that person."

Although Victor felt that the CIA hadn't paid any attention to his warning during debriefings in 1980, he tried to be objective. When asked: "If the CIA knew about the assassination plot on the Pope, why didn't they take measures to protect him?" Victor wanted to say, "Ask the CIA," but said instead: "I cannot speak for the CIA, but I can guess that you have to classify the information that you receive. You need to have the time, date, place, and how. But I knew only the fact."

"Could you tell us more about what the US authorities could have done better in debriefing and welcoming you?"

"I've been treated extremely well by the American people, I can tell you that. Speaking of the CIA, I didn't have too long a relationship with them. I think I've been treated like everybody else."

Exiting the press conference would be the tricky part. Victor ended it politely but a little abruptly, and walked rapidly to the elevator. The next day he would laugh when he heard that the press blamed the CIA for their bodyguards' heavy-handed treatment of reporters. The irony of the situation was that everyone, the KGB included, assumed that the CIA would provide tight security protection during the press conference. In fact, there was none.

So much for assumptions.

Victor underwent a "dry-cleaning" by riding different taxis for half an hour. Now his disguise was more a burden than help because so many people had seen him at the Press Club and on television. He got out of a taxi in Georgetown, strolled through the entrance to an underground garage on M Street, and quickly went to the elevator. Alone there, he removed his disguise. He exited the elevator at the mall level and took a taxi to the McPherson Square metro station.

Suddenly Victor had a problem. Standing next to him in the train was a reporter who'd sat in the first row at the press conference. Victor held his breath, trying to think of a way to get out of the situation. Unexpected relief flooded through him when the reporter's scan passed over Victor's face several times without so much as a flicker of recognition in his eyes. Victor's disguise had passed the toughest test of all. The next morning Victor would smile when he read reports that his CIA-supplied wig was absolutely horrible.

Victor retrieved his car at Union Square, and took a circuitous scenic route. Spotting no signs of a tail, he drove directly home.

Olga was excited. "You're all over the news! How did it go?"

"Well, okay I guess. I don't think I said anything stupid."

"I was so worried about you. I thought you had taken those CIA threats too lightly."

"I wasn't worried about them, but more about myself. In a charged atmosphere like that there's always the danger you can mess up and say something secret."

That evening Donald stopped by. "Victor, you did very well. We have no quarrel at all."

"I didn't see you there."

"I was in the overflow room. Anyway, I can tell you for sure that there are no complaints about security breaches from any quarter. The whole Intel community's relieved."

So was Victor.

28

One day Victor got an unexpected request for a meeting. A mutual friend called and said that Leonid Milgram, the principal of the Moscow school that Victor had attended, was coming to Washington, and wanted to meet with him. Leonid Milgram held a special place in Victor 's memory. The school was probably the best, and definitely the most prestigious school in the country. It required stiff entrance exams, and an unofficial but firm prerequisite was that students come from very prominent families. Most were children and grandchildren of the country's elite.

Leonid Milgram was the Principal. Leonid Milgram *was* the school. Milgram was a superb history teacher; his encyclopedic knowledge was complemented by his considerable oratorical skills and a passionate style of delivery. His students were mesmerized. He never had any discipline problems in his class. Among students he had a reputation as a tough but fair man; his integrity was unquestioned. No student ever wanted to be called to his office. Most of the school graduates ended up in the highest echelons of the country, and practically all of them were very fond of Milgram, staying in touch with him for many years after the graduation. He was honored as a Distinguished Teacher of Russia, and as an Honorary Citizen of Moscow.

He was extremely well connected, and could get into any office he wanted. He was a master of PR, at a time when nobody there understood what PR was. No one knew exactly how he managed to get all those connections, but everyone knew he had them. Milgram was also a consummate socialite, and very popular with women. Unusual for a Soviet, he was married to a daughter of the chief editor of *L'Unita*, a well known Italian and international communist, and traveled abroad often. Due to Milgram's connections the school had a great gymnasium, a stadium, a movie theater, and an indoor swimming pool—unheard of luxuries for a Soviet school. Students were taken on frequent and interesting field trips, and foreign delegations very often visited the school.

Victor had attended that school from the sixth grade through graduation. He did well academically, but his somewhat rebellious attitude meant quite regular meetings with Milgram. Strangely, Milgram did not expel Victor, even though he did expel some of Victor's friends. During these sometimes contentious meetings they came to like each other.

One event at the end of Victor's tenth grade particularly impacted their relationship. Victor happened to be in the movie booth upstairs where projectors were running a movie for the kids in the theater. The film was old, made of easily ignitable cellulose film. Something malfunctioned during the rewinding, and the film caught fire, instantly engulfing the room, with a lot of film spaghettied on the floor. Miraculously, all four boys in the room got out, but the fire spread to another room where there were many ignitable films on the shelves, which threatened an explosion. Two of the boys just ran away, as Victor quickly grabbed a fire extinguisher, trying to subdue the fire. His friend unfolded the fire hose and managed to turn it on. They were fighting the fire together when Milgram ran up and tried to help. Milgram had just had a heart attack and was very weak. Victor yelled at him to go away, and seeing that Milgram didn't react, Victor literally threw him down into the hands of a group gathered on the staircase below. This showed the utmost disrespect in front of a few teachers and students, but it was simply a reflex. Miraculously, the fire was very soon extinguished. When things calmed down, Milgram came to Victor and thanked him. Victor knew his gratitude was wholehearted. They never mentioned the incident again, but Victor felt that their bond had strengthened.

Naturally, Victor discussed the approach with Robert. Robert was not thrilled at the prospect, but didn't object, and Victor agreed to the meeting. He suggested that somebody should pick Milgram up at his hotel and bring him to a restaurant, but Victor declined.

When Victor pulled up to the hotel entrance, Milgram was standing there. He had hardly changed during the fourteen years since they last met. Victor got out of the car, and they hugged.

"Good to see you, rebel." Milgram chuckled. "I knew you'd come yourself."

"How did you know?"

"I was your teacher, remember?" Victor just laughed.

They went to a nice restaurant in Bethesda, and had a delightful dinner. They quickly recounted the history of most of their mutual friends, and Victor was filled in on who was where and doing what. They were not in a hurry, both enjoying the conversation and each other's company. They carefully avoided the minefield of ideology.

At some point Milgram suddenly asked: "You probably wondered how I made all my connections?"

"Everybody wondered about that."

"Well, I can tell you now." He took a picture out of his pocket and showed it to Victor. Victor saw it was Dzerzhinsky, the dreaded founder of the KGB, with a toddler on his lap sitting next to another man. "This is my father. He was the right-hand man to Menzhinsky, and this is me, on Dzerzhinky's lap." Menzhinsky was Dzerzhinsky's number two, the head of Intelligence.

Victor could only say, "Wow"

"My father was later arrested and executed during the Stalin purges." Milgram paused. "He was later 'rehabilitated' by Khrushchev."

Later Victor did some research and found out that Milgram's father, Isidor Milgram, was a notorious communist operative in the West and in China, sometimes posing as a Soviet diplomat. He was the communist executioner of the enemies of the state abroad. He was apprehended, tried and convicted for murder in Europe and later exchanged for some spy in the Soviet Union.

Little by little the conversation turned to the current events in Russia. After briefly describing what Victor already new, Milgram said: "Everybody is so confused now. We don't know what's good or what's bad, we don't know what to do."

"But you are a teacher. No matter what, you must be proud of how many people you reared. You gave them knowledge, and you taught them decency. What can be more gratifying than that?"

"Well, that's what makes my life tolerable. However, some problems are so daunting morally." He sighed. "Just one example. We were collecting funds for a memorial to the victims of Stalin's Terror. I mentioned that to my son, fully expecting him to contribute. He refused."

"Why?"

"He said: 'Dad, Stalin executed a lot of innocent people, true. But he also executed a lot of the Old Guard communists who executed millions of innocent people. Which victims is the memorial going to be for?"

Victor just nodded. He understood that Milgram's son's remark was a direct reference to Milgram's father. *Must be very painful for Leonid. For me it's a rough approximation of justice—those commissars who murdered millions of innocent people were exterminated by Stalin, just like roaches. Good. I wish I could contribute.*

After some more chat, Milgram turned serious. "Victor, I do not want to discuss what you did. I can understand why you did it, now more than ever."

Victor did not react, and he continued: "But that's over. It was another country, another era. The Cold War is over." He paused, and purposely said: "It can be forgiven. But please stop doing what you are doing now."

What? Very few people know that I am working for the NSA, fewer yet know what I am doing there. He can't mean that.

"What do you mean? A few public appearances here and there do not amount to much. Besides, I cannot just shut down my ideological convictions."

"It's not what I mean. Your appearances are not a problem, you are entitled to your opinion like anyone else." He looked Victor straight in the eye. "I mean what you are really doing now." He paused and chuckled. "We have our people here too, you know."

Victor was shocked, so few people knew, even generally, what he was doing with NSA that the thought was frightening; he hoped that his face did not betray him. *My God! They know. How?* He became preoccupied with his desert, and changed the topic. Milgram quipped: "Just think about it, OK?"

At the very end, just before leaving, Victor said:

"I know things are hard in Russia, but I probably do not comprehend the depth of it."

"Yes, it's very difficult, especially for older people. Their values are gone, and their valuables are gone. They have nothing. Total crash."

"I do not want to offend you, but is there any way that I can help you? I mean strictly personally."

Milgram gave Victor a long look.

"Victor, please do not spoil our beautiful friendship."

Victor understood, and he just nodded. Later, he wondered if it was an original phrase or a quote from "Casablanca" with a hint. He never figured that out.

Victor described his worries to Robert who was intrigued, but said that most likely it was just a bluff. Victor was not so sure.

29

Victor's sudden celebrity meant he was effectively working a second shift in addition to his regular NSA job. It was pretty stressful, and Victor somehow had to balance all his activities. The Sheymovs kept their resettlement identities, but for public appearances Victor used disguises and made sure that he wasn't followed when transiting between the two identities. Their neighbors had no idea that the Schwartz family were in fact the Sheymovs. The NSA work, of course, was the most important, and took the most time. All the other people Victor worked with had no idea at all that Victor still worked at the

NSA, and assumed that he had retired from the intelligence community altogether.

He could not possibly accommodate all the requests for appearances and lectures. Olga quipped that Victor has been on all the major TV shows except Dr. Ruth. Victor learned pretty quickly that the main purpose of many of the shows was either advancing somebody's political agenda, or pumping up the image of the host. He limited his acceptance to only those who agreed either to a live interview or to broadcasting the taped one in its entirety. That trimmed the volume of requests significantly.

One request came from a reporter from a major Soviet newspaper. The Soviets were embarrassed by the public disclosure of Victor's defection with his family; it was egg on the face of the KGB, and they needed to do something about it. Victor understood very well that the goal was to distort what Victor was saying and present him in a very bad light to the Soviet public. It wasn't a big secret that the "reporter" also happened to be a KGB operative. Some people were concerned that he would try to kill Victor with a poisonous handshake. Victor didn't believe that—he assumed the main goal was just propaganda. Against all advice Victor decided to grant the interview. He talked to Herb Romerstein, who had introduced him at his press conference. He was an old hand in Soviet affairs and a very intelligent man with a great sense of humor. They concocted a plot.

The reporter was ushered into a conference room at the National Press Center. Victor was sitting at the far end of a long conference table; the other end was reserved for the "reporter." Access to Victor's end of the table was blocked wall-to-wall in the middle by heavy chairs, so it was not physically possible to approach Victor closer than five or six feet. To the great surprise of the Soviet reporter there were two other reporters sitting at the "media" end of the table: one from Radio Free Europe and another from Voice of America. There were microphones and tape recorders on the table.

When Herb introduced the Soviet reporter to the others, he was outraged. "What is this? I asked for an exclusive interview, and this is not exclusive."

Herb, with all the innocence of a young lamb said: "You never mentioned 'exclusive' when I spoke with you."

The reporter raised his voice. "I did! And you promised it to me! I want an exclusive!"

Herb, the peacemaker, humbly said: "Well, there must have been a misunderstanding. Victor is so busy these days that it's very difficult for him to grant exclusive interviews. If you insist, we can get back to you with a date that's possible, but I can tell you that it won't be any time soon."

The man thought for a moment, then gave in; this was obviously better than the alternative, i.e. nothing. "OK, but this is outrageous." He looked straight at Herb. "And you're responsible!"

Herb, never at loss, quipped: "Well that's typical Soviet chauvinism— if something goes wrong, blame it on a Jew." The other reporters cracked up, and the Soviet man just took a seat.

Victor spoke: "Thank you all for coming, and for your interest. Given the Soviet record of..." he paused, "slightly biased reporting, here is the ground rule. I'll answer your questions as best as I can for the record. You can report any part of what I say that you find fit. However, if any distortion is detected in the report in the Soviet Union, both the Voice of America and the Radio Free Europe will transmit a true and complete record of this interview. Agreed?"

Everybody agreed. In an hour the interview was over. The Soviet reporter knew that he had been outplayed and radiated fury. He couldn't resist a threat as he left. He turned to Victor and pointedly said: "You have yet to hear from us." Victor smiled. No word of that interview was ever published in the Soviet Union.

Olga and Victor knew that the Moiseyev Dance Company was in Washington and would perform at the Wolftrap. After a short discussion they felt that it would be too risky to attend, and decided to pass. Then Bob Hanssen dropped by. After some small talk he and Victor went to the back porch of the house and Bob said: "I have a treat for you guys. The Bureau is grateful for your help and wants to say thank you. Let's go see the Moiseyev performance at Wolftrap tomorrow. I got great seats through the Bureau for all of us."

Victor was taken aback. "Bob, are you saying the Bureau is comfortable with this?"

"Sure, why not?"

"Well, half the Soviet Embassy will be there."

"So what, we'll sit close in, and they'll look at you from the back." He chuckled. "Besides, I'll be armed."

Something does not compute here. Why would the FBI want me to go there? They must be up to something. Victor shook his head. "All right, we'd certainly be delighted. If the Bureau is comfortable, why wouldn't I be?"

Olga was surprised too, but with the FBI behind it, she was ready to enjoy the performance.

The next day Wolftrap, as expected, was packed with Soviet embassy staff and Intelligence Community officers, and surveillance. The rest of the seats were occupied by the innocent public. The air was filled with excitement, although for different reasons for different people. Their seats were really perfect. As Victor insisted, they were almost late, taking their seats when almost all the seats were already occupied, so the audience saw only their backs.

As always with the Moiseyev, the performance was great. During the long intermission, Olga and Bonnie Hanssen stayed in their seats, but Bonnie wanted some candy, so Bob suggested that he and Victor get it. Victor agreed, but again he wondered about the Bureau's intentions. That wondering turned to astonishment as Bob, making excuses about the crowds at the food stands, went further and further around the huge theater.

What's going on? He is literally parading me around. With all these hundreds of cameras flashing everywhere, we'll be in quite a few pictures together. This is especially puzzling because Bob is in the analytical unit, he is not an operative. Then why?

He turned to Bob and said quietly, "This is quite a stroll."

Bob was obviously enjoying himself. Uncharacteristically, he was clearly excited. He gave out a short laugh. "Oh, don't worry. Here's a stand with only a few people." They bought the candies and made their way back, taking their seats just in time.

Victor watched Bonnie. She did not eat the candy.

Weird. OK, we'll find out soon enough.

Victor wondered about that parading trip for a while. He felt that the FBI was playing some game with the KGB at his expense. However, he figured that with him going public very soon it didn't matter security-wise. With that, he put it out of his mind.

One evening Tim, the family dog, suddenly gave a very loud howl on the back porch. Victor rushed there and found him unconscious. They quickly put him in a car and drove to the emergency animal clinic nearby. The doctor saw them right away. He declared Tim dead and, having examined his tongue and a swatch from his mouth ruled it poisoning. That was bad news. It was a hard blow for Olga, Victor and Elena—Tim was a full member of the family.

Back home Olga was trying to cope with the loss. After a while she asked a logical question: "Victor, are there other implications in this? The only reason to kill Tim was to get at you."

"I don't think so. It makes no sense. If an intelligence service wants to kill or kidnap me, they would be crazy to try it at my home. They'd do it somewhere else, not on my turf."

Olga shook her head. She was not convinced.

Victor went on: "Look, if this is against me it really is some very crazy, amateurish stuff. Not to mention that Tim's not a guard dog at all."

"Any other ideas?"

"I don't know. Sometimes next-door neighbors do nasty things like that, but only when they are annoyed by the dog. And even then, they must be unstable people. A reasonable person would be wary of retaliation. Besides, I haven't noticed any animosity from our neighbors. Have you?"

"No."

The next day Victor brought that up with Robert and asked if he saw any security issue there.

"No. Sometimes people are annoyed by the wild animals in the neighborhoods, so they put out poison out to deal with them, and sometimes dogs and cats get poisoned as well. That's probably it."

Without Tim the Sheymovs' home became a little darker, and it was a long while before they came to terms with it. But life went on.

30

Now that Victor's existence was no longer a secret, he was free to communicate with numerous contacts, including many in the Soviet Union. As a result, he rapidly became attuned to the latest events in Russia and, more important, to the mood and shadowy political currents there. Then Victor received an offer from Salomon Brothers, the big Wall Street investment bank, to become a personal consultant to its Chairman. This offer was too good to pass up. In addition to working with the Chairman, Victor also consulted with the heads of the company's Equities and Bonds departments, effectively working with the top three executives of the firm. The work was not time-intensive, and involved just occasional day trips to New York and a few conference calls, but the issues were very important and the stakes were very high.

In the second half of 1990 events in the Soviet Union and Eastern Europe took increasingly dramatic turns: the Soviet empire was crumbling, along with the power of the Communist party. Mikhail Gorbachev became hyperactive. Victor clearly understood Gorbachev's role. A master of political maneuvering, Gorbachev was doing his best to salvage what he could of the Communist party and the Soviet Union. His main virtue was that he was grossly misunderstood—by the White House, who took him at face value, and by communist hard-liners, who feared he was abandoning the interests of the party. The ironic truth is that Gorbachev was a more devout Communist than the hard-liners who criticized him. He tried to save the Communist Party with smoke and mirrors. He was smarter than they were, and possessed an acute understanding of the gravity of the situation in the Soviet Union. In true Leninist style, he demonstrated his "flexibility" by saving what he could of the communist system rather than losing it all. But Western leaders saw Gorbachev as an ebullient, energetic catalyst for change who welcomed democratic institutions and capitalistic notions. A darling of the Western media, Gorbachev charmed his way through, thereby softening the fall of his beloved communist system. So, ironically, as he succeeded in duping the West into believing in his announced democratic and humanitarian intentions, he failed to have his cohorts understand his real goal of saving Communism, and became their poster enemy.

During the summer of 1991, tensions ratcheted up in Moscow. Victor's contacts felt that "something's about to happen." If one considered the lessons of Soviet history, it was not difficult to foresee that Gorbachev needed a strong push from the hard-liners toward a military-emergency regime to give him two alternatives, either one desirable. If the hard-liners pushed hard enough to precipitate a major political "crisis," Gorbachev could strengthen his position by declaring himself an emergency leader with greater powers. Or, if the crisis were less severe, he could use it as a bargaining chip with the West, to whom he'd say, "See, we just can't move too fast. You've got to be patient. Meanwhile, please give me your support as we prepare to take our next step towards democracy."

August, 1991

The phone rang. Victor looked at the clock. 3 AM.

"Hello."

"Victor?"

"Yes."

"Hi. This is Stanley, the head of Equities at Salomon."

"Hi."

"Do you know there's a coup in Moscow?"

"No."

"Why?"

"Because I was sleeping,"

Stanley probably realized that his assumption was unreasonable. He slowed down, but still was clearly excited. "Well, some guys took over. I got one name." He paused slightly. "Kryuchkov. Do you know him?"

"Yes." Victor was waking up.

"OK, the long and the short of it is that the markets open at eight. It's gonna be a blood bath. The question is, what do we do."

"I understand."

"All right, can you snoop around and find out what this coup is about, what the outlook is, so we can concoct a strategy. I need that by seven."

"I'll try. The good news is that I still have a few friends there who are very well wired and should know what's going on. The bad news may be that there are no communications with Moscow or even the whole country. If that's the case, I can only know what comes from the media, and that's not going to be much."

"OK, do the best you can."

Olga was not sleeping. "What happened?"

"Coup in Moscow against Gorbachev."

They went downstairs and turned on the TV. Olga was making notes of what was on the news, which wasn't much. Mostly, panicky statements from some just-awake talking heads saying that democracy in Russia is over. Victor quipped: "There never has been any in Russia."

Victor went to the phone. He was pleasantly surprised that the lines to Moscow were busy but not cut. That in itself was significant information. It took him a good half-hour to place the first call. He managed to talk to several people. Some of them were caught completely off guard, but two of his friends were not. They talked in Aesopian language, and by six the picture began to clear.

Olga made another brew of coffee and gave Victor a summary of all the network news. Together, they reconciled all they had.

At six-thirty Victor called Stanley. He was put though instantly. "Victor, what's up? Did you find out anything?"

"Yes, I think I have a pretty clear picture of what's going on." Victor chuckled. "The executive summary is that this is not serious and is going to fold in a few days, no more than a week."

"Are you serious? Did you see all the networks? Are you saying they're all wrong?"

"Yes. True, on the surface the coup looks very impressive: the Prime Minister, the Ministers of Defense and Interior, and the head of the KGB as a leader of the coup." Victor took a breath. "However, this coup failed to implement the fundamental requirements of a

successful coup. Of all people, Kryuchkov knows how to make a successful coup–the KGB has a great deal of experience with that. He
knows very well that certain things must be done, otherwise the coup
will fail."

Stanley interrupted: "Like what?"

"August's a good month for a coup because everyone's on vacation—but the day is wrong. Today's Monday. The best time for a coup
is Friday night, when everyone in power is tired and has gone to his
summer dacha, where communications are usually limited and their
ability to counter the coup is hampered. Secondly, all communications
in the country are cut except those controlled by the coup. The communications were not cut, and the minister of communications was
not part of the coup. Further, some potential adversaries are arrested
or killed–none of that happened, as far as I know. Finally, the target of
the coup must either be killed or arrested and kept under immediate
control of the coup leaders. At the very least he is their life insurance
policy. Gorbachev, as far as we know, is resting comfortably at his summer villa by the Black Sea."

Victor took a break, and Stanley did not reply. Victor went on,
point by point.

At the end of the speech he said: "So, what we have so far is just a
bunch of declarations, no real actions. I think all the indications are
that Gorbachev orchestrated that coup, and he will double-cross these
guys pretty soon. That's all."

"Are you sure?

"Pretty much so. See, you have all the major players, the top key
guys on board."

"Yes, and that's why everyone thinks it's a success."

"No. First, these guys compete fiercely, and they cannot agree to
anything on their own. Mysteriously, they all agreed. Second, they are
all Gorbachev's people, handpicked by him. So, only he can bring
them to a consensus."

After a pause, Stanley was doubtful. "Victor, I don't understand,
why would Gorbachev do something like that?"

"Stanley, I can only guess at that. He's been pulling rabbits out of his hat for a while now, trying to extract economic help from the West without giving away much politically."

"He definitely has been."

"Well, now he's running out of rabbits." Stanley chuckled, and Victor continued. "He wants to show that he's under tremendous pressure from the right, i.e. from conservative elements of the Communist Party, so the only way he can withstand that pressure is for the West to help him, without demanding too much in return. In other words he's saying 'guys, you have to adjust your expectations and be happy with what I offer you. Otherwise, the really bad folks here will take over, and you would be most unhappy with them.'"

Stanley said: "Victor, thank you very much, we have to digest everything you said. You do realize the stakes? Do you know how many millions we're going to lose if this is a real coup and the whole *perestroika* business goes down the drain. If we start buying in a sinking market on our scale, we'll end up either making a real fortune or losing a lot."

"I know."

"And you still stand by your recommendation?"

"Yes, this is my best judgment. That's where I'd put my money if I had any."

"All right, call me at quarter of eight if you have anything else."

Victor made two more calls, not to Moscow but to St. Petersburg. Everything was corroborating his analysis. At a quarter of eight he called Stanley again and confirmed his recommendation, reiterating that if looked at objectively, everything the coup leaders had done in the first hours of the coup was a TV production. No real actions.

Stanley said: "Well, Victor, we've made a decision to follow your advice. I sure hope you're right. Wish us luck."

By mid-day Washington was boiling. Victor received a call from PBS inviting him to participate in a panel discussion with a famous female anchor. He accepted.

When he arrived at the studio, in the green room he was surprised to see General Odom, the just-retired Director of the NSA, on the monitor. He was passionately describing all the upcoming horrors of dealing with the new administration in Russia when all the democrats had gone with Gorbachev. *Oh God, another expert on Russia.*

In the studio he saw two former Soviet intelligence officers and one expert with a lot of experience in Soviet politics. The discussion was somewhat heated, also prophesying gloom and doom. Victor avoided jumping in, hoping that the anchor would manage the discussion. With very little time left the anchor noticed Victor and invited him to express his opinion. Victor briefly repeated what he had told Stanley that morning. There was an instant and very uncomfortable silence in the studio. The anchor was off guard and clearly did not know what to do. She looked as though she'd just heard something extremely outrageous, and mumbled something like "Well you see, we are open-minded here and any opinion can be expressed." In the break at the end of the program nobody said a word to Victor, and he quietly left the studio.

At home Olga was concerned. "It looks like everyone has the opposite opinion. What if you're wrong?" She sighed. "It's so crazy here in Washington. But the real question is, what will happen to our relatives if the coup's successful?"

Victor shook his head, not wanting to think about it. "Only God knows." He sighed. "But I agree with you about the craziness. Proof again that the CIA's a useless chunk of bureaucracy. If they'd done their job, there wouldn't be an uproar."

"How come?"

"Very simple. Just look what happens here when something like a coup takes place abroad. Everyone starts running around like a chicken with its head cut off. Everyone's glued to CNN. This means only one thing—that the event was totally unexpected. And that means, in turn, that the CIA's not doing the job they're paid to do. Their primary job is to develop good, reliable sources who can find out about such events before they happen, not after. With the huge amount of money this country's taxpayers pay them, this shouldn't be too difficult. If they're worth a damn."

"I'm sure cables are now flying back and forth between the CIA station in Moscow and Washington."

"Sure. But they're reporting news, not intelligence. But CNN's much better at it than they are."

"Aren't you being a little harsh?"

"Not a bit. This is the naked truth—which they try to obscure with a bunch of rhetoric. They always try to drag truth into muddy water, where they're comfortable. They hate clear water…. Anyway, real intelligence precedes news. There's no way around it."

Olga shook her head. "You know, I've never heard anybody say a neutral word—forget a kind one—about the CIA."

"Neither have I. But they're still alive and well in their swamp."

The next day, with the coup obviously falling apart, he got a call from the PBS producer, apologizing profusely and saying that the anchor asked to convey her apologies as well for last night's treatment and asking him to return to the same show. Victor politely refused, blaming his schedule. The girl insisted, and then asked, "How did you know?"

Victor chuckled: "I read a lot."

Although Victor was reluctant, another producer persuaded him to appear again that evening.

The show's anchor remarked that Victor had made a lucky guess. Victor responded by pointing out that the designers of the coup had totally miscalculated the reaction of the Russian people and the strength of Yeltsin's personality. Victor's earlier remark about Gorbachev's behind-the-scenes involvement in the coup was politely ignored. When Georgian President Gamsahurdia, of course independently of Victor, expressed the same opinion, he was publicly and rather rudely rebuked by President Bush. But that Gorbachev's complicity was suspected by many informed Russians at the time and later became a fixture in Russian social media. At the time, however, nobody wanted to comment.

There was a rumor on Wall Street that Salomon made a few hundred million on the market move. A week later Victor received his fee for consulting Solomon during the crisis. It was a check for five thousand.

31

Victor and Olga were sitting after dinner and enjoying a quiet evening, the first in a week. The coup was over, and they both vividly remembered CNN's coverage of the dismantling of the statue of Dzerzhinsky—the infamous founder of the KGB—in Moscow's Dzerzhinsky Square. Yeltsin had become a folk hero and it was obvious that Gorbachev was out of a job.

"I remember when you said in your television show about Gorbachev. He's like a magician who pulls rabbits out of his hat—but he's running out of rabbits. Now I know exactly what you meant. It looks now like communism is dead, at long last. That was our primary goal. Frankly, I never thought that I'd live to see it."

Victor thought for a while. "It will be dead, eventually. But it'll take a long time."

"How come? You can see that everything's falling apart in the communist camp."

"Sure, communism as a political movement and ideology is dead all right. But the point is that communism is not just a political movement, it's not just ideology. It's also a mindset, one of the main components of which is the denial of morality. In that form communism's still alive and well, unfortunately. It'll probably go through different stages: decentralized communism, then some type of private communism, and finally some form of personal communism. Only then will it finally be dead."

"Do you mean that people in power over there are no different than those who preceded them?"

"Precisely. They may use the same words we do, but they mean different things by them. Even their idea of democracy is based on communist propaganda, which has been poured into their minds for many years. It'll take a long time to cleanse this evil from our planet."

"So, what do you think's going to happen in Russia?"

"Since the 1917 Revolution Russia's been an ideological criminal state. Now it's about to become a non-ideological criminal state, which will go through the stages I mentioned. Only then will they turn back to humanity." Then Victor added: "If they don't kill each other in the process."

Victor's gamble with the press conference paid off. The KGB hadn't dared to secretly detain his parents. But the KGB wouldn't allow them to visit the United States. By carefully using Aesopian language in their telephone conversations, Victor learned that the KGB was giving them a hard time in other ways, and that their health was deteriorating quickly. This treatment by the KGB was in violation even of Soviet laws.

Victor began investigating ways to assist his parents. He discovered that of all the defectors to the West, only the families of five—four who defected to the United States, including Victor, and one to Great Britain, Oleg Gordievsky—were persecuted and prevented from leaving Russia by the Gorbachev government. On the one hand, Victor was proud of this high assessment of his work by the Soviet government; on the other, he had to find a way to protect his parents.

Luckily, Victor received help from the Jamestown Foundation and its head, Bill Geimer. His unrelenting lobbying efforts in the Congress and the State Department resulted in putting substantial pressure on Gorbachev. After numerous low-profile attempts to help, the U S Senate sent Gorbachev a letter signed by 20 Senators; the House sent a similar letter signed by 43 Congressmen. Even President Reagan appealed to Gorbachev, but the "great humanitarian" snubbed them all, not even bothering to answer. Victor was enormously grateful for this strong support. All four families remained firmly held inside the Soviet Union. Margaret Thatcher, however, did achieve success by forcefully appealing to Gorbachev, who released Oleg Gordievsky's family.

Shortly after the coup, it became obvious that the Soviet Union was falling apart. As a consequence, its formerly impregnable borders had become porous. Victor realized that this presented an opportunity to liberate his parents from the grip of the KGB. Because he knew that their personnel were now worrying mostly about protecting their own hides, Victor figured the KGB would be unusually slow to react to a fast-moving operation.

When the Baltic Republics of Latvia, Lithuania, and Estonia declared their independence with no substantive challenge from Russia, Victor decided to make his move. He called his parents and told them in Aesopian language to go immediately by train to Vilnius, Lithuania. Even considering his parents' wartime experience and their strong characters, Victor was amazed that they did so without any hesitation. They took off, despite the risks they were taking with the KGB. The border between Lithuania and Russia was open, and the borders of countries to the west had quite liberal regimes.

Victor asked the CIA to meet his parents in Lithuania, but they refused. So Victor had no choice but to go himself. When he mentioned his plans to the NSA, they were less than enthusiastic, believing the danger to Victor was unacceptably high. The issue was quickly elevated and the CIA was ordered to escort his parents from Lithuania to Washington.

Two days later Victor joyfully greeted his parents at Dulles International Airport.

32

Victor's meetings with the FBI became less and less frequent. But personal relations with Bob Hanssen and his family were a different story. The Sheymovs had become close to the Hanssens since they moved to a Virginia suburb of Washington.

Bob and Bonnie had been very helpful with the move, and particularly with finding a school for Elena. Everyone was concerned about her security, and Bob suggested placing her in Oakcrest, a small Catholic school for girls. The Hanssens' two older daughters went there, Bonnie taught there part-time, and Bob was closely involved on the Board. The school turned out to be wonderful, far exceeding their expectations. Academically, it was very strong. No less important, the school maintained a perfect balance between individual attention to every girl and good discipline, between encouraging individual performance and the common good, between strict adherence to Christian values and facing the real world. Having daughters in the same small school inevitably brought the Hanssens and the Sheymovs close together as parents, in addition to Bob's being the FBI liaison for Victor.

The two couples liked each other. Both Bob and Bonnie were interesting to be with. Bonnie was more subtle, and Bob more outgoing, telling a lot of jokes, but casually making many intellectually deep observations.

At Olga's birthday party Bonnie gave her a book, *The World of Jeeves*, by P.G. Wodehouse, saying "This is Bob's favorite. You'll love it." Olga laughed at the quote from the Atlantic: *"There is a controlled lunacy in these parodies of life among the British aristocracy."*

Bob was tall, slim, dark-haired, with very dark eyes. In an office meeting environment his eyes would not attract anyone's attention. However, his eyes sometimes became really penetrating, in a way that would make most people uncomfortable. In a casual social situation Victor sometimes noticed an instant dark sparkle that would be very difficult to read–whether it was a sparkle of humor or a sparkle of a darker mischief. Bob moved very smoothly, with no sound at all. This could be disturbing, as he would quietly enter the room from behind and just stand there. When one noticed him, one would never know for how long he'd been standing there. Victor was impressed by Bob's hands, fine and flexible, with long fingers, the hands of a concert pianist. Olga as an artist of course noticed that, and once commented that those were the hands of an eighteenth-century cardinal.

The Hanssens lived a modest lifestyle. Having six children must have been financially difficult, but they never complained. The only luxury item Victor ever saw in the Hanssen home was Bob's Nikon camera. Olga and Victor were particularly impressed when Bob casually mentioned that he had received a payment of some seventeen thousand as compensation from an insurance company for an accident that seriously damaged his hand, when some teenager made a wrong turn and rammed Bob's car. Olga had jokingly suggested, "Bob, now you can take Bonnie for a nice vacation." Bob replied: "No, that has to wait. I gave that money to the Church." That generous gesture earned a lot of respect. Bob was an openly devout Catholic. He made sure that the whole family went to church at least every Saturday—and usually more often than that.

Bob was an ideal father. It was pointless to call him during the hour that he would read nighttime stories to his boys. He would not interrupt that for anything. He was very protective of his daughters as well. Once he was late for supper at the Sheymovs, and came in laughing. He explained that some jerk had been bothering his daughter, making questionable compliments and apparently trying to recruit her. When she complained to him Bob quickly realized that the guy was a pimp. So he went to the bar where she had arranged a meeting, and sat nearby. When the guy started making his pitch, he came up to him and said: "Bob Hanssen, FBI." Before he was able to say anything else, the guy was gone, and never bothered his daughter again.

The only member of the Sheymovs family who did not like Bob was Elena. She always tried to stay away from him. Responding to Olga's question she said: "He's just so proper, so right. He tries to make you feel inadequate. But there is something dark in him. I don't know, but I am uncomfortable when he's around." Olga and Victor felt that she was entitled to her opinion and she was never asked to be around him more than she wanted. Olga helped her make excuses.

Once the two couples were having supper on the Sheymovs' veranda, and Olga asked sociably, "Where did you guys meet?

Bob gave out a short laugh accompanied with a dark sparkle in his eyes, and said: "In a madhouse."

Victor and Olga just cracked up. Bonnie looked slightly uncomfortable. Bob went on. "Bonnie's father was a well known psychiatrist. He was the head of a mental institution, that's why Bonnie was there." The implication was that the family lived on the premises.

Victor laughed: "That's fine, but what in the world were you doing there, Bob?"

"I was in medical school at the time, so it was my summer internship."

"Oh, I didn't know you were in medical school."

"Well, I studied dentistry, almost became a dentist. Bailed out at the last moment."

Olga intervened: "But where did you actually meet the first time?"

Bonnie said: "Bob was doing some gardening work when I first saw him."

Olga nodded, but an automatic truth checker threw a little red flag in Victor's head. Suddenly Elena came in, and the conversation shifted to something else, and the subject of the funny detail of the Hanssen's family history was abandoned and forgotten. Years later that red flag popped up again in Victor head, and Victor realized what had been the discrepancy: medical interns do not do gardening in a mental institution, but the patients do.

Bob Hanssen was a very righteous man. He would never miss a chance to make a religious reference regarding "wrong" current events. He was a proud member of Opus Dei, and was always at the most conservative end of any religious discussion. He sometimes quoted one of his favorite Catholics, Mother Teresa. Naturally, this made him ideologically very conservative, and he was outspoken in his political opinions. In his own slightly ironic manner he often expressed "admiration" for both Stalin and J. Edgar Hoover. It was often difficult to know if he was praising them or mocking them. He would often tell stories on Hoover, like the one that Hoover had a slight fender-bender when his car was making a left turn, after which his driver never made a left turn again, always choosing an alternative route. Another "funny" story was that after hearing a group presentation, Hoover quipped to his handlers: "Fire that pinhead." The men allegedly had no idea who he meant, and did not dare ask. So, they measured the hat sizes of all attendees of the meeting and fired the one with the smallest head.

Victor felt that Bob's admiration for autocrats was not ideological, but rather related to their ability to solve problems efficiently. However, there was one interesting aspect of Bob's tirades about the autocrats: while he found such rumored stories very funny, he never expressed any sympathy for the people who had been on the receiving end of their eccentricity.

On a couple of occasions Bob invited Victor and Olga to the FBI firing range at Quantico, when Victor gave a lecture to the students at the FBI academy. It was fun; they could try different weapons, and the instructors were happy to teach Olga to shoot. Interestingly, Bob himself never fired a weapon there, and never even handled one. Victor had the impression that Bob shied away from weaponry altogether, preferring intellectual work.

Bob had an exceptional ability to focus, and to compartmentalize. Victor once jokingly quipped to Olga that Bob had more than one personality. At small social events Bob was sociable and engaging but assertive and dogmatic. In the office he was quiet and in meetings he stayed quietly in the background and said little. Victor noticed that when they were alone, Bob was fluent, and never referred to the FBI as "we," as was common with many FBI agents. He always referred to "the FBI," or "they." Quite often he displayed little respect for the FBI's intellectual and analytical abilities. However, he had a lot of respect for their criminal investigation capabilities. And he often expressed his opinion that all the criminals were utterly stupid since they did not realize that they'd be caught, sooner or later. He loved to tell funny stories about the average criminal's stupidity.

There were certain things about Bob that Olga and Victor found objectionable, but their general attitude was "well, nobody's perfect." Once Bob and Bonnie were a little late for a supper at the Sheymovs' house, which was unusual. When they arrived, Bonnie apologized, and Bob said "Well, things happen when your daughter learns to drive."

Victor asked: "I hope everything is all right?"

"Yeah, no problem. We have a CIA guy in our neighborhood. So, she was turning around in his driveway, and drove over his dog, and killed it."

"Oh, that's terrible."

Bob just laughed. "No problem, the dog was old anyway, and the guy wouldn't quarrel with me. Nothing to worry about."

Both Olga and Victor felt very uncomfortable, feeling more for the dog than the CIA guy. Victor noticed that Bonnie did not react at all.

Bonnie was also religious, but in her inward, quiet way, in contrast to Bob who did not miss an opportunity to advance his Catholic views. Once Victor was careless enough to make a joking remark about the convenience of forgiveness of all sins by priests. Bob immediately became agitated. He gave a good ten-minute lecture on the subject, concluding it by saying that no one can question the greatness of God, no one can question that God's love and forgiveness is bigger than any sin by any mortal. During that time Victor was staring at his shoes, deeply regretting having made the remark. By the end of the tirade, Victor became slightly irritated at being lectured like that and was about to say that he meant priests, not God, and was going to ask about who then is hell populated with. Olga sensed what was coming, and when Victor caught her warning look, he just shut up, allowing her to tactfully change the subject. After that Victor was careful not to provoke religious discussions, though Bob frequently found a reason for delivering a sermon.

Both Olga and Victor were surprised and grateful to Bonnie on one occasion. Olga needed surgery, and the hospital required that she provide blood, just in a case it was needed. That would delay the surgery. When she mentioned that to Bonnie *en passant*, it turned out that Bonnie had the same blood type. Bonnie absolutely insisted on donating her blood, and was adamant when Olga hesitated. Needless to say, both Sheymovs were impressed and grateful.

One remarkable thing about Bob was his tendency to look at real-life human situations, professional or otherwise, in an abstract way, as though he were analyzing a chess play where people were the chess figures. It reminded Victor of a mediocre movie on Greek mythology that portrayed Zeus presiding over other Gods on Mount Olympus, watching the humans below, amusing themselves by manipulating them for their entertainment.

In essence, Victor thought Bob might well be described as intellectually arrogant; there were very few people who were worth his while to talk to seriously.

33

Victor finally finished one project that he had started back in 1986–writing a book. He absolutely did not want it to be an autobiography. He felt strongly that the longtime horror of communism was generally underestimated. Most writers concentrated on the external expressions of the system, such as mass murder. Victor wanted to emphasize that the damage of communism to people was even more severe, because communism corrupts people's souls, and that damage would last for generations. Mindful of the realities of the readers' market he wanted to avoid an academic book, and decided to write about his own experiences, concentrating on events that could illustrate specific issues. He felt that this way he could deliver the message to more people. Additionally, he wanted to write an account of intelligence operations that was based on the reality he had experienced at first hand. This would counter the numerous spy books that were the products of someone's imagination based on at best questionable and usually distorted hearsay, thrice removed. Victor's book was called *Tower of Secrets*.

When Victor finished the book he realized that the book would have two enemies–the KGB and the CIA. Accordingly, he started marketing the manuscript relatively quietly. Publishing was generally outside the KGB sphere, but the CIA had long been involved in it. The KGB would not want their operational embarrassment to be publicized again, and the CIA wanted to have full control over Victor's writing, as they had over everyone else's writing connected to the agency. Victor had refused to sign a paper to that effect. Victor had no illusion that the CIA would not get wind of his book, but he hoped they would be too slow to interfere before publication was under way.

The manuscript was enthusiastically accepted by the Naval Institute Press, NIP – the same publisher that discovered Tom Clancy. NIP liked the manuscript and paid far more for it than they had ever paid for any other title, and wanted it to be their major book of the year, and put it on a fast schedule.

The book was accepted by Tom Eppley, NIP's Editor in Chief. Six months later and not long before the release of the book, he was fired, and the NIP marketing director also left the company. The marketing budget was cut, and by publication date advance sales were minimal. Victor immediately smelled a CIA rat. His suspicions grew when during his scheduled promotional appearances all of a sudden book deliveries were messed up. This failure inflicted significant financial damages on the small publisher.

The consolation for Victor was a large number of wonderful letters from readers. Victor was surprised, and gratified. Nobody forced these readers to write to him, but they did. They expressed so much kindness and appreciation that he felt guilty that he physically could not answer all of them. That was a reward that neither the KGB nor the CIA could take away from him. Most gratifying was that a parent organization placed the *Tower of Secrets* as the number 2 recommendation on its reading list for teenagers. Victor was amazed that readers continued to write him many years after the publication of the book.

Soon Victor encountered another example of the continuing CIA viciousness. His sister and her husband felt very uncomfortable in Russia, given Victor's activities in the United States. They decided to emigrate to the US, and permission was granted. It would not be difficult for Helena and her husband to find a good job. She was an engineer with strong TV broadcasting experience, and Sergey was a good mathematician, and a senior editor in the principal Russian scientific publishing company.

When the family arrived in Washington, they promptly hired an attorney to help them with immigration and Green Card issues. Victor was called to the attorney's office to sign some papers. His schedule was pretty tight, and the process was quick. The lawyer was very efficient, and Victor was out of his Alexandria office in no time.

A few days later Victor got a phone call.

"Do you recognize me?"

It was a familiar voice.

"How about a drink?"

"With you, any time."

"Remember the place we had lunch last time?

"Yes."

"See you there in half an hour."

"OK."

Victor met the friend at the restaurant. Almost right off the bat, the friend said: "I understand your sister is settling here."

"Yes, I think I mentioned that to you."

"Well, they set you up."

"What do you mean?"

"You signed a paper describing how she and her family were severely persecuted in Moscow."

"I did not."

"Yes, you did."

Victor thought for a second. "You mean those papers their lawyer had me sign?"

"Yes. One of them, which you probably didn't bother to read, was exactly that, signed by you and stating that you know for a fact that they were *severely* persecuted." He chuckled. "I don't know exactly what they've got, but they're going to show that they were not 'severely persecuted'. He paused. "And they are planning to charge you with perjury."

Victor was stunned. "Let me guess. That lawyer is a former CIA man."

The friend nodded.

Victor just said: "Thanks. I owe you one."

The friend grinned. "You do," and laughed. "That's what friends are for."

They parted in a few minutes.

The next day Victor sent a letter to the lawyer, saying that he may mistakenly have signed a memorandum claiming severe persecution of his sister's family. To clarify the issue he stated unequivocally that he was not in a position to witness any such persecution, that he never wrote that memorandum, so his signature is null and void.

He soon received a call from the lawyer, who was furious, saying that the paper was just a routine thing that everyone files. Victor asked to see a copy of it. The lawyer declined saying that Victor is not his client, and went on yelling that Victor cannot withdraw his signature. Victor just said: "Be advised that a copy of my letter was sent to the appropriate place." The lawyer hung up, and Victor never heard from him again.

Following this incident Victor called Bill Camp, the highest-ranking CIA man he knew. They were on friendly terms personally, and Victor kept his emotions down. He simply said: "Bill, this is not a personal call."

Bill immediately reacted. "Oh-oh, something bad is coming."

"Not yet, but it may be. Despite all the assurances, the Agency is still interfering with my life." Bill tried to interrupt, but Victor did not let him, and went on. "Two recent incidents were the last straw. Please make sure that the CIA is advised that if I see any sign of interference, I will make sure that they regret all they have ever done to me. There will be no further warnings or discussions."

"Victor, would you be kind enough to give me the courtesy of an explanation, please?"

"Bill, this is not personal, I already said that. This is a message and I'm not in the mood to discuss anything any further."

Bill chuckled. "The shortest messages are always the nastiest ones."

"Bill, I hope that personally we remain friends." They would, until Bill's death a few years later.

When Bill retired he and his wife Jean moved to Watsontown, Pa. Everyone was surprised. Watsontown, a really small town about 10 miles South of Williamsport, was definitely not one of the bustling political centers of the world that Bill was used to living and working in. Olga and Victor visited the Camps occasionally, visiting nearby antique shows. During one of their visits, Victor was even more surprised when Bill mentioned that he was going to run for Mayor of Watsontown. Victor thought Bill was joking, but he wasn't. Unfortunately, this plan did not materialize. Many years ago Bill had suffered from a terminal cancer that to the doctors' astonishment suddenly stopped. All these years Bill felt that he was living on borrowed time. He took his diabetes stoically, and never complained.

One day Victor got a phone call. Jean's voice was soft, and the tone was revealing. Instead of the usual greetings, Jean said: "Victor, here is Bill, he wants to talk to you."

Bill's voice was weak, and he was obviously in a lot of pain. "Victor, my cancer returned, I have a bad blood infection. Just calling to say goodbye."

Victor did not know how to react. "Bill, I am sorry to hear that, but you're a tough guy, come on. You've beaten this thing before. You're going to be the Mayor of Watsontown, remember?"

"Victor, this is serious. Give my love to Olga, we love both of you." He slightly paused. "Difficult to talk. Goodbye."

"Goodbye, Bill."

A day later Bill passed. He was a good man. At his funeral there were some people from Washington, but Victor was surprised how many local people were paying their respects. People whose hearts he attracted during his short time there.

Ian, Victor's old MI6 colleague, came to Washington. It was Victor's chance to play host. On his day off Victor took Ian to Annapolis for a tour of the Naval Academy. Ian was very interested in American history, since some of his family had settled there a couple of centuries ago. And Annapolis was different. When they were walking along the Annapolis waterfront, Ian asked Victor how he felt about his security in Washington.

"Well, I think that I'm reasonably secure here. Mainly because of my public position. They have a lot of things to worry about, so I think I'm not too high on their worries list."

Ian chuckled. "Yes, they have enough problems now."

Victor hesitated, and then said: "But something is not right here." He knew that Ian was so good professionally that he would not discount a sixth sense.

Ian looked at Victor very intensely, and Victor said, "You know, I have this strange feeling that I am walking next to something very big and very ugly." He paused. "Don't know how to explain it."

Ian said quietly. "Victor, don't disregard it. You have good instincts. It may be very serious." He understood exactly what Victor meant.

Victor nodded. He had nothing else to say. Ian asked: "Have you taken a good look at your immediate surrounding, people you are in more or less constant contact?"

Victor smiled. "Of course. That's the irony. Every one of these contacts has the highest clearance, and have been scrutinized so many times that every new review looks ridiculous."

Ian nodded. "Just be careful, don't trust anybody. Just keep your guard up all the time."

34

The CIA's attempts to write off all its failures in Russia on Edward Lee Howard, a would-be CIA agent dismissed before his first assignment—were laughable. Most professionals took it for what it was—an attempt by the CIA to use a method known to be used by police worldwide—the so-called crime-clearing technique. When police cannot solve a series of crimes they blame them all one suspect.

When one of his colleagues at NSA made a joke about that CIA ploy, Victor said: "That's nothing compared to what the KGB has done."

"What do you mean?"

"Well, when we disappeared in 1980, they had little to go on. But they knew that heads would roll if they didn't find out what happened to us. So, with no indications of us being in the West, they 'investigated' our disappearance, and very successfully. Not only did they declare us all dead, but also found the murderers, who confessed with details. That made everybody there happy."

Everyone laughed, and Victor continued, "that is, until they found out from a mole in the CIA that we were here. However, by that time most of those involved were in some other job and the blow was softened. Likewise with Howard the CIA could write off a lot on him, saying that they're clean now, and the FBI was to blame for his getting away. Bureaucracy at work."

The consensus in most of the intelligence community was that Howard was a red herring. A key security concern was that it was becoming clear that the CIA had been penetrated by the KGB, and badly. The only question was the identity of the mole. Though the NSA was a separate agency and focused on its own interests, it had a vested interest in CIA security because of its interactions with the CIA. But the "turf" concept is well entrenched in any bureaucracy, and no one was particularly eager to step on some toes in a "sister agency."

The search for the CIA mole was at full throttle. Then, there it was, the announcement of the arrest of Aldrich Ames. The intelligence community was elated.

Victor did not participate in any of the process, and learned about what happened mainly from the media. In a short time a lot of information about Ames' actions had become public. Other information floated through the intelligence community. Everybody was shocked at the sloppiness of Ames' tradecraft. A lot of folks were making fun of the CIA's professional training. But the bigger implication was that even with his lousy tradecraft Ames had not been caught for very long time. That was a very legitimate concern.

As Victor read the information about Ames, he became uneasy. Some dates and names did not make sense, and certainly did not match Victor's experience. When the dust of the Ames arrest had settled, Victor started looking into the case.

Over the past several years the name of Victor Cherkashin kept popping up in counterintelligence circles. Cherkashin was the KR line Chief in the KGB Washington station. KR was the acronym for counterintelligence (*Kontrrazvedka* in Russian). It was one of the cardinal divisions of the KGB's First Chief Directorate, responsible for foreign intelligence, that was later renamed SVR, a Russian acronym for the External Intelligence Service. The KR Division handled a number of tasks, the most important being preventing recruitment of KGB officers by foreign intelligence services, and recruiting officers of foreign intelligence services, the CIA being the prime target. Victor Cherkashin was probably the most successful officer in that Division. He had much experience working against Americans, working at the Moscow Center as well as in postings abroad. He had recruited some important assets, and was universally feared by all KGB intelligence officers, who knew that the slightest suspicion from Cherkashin, justified or not, could at the very least cost them a career.

Victor clearly recalled his last meeting with Cherkashin, then head of the KR line at the KGB Washington station. It was in early

1980. Victor was slightly puzzled by a friend's invitation to a small dinner party. This dinner was at the friend's apartment, where Olga and Victor would meet Cherkashin and his wife, dinner for six. Cherkashin's wife could not attend, so it became a dinner for five. Victor had not met Cherkashin socially before, and he could only guess at the reason for the invitation. Often KGB officers were curious about Victor's unit and what they were doing. During the evening many topics were covered, but neither Cherkashin nor Victor's friend asked any direct questions. All they knew was that Victor was involved in all aspects of cipher communications security. At the end of the evening Cherkashin said he was looking for a head for the communications unit at the KGB Station in Washington, the *Residentura*, and asked Victor if he was interested. Victor replied that it was not exactly what he was doing, ducking softly the suggestion of a prestigious posting. Cherkashin just nodded.

Victor also knew that Cherkashin's posting to Washington was not a routine rotation, but was based on the urgency of a certain problem, and his remarkable record made him the best man to deal with the situation. Victor also knew that Cherkashin had made a spectacular recruitment in his previous posting in India, and that his Washington posting was related to that, to manage that supermole he recruited in India.

The most interesting aspect of the meeting was that it had occurred after Victor's visit to the American Embassy in Warsaw. Victor figured that if the KGB had the slightest suspicion in that regard, he'd be sitting in a different place, and talking to nastier people than Cherkashin. This fact added some excitement to the occasion. Victor mused that he knew more about Cherkashin than Cherkashin knew about him. Hopefully.

Because Cherkashin's cover was as a diplomat accredited in Washington, all his arrivals and departures were registered. Victor secured the record, and made a graph of Cherkashin's arrivals and departures. This was a classic example of the usefulness of visual aids. The result was so obvious that Victor was mad at himself for not having done it earlier.

Normal vacation leave for senior KGB officers was forty-five days plus travel time. Occasionally some saved two weeks for a later time. Cherkashin took that regular leave time in 1981, 1982, 1983 and 1984. The only odd vacation time was in 1980, when he was absent from Washington for 75 days. That was really unusual, and Victor decided to return to that later. The only other trip in 1980-81 was his trip Moscow at the beginning of 1980. Victor remembered that trip, because of his dinner with Cherkashin in Moscow. The normal one vacation trip per year was pretty much standard, and Cherkashin's schedule was fully compliant.

Then, in 1982, there was one additional short trip. In 1983 his schedule really stood out: Cherkashin made five short trips within the first five months of the year. That was truly extraordinary.

Victor stared at the graph, knowing that that was a revelation of some sort, but he couldn't figure out what. He decided to compare it with other known events of that time. When he compared it with the FBI's work with Martynov and Motorin it all became obvious. Martynov volunteered to the FBI in January of 1982. Cherkashin flew to Moscow on January 28, 1982.

The important point for Victor was that Cherkashin did not need to go to Moscow if an officer was known to have been recruited. All procedures for such an occasion were in place. All he needed to do was send a cable, and put the man on an Aeroflot plane under some pretense, or have him drugged. The only reason for Cherkashin to go to Moscow was to do something non-standard. What could be non-standard in such a situation? Probably, Victor reasoned, a personal plea not to sack the officer in order to protect the source. Cherkashin was probably successful, because Martynov worked and lived out of the Embassy, and was rarely there, and no one would notice his absence. So "neutralizing," i.e. preventing him from learning anything beyond what he already knew, would not be too difficult.

Victor realized the next point was crucial. The FBI started compromising Motorin in December of 1982. It was a multi-stage process that ended with his firm recruitment in April 1983. Cherkashin made five short trips in 1983, between January 7 and May 23. That was truly

extraordinary and looked like an operational mistake. He was probably desperately trying to protect his source and was facing a very difficult task. Kryuchkov must have said something like: "You've got an
American spy in your Station, and you convinced me to let him be,
and now you are trying to get me to agree to your having two American
spies there. What's your limit?"

Victor felt that Cherkashin's trips were clear evidence that the KGB
was monitoring the FBI's work with Martynov and Motorin practically
in real time. Furthermore, their source in the FBI was so valuable that
it was agreed to let them be until a solid decoy source was found so
they could be safely sacked.

Victor had already looked at Cherkashin's trip to Moscow as
it related to Ames, and the graph just confirmed the correlation.
However, Cherkashin's 75 days "vacation" in 1980, ostensibly in
Moscow, was something that needed analyzing.

What caught Victor's eye now was that fact that the KGB's roll-up of
the CIA assets in Russia in 1983-86 did not match the timing of Ames'
disclosures. Ames' first contact with the KGB took place on April 16,
1985, and his first transfer of information was on May 17, 1985. That
was also the date the KGB started the roll-up with the recall of Oleg
Gordievsky, the Chief of the KGB London Station and a British double-agent. That was way too soon for even the most neurotic reaction,
even if Ames had provided that information on April 16.

Clearly Ames' main consideration was money. Given that, Victor
figured Ames would withhold the most valuable information until his
pay was assured. Initially, he'd provide just enough to get the KGB's
attention. The first confirmed payment was May 17. If Victor was right,
Ames would deliver his most valuable information no earlier than his
June 13 meeting. However, even if Ames had given all his information
to the KGB on the first contact, it still did not correspond with the
timing of the recalls and arrests of the CIA assets. Victor knew the
KGB received such claims regarding its officers all the time. Many of
them were checked out, and that took a long time. If the KGB reacted
as it was claimed in the Ames case, it would have lost all its operations
officers a long time ago.

This point was reinforced by the details of the arrests of the CIA assets. In all the accounts Victor read the arrests were bundled in one batch. However, when he looked into it further, it became apparent that there were three different strings of arrests. The sequence and timing of these arrests showed a pattern of diminishing importance. The first string included only the most damaging penetrations: the Station Chief in London, KR officers, and First (American) Department officers. The second string included less damaging penetrations. The arrests of these two strings were completed by the end of 1985 and included all the essential and currently active assets. The third string comprised old cases, including agents like General Polyakov, who had retired and had been out of communication for years. Investigating tips of this nature takes time, and it is impossible to predict how much time a particular case will take. So, Victor reasoned, it was highly implausible that the KGB had completed all these investigations in the order most convenient for their interests. The sequence was a firm indication that all those arrests were planned well in advance.

Victor realized there was a further point to be made about the third string of arrests. The KGB started arresting all non-essential CIA assets in 1986. This totally contradicted the usual KGB care for its sources, and was an indication that the KGB was deliberately showing its full knowledge of the CIA operations, flagrantly challenging the CIA. This point was strengthened by the fact that some of the CIA case officers were arrested going *to* the meetings with their assets. The usual KGB practice was to make an arrest either at, or after the meeting. The case officer could well have been under undetected surveillance while going to the meeting, and that would have made analysis of the case more difficult. And yet, the KGB chose to arrest the case officers while they were going to the meetings, clearly demonstrating its prior complete knowledge, once again rubbing it in to the CIA. Furthermore, The KGB had gone one step further in this operation, arresting a case officer of a double-agent, which made no sense if the KGB had cared about the source.

Victor noted that at the time of these highly uncharacteristic actions the KGB had also made several totally unexplained and very serious operational errors in handling Ames. First, just two days after

Ames' walk-in on April 16, Cherkashin went on an unprecedented clandestine trip to Moscow. The trip to Moscow was not formally registered by the State Department. Obviously, he could not go openly, as that would be a gross violation of fundamental security procedures, and could connect him to the Ames contact and offer to the KGB. But he did not have to go to Moscow in the first place. Victor knew that there were fully secure, well established procedures for a case of a walk-in of any level of sensitivity. For instance, Cherkashin could have written a sealed personal letter to Kryuchkov to be opened personally. With the twice-weekly diplomatic pouch service to Moscow that would be faster than his difficult and politically risky clandestine trip. Victor reckoned this meant that Cherkashin had another reason to go to Moscow—to see Kryuchkov personally. It would have been to make a plea of a highly unusual nature. The hint as to its nature could be that the third participant of the meeting was Vadim Kirpichenko, whose support Cherkashin probably enlisted for his plea to Kryuchkov. Importantly, Kirpichenko had been the head of Directorate S, handling 'illegals' and extremely important moles.

All those events were happening in the background of a major power shift in the Soviet Union. Andropov had been an old intelligence hand. He knew how important highly placed agents could be, and probably decided to be deliberate with the roll-up of the CIA network. Gorbachev, on the contrary, did not understand intelligence at all. Soon after Gorbachev came to power in 1985, KGB chief Kryuchkov would have had to report the existence of the CIA network. Gorbachev probably demanded that it be dismantled completely and quickly. Naturally, this panicked the KGB, understanding that this would ruin their own network in the US. They were looking for a way to save their own network in the US.

Going through all the conceivable scenarios Victor was leaning to the idea that the situation, urgent and unusual, demanded a personal plea to Kryuchkov, and that Cherkashin's plea to Kryuchkov was about burning Ames to protect their prized agents. If this scenario was correct, Kryuchkov probably agreed to sacrifice Ames. The KGB knew Ames with all his weaknesses, and understood that he would not last long as a source.

Whatever the motivation, Cherkashin returned to Washington openly, clearly alerting the CIA and the FBI that something extraordinary had just occurred at the KGB station in Washington. One such giveaway should be enough by KGB standards, but after realizing that the CIA did not pick up the hint, they went further.

The second event was on May 17. Defying all operational security rules for no apparent reason, the KGB invited Ames for a brief visit into the Soviet Embassy building. That visit was immediately followed by an outside meeting with Soviet diplomat Sergey Chuvakhin, where the money was handed to Ames. Furthermore, inexplicably, Cherkashin openly went to Moscow three days later. This performance would be unacceptable for any intelligence service. By KGB standards it was simply unthinkable. The CIA still did not get it. Victor wished he could have seen the astonishment on Cherkashin's face.

So Cherkashin had to shout even louder. He dropped in on a meeting between Ames and his courier on July 31. Judging by Cherkashin's prior stellar operational performance, he would never do that even if he had been sure that he was not under surveillance. But he knew that in Washington he was under FBI surveillance all the time, and still did it.

35

One day Bob Hanssen asked Victor for a meeting.

"Victor, the F BI wants you to participate in an operation in New York. Would you agree?"

The memory of Bob's invitation to Afghanistan, and the fact that he rebuffed him very directly, instantly popped into Victor's mind. "Conceptually, yes. Subject to particulars, of course."

"Good. Your participation would be operationally small, but essential for the operation. It would take a day, two at most. I'll let you know.

"Sure."

About a month later Bob told Victor that the operation was a go, and invited him to the final clearing meeting at the Headquarters.

Accompanied by Hanssen, Victor entered the conference room; he was surprised. High-level counterintelligence people from New York were all there, along with the Headquarters people. Victor knew most of them, and was on good terms with the Counterintelligence supervisor from New York. The head of the operation started his presentation. By the end of the presentation Victor was shocked. Incredible in its operational complexity, with dozens of people involved, the operation was fundamentally doomed.

The top supervisor from New York thanked the presenter and asked for comments. There weren't many.

Then Victor said: "Well, it's pretty complex operationally, I think it can be done in a much simpler way. More importantly, the underlying assumption may be incorrect; I think it needs to be verified."

Ignoring the assumption remark, the New York supervisor said in a slightly sarcastic voice: "Well, do you have a better suggestion operationally?"

"Offhand, something like this looks more efficient" – and in a few sentences Victor described a different, mush simpler and more secure approach.

Bob Hanssen, as usual in such meetings, kept a very low profile, almost as though he was not there. Victor looked at him, but Bob turned away. Victor took it as a career concern–don't stick your neck out. The supervisor was really irritated. "Look, we spent some time designing this. What do you want to do, run our operations?"

Now Victor was irritated. The flaw looked too big to agree. "I am not trying to run your operations, but I would prefer not to participate."

Suddenly, there was a total silence in the room.

The supervisor went ballistic. "Victor, you're holding a gun to my head. This operation is designed with your participation." He made a pause. "Frankly, I think you're playing Russian Roulette with your relations with the FBI."

That was too much. "Actually, I prefer Jewish Roulette."

"What's that?"

"Same as Russian Roulette, except that you hold the gun to somebody else's head."

Everybody cracked up.

"Victor, I am very serious."

Victor had no room for maneuver. "All right, than let me get serious too. I am not going to participate in something like this. This operation is designed to fail." He took a breath. "Let me make a prediction. If you go ahead as planned, this thing will fall flat on its face. You will have a nasty stink in Russian media that will probably be picked up by American media, and you will end up with egg on your face. Good luck."

There was not much else to do there, and Victor left. Victor's words proved to be prophetic in more than one way.

Sure enough, two weeks later a major Russian newspaper ran a series of two articles on the matter, and it was picked up by American media. Interestingly enough, the Russians blamed the CIA for the operation. When this came up with the NSA counterintelligence, everybody was making jokes about the CIA being a fire hydrant in a dog show, and FBI being Teflon-coated. What they did not know at the time was that the operation was concocted by Bob Hanssen.

After that encounter, naturally Victor had little interaction with the FBI, except for the occasional discussion with the counterintelligence analysts.

36

In intelligence, perhaps more than in any other business, a clear picture of a situation can only be seen years after the event. Victor recalled how, when years ago he was walking down the street with one of the top experts of British intelligence who had superb tradecraft skills, he took advantage of the moment to ask, "Richard, what makes you so good at street work?"

Richard smiled. "It's all in the fundamentals. Never mind how they look. Never mind what they say. But watch what they do, what they really do."

Victor didn't answer—this seemed obvious common sense.

They were passing an old cathedral overlooking a square. Richard looked high above the steps up to the entrance. "See that man sitting on the steps? What's he doing?"

Victor saw a panhandler. "Begging for money."

"That's an assumption. All you can really say is that he's sitting there, in a position to observe everything going on in the square." He paused. "Perfect position for area surveillance, by the way."

"Thank you."

Richard chuckled. "Just remember that, always. Most people don't." The fundamental depth of the remark then dawned on Victor. He remembered this adage, and came to realize that its application went much broader, well beyond surveillance street work.

Victor occasionally raised his concern about the CIA with his NSA counterintelligence colleagues.

"Look, fundamentally, CIA clandestine operations are not doing well at all."

One of the guys said, "Well, they say that all their failures are public but all their successes are classified."

Victor laughed. "We constantly hear about them recruiting agents. This is just not true. They probably never recruited anyone. Defectors, so called "walk-ins," come to them as a matter of course, whatever their motivations—but mainly they act on their image of this country. They are defecting to the United States, not the CIA. The CIA just happens to represents this country to them."

One of his colleagues said: "That's probably true, but you're really talking about ideology. What do you want us to do? Straighten out the CIA? That's just not doable. They're so political, they try to manipulate everybody, even their own wives." Everybody laughed.

"No, I'm not trying to lecture you on the obvious. I just want to take a look at the fundamental assumptions here. The bottom line is that volunteers, defectors, account for most if not all their human intelligence."

"That's definitely correct."

"All right. Then why do they treat them so badly? It just doesn't make sense."

"Well, that's a good question."

"What I mean is that they consistently mistreat their own assets. This hurts their own interests, this country's interests."

"Well, they blame it on the defectors themselves."

"Of course. But it just cannot be that all defectors are no good, drunkards, mentally unstable, and so on. However, the CIA treats them all badly. At least, I haven't heard of any defector saying a good word about their treatment by the CIA." Victor chuckled. "All right, without disclosing any secrets, can you tell me that you ever heard of a single satisfied defector?"

"No, not really. But I still don't get it. What are you trying to say?"

"Well, I'm trying to say that something is fundamentally wrong with CIA security, big time." Victor took a breath. "My hunch is that they've been penetrated badly, and that the moles inside the CIA manipulate the Agency into treating the defectors badly."

The reaction was very skeptical. "That's a real stretch."

"Not really. Suppose they do have a mole or two in the Agency. What's the biggest danger for those moles?

"Defectors, definitely."

"So, what's the best defense for a mole? To discredit defectors and to discourage future potential recruits against defecting. How you do that? By treating those that come badly. Simple."

"That makes sense theoretically, but how would you do it in practice?"

"The easiest people to manipulate are usually the manipulators. The CIA's idea of intelligence is a competition for who can be the biggest crook."

Laughter. "There's a lot of truth in that."

Victor went on. "Did you notice that one of Yurchenko's debriefers was Ames?"

"Yea, that was unfortunate."

"Can you imagine that Ames wasn't trying to discredit Yurchenko? Did anybody look specifically into that possibility?"

"Not as far as we know."

The discussion went on for a little longer, but the consensus was traditional: the NSA could never investigate its sister Agency.

Olga and Victor saw there was a great deal of misunderstanding of Russia in the US. Immediately after the fall of the Soviet Union numerous "experts" on Russian affairs and business had popped up everywhere. Most of them had no idea what they were talking about, didn't speak Russian, had little knowledge of Russian or Soviet history, and no real experience at all. Many businesses and Government organizations were falling victim to these "consultants." As always, truth competes with lies on equal terms.

Olga had never lacked creativity. She had been interested in television production for a while, and now she came up with the idea of becoming a TV producer. She quickly completed the required educational credits and received her producer's license. The pace of the Sheymovs' family life became even more interesting. Olga started a talk show on a local public TV station, which she called *Russia Today*. The show was in English, for an American audience. The idea was to provide viewers access to top-level experts on Russia, both Russian and American, to discuss and compare their views on current political, economic, cultural, and technical issues. The show quickly became a success. The impressive guest list included such figures as James Billington, Vasily Aksyonov, Sergei Bodrov, Nikolay Getman, Boris Grebenschikov, Michael McFaul, Paula Dobriansky, and Oleg Kalugin among others.

At the end of the show's first year the station encouraged Olga to enter the show for the prestigious Telly Award. About nine hundred stations from all over the country entered shows for the competition. Everybody was stunned when Olga's *Russia Today* won two Telly awards: *Best Talk Show,* and *Best Set Design.* Olga was told that this was the first time that a show won the *Telly* in its first year of production.

In a meeting with Jim Millhorn, a very experienced FBI analyst, Victor mentioned the implausibility of Aldrich Ames burning Motorin and Martynov, the two prized FBI assets in the KGB Washington Station. He referred to the well-publicized fact that Cherkashin, Ames' handler, took down the KGB operational map in the Station corridor. That was cited as Cherkashin's heightened sense of operational security.

Jim said: "That's well known. So what?"

"Well, the important thing here is not the fact, but the timing. First of all, this kind of map in the corridor of the Station is common in KGB stations all over the world, including where Cherkashin was posted before. Every morning operatives that are going to have an operation that day mark the general area of the city, so that other operatives stay away from it, to avoid inadvertently bringing their 'tails' there."

Jim just nodded impatiently, and Victor went on. "Now, Cherkashin had seen this kind of map before, but all of a sudden he starts bitching about it in Washington."

"Yeah, it's a high security area."

"Did you look at *when* he started bitching about it?"

Jim thought for a second. "I think around 1983."

"Precisely. Right at the time the FBI was recruiting Martynov and Motorin."

"What are you saying?"

"Just think about it, OK? To me that suggests that was when he learned about Motorin and Martynov. And the question is, how did he learn about them? Ames was not even on the horizon at the time."

Millhorn did not respond.

Given the skeptical reception his ideas received, combined with the uneasy feeling that Ames was not the main culprit in the American troubles, Victor decided to do some more digging. He just could never forget how badly not only he, but also his wife and daughter had been treated by the CIA when it was totally contrary to the interests of the United States. And he still had his suspicions about Jack's 1985 "suicide."

Victor's research quickly led him to concentrate on a small number of CIA officers, based on their exposure to the list of the CIA agents lost in 1985, the so-called "Year of the Spy." In his research Victor started comparing the timing of these officers' postings. The information was publicly available, but not easily accessible by mere mortals. Victor turned to Olga for help in some research at the State Department. With her media credentials this was easy for her.

Olga came back laughing. "Victor, Bob Hanssen really gave me a scare."

"How come?"

"Well, I was sitting at the monitor in the public research room at the State department. Naturally, I was pretty much concentrating on the screen. It was very quiet in the room and I hadn't heard a sound. Then, all of a sudden, I saw a reflection of a dark figure leaning over my shoulder to read my screen. It was really spooky. I quickly turned around, trying to stand up." She took a breath. "And guess what, it was Bob Hanssen, smiling with his strange smile. You know how he moves, no sound at all. I was really scared. So, he asked what I was researching, and I told him it was some information you needed. We chatted a bit and I left."

Victor laughed. "I know very few people who move like that. Did you tell him that you were going there?"

"No. It must have been a coincidence."

"Not likely, somebody must've tipped him off. He was probably a little puzzled and decided to take a look personally."

During this time Victor had several meetings with the FBI analysts, mainly with Jim Millhorn. He used this opportunity to question the rationale for writing off all the American losses to Ames, and raised the possibility of other penetrations of the CIA. On one occasion Victor said, "Jim, you know, everyone traditionally concentrates on the time of a subject's access to information."

"Sure, what's wrong with that?"

"The interesting thing here is that we concentrate on the *beginning* of the access. Actually, that's a false assumption. See, with perishable information that's perfectly all right–if you don't report it quickly it becomes useless. But with really sensitive information of long-term value, such as a mole's identity when very few people have access to it, it's just too dangerous for a mole to pass on. His masters are likely to act on the info, and that would bring the mole squarely into the focus of the CI."

"What are you driving at?"

"Well, a really careful mole would report this kind of information only after *leaving* a particular position of access. Nobody's looking at the time when a subject of interest *leaves* the position of access."

Jim was surprised. "Come to think of it, you have a point. Let me think about that."

Victor's work with NSA was becoming less intense. Some of his work was not too sensitive, and given the worsening traffic situation around Washington, Victor wanted to do some of the work at home, with proper security precautions, of course. The NSA agreed.

One day Victor was working at home when the phone rang. It was Bob Hanssen. "Victor, I'm home and need a ride to the hospital. Can you help?" He sounded like he was in pain. Victor was a little puzzled, but he knew that Bonnie was probably at the Oakcrest School, teaching.

It just happened that Victor's car was in the shop. "Bob, I have no car now, it's in the shop, but Olga is at Tysons now, she can pick you up in a few minutes. Let me call her, I'll call you right back."

Victor called Olga and asked her to give Bob a ride to the hospital. He called Bob.

"Bob, Olga will be there in a few minutes. You sound like you're in a lot of pain."

"I am. Probably kidney."

"Are you sure you don't want an ambulance?"

"No thanks."

Olga returned home in about an hour. "Well, it looks like Bob has a kidney problem. I can't understand why he didn't call an ambulance. He was in so much pain that he told me a few times to drive faster."

"Where did you take him?"

"Fair Oaks. I pulled up to the Emergency entrance, and he got out, struggled to get his briefcase and finally pulled it out, and almost ran to the entrance, limping very heavily. I never understood why he'd take his briefcase with him from home to the hospital. I offered to go in with him, but he refused."

"Briefcase?"

"Yeah."

"Strange." Victor paused. "Call Bonnie at school in case he didn't."

37

The depth of the CIA's malevolence never failed to amaze Victor. In 1996, after *Tower of Secrets* had been published, the agency tried to get him to sign a piece of paper stating that he would never publish anything without prior approval of the CIA. When Victor formally refused, the CIA stopped his pension. Victor wrote to the IG to note that this was a breach of their agreement. Resettlement demanded a meeting. Victor agreed, on condition that Robert Holderman of the NSA was present, that the meeting was recorded, and that the NSA would keep one copy. Very reluctantly, the CIA agreed.

Before the meeting Victor met with Robert.

"I heard through the grapevine that the current head of Resettlement is Amy Tabzi. Interestingly, every response to my questions about her contained three words. The first two were various expletives, but the third one was 'bitch.'"

Robert laughed. "Well, I can confirm that she's a pushy specimen."

At the arranged time, Victor pulled into the parking lot in front of the Tysons Corner Sheraton. One didn't need intelligence training to spot the heavy presence of security—although there was no need for it. Two obvious security black Suburbans with dark windows were standing conspicuously by the entrance, with their drivers at the wheel. It only attracted attention to a rather unimportant event. *Yet another case of putting psychological pressure on me. This time they want to demonstrate that I'm dangerous—a threat to their employees, who must be watched.*

After Victor met Bob in the parking lot, Victor indicated the Suburbans with his eyes, and Robert just smiled and shrugged. They went to the lobby, where two men escorted them to a suite. Its conference room was furnished mainly with a large round table ringed by chairs, and a couple of armchairs to the side. The door to the adjacent room was shut. When the door opened two women emerged, and one decisively shut it—a signal to Victor that others were in there; must be armed security guards.

Victor sat down opposite a dark-haired, short heavy-set woman in her late middle-age. Her attire was typical of that worn by CIA women: an executive business suit that was a pretentious imitation of Wall Street pinstripe. Her deliberate, efficient movements were those of a busy executive, and her steady dark eyes communicated unshakable self-confidence.

While Victor waited for the meeting to begin, he mused on their respective reasons for attending. *They want to undo the mistake they made, and provoke me into making one of my own. I want the opposite—to nail them on their mistake. My existence was so secret back in 1980 that the Resettlement people responsible had no access to me, so I never signed any promise not to publish anything without their permission.*

When everyone had introduced themselves for the record, the woman referred to herself as "Amy" and stated, "I represent the United States Government here."

Not only was her sweeping assertion immodest, but it was also incorrect. Besides, Robert was far senior to her. Victor smiled. "To be more specific, don't you actually represent NROC, the National Resettlement Operations Center?"

Amy nearly shouted: "I said that I represent the United States Government!"

Feigning surprise, Victor said, "All of it?"

"All of it, sir!"

When Victor said nothing further, Amy began talking rapidly. Suddenly, he became fascinated by his strong impression that Amy's mouth operated independently from the rest of her face, which was as immobile as a bust. Although the mouth constantly interrupted others, no one could interrupt it.

While listening to a lengthy discourse on how well-intentioned and caring the CIA was, Victor saw the mouth take a gulp of air and instantly seized the moment by interjecting, "Excuse me, Madam. You can save time by skipping the propaganda part."

Amy became indignant, and Victor was a bit taken aback when the rest of her body started functioning. She tried to stand up, but then realized that she was stuck between the arms of her chair, and gave up. Fuming, she screamed: "Why am I taking this abuse? I don't have to take this abuse!"

Gee, all these folks come from the same school. Just the same way Nedrof tried to pretend enraged innocence.

In a low voice Victor said, "This is a free country. So you may leave at any time. I don't mind ending this charade."

At that, Amy's fake indignation evaporated. "Well…we'd better get down to business." Victor glanced at Bob, who was obviously laboring to keep his face expressionless.

Soon Victor found an opening. "I asked to see the agreement signed by me and Bill Camp after the IG investigation, with its addendum. I also asked to see Bill's affidavit on the matter, which he wrote not long before his death. Those documents are the keys to the present situation." Victor had never been given copies.

Smirking, Amy stared at Victor. "We couldn't find any of those documents." Again the message was loud and clear: *We can do to you whatever we want, and there is nothing—absolutely nothing—you can do about it.*

After a brief argument, Victor was faced with a disturbingly familiar situation. The CIA sought to break its promises to him by cutting off the money they owed him unless he signed a quitclaim officially declaring that he had no claims whatsoever against the CIA. If he signed it, his payments would be restored, with a thirty percent reduction—and then only for five years, instead of until retirement age.

Amy took another document out of her briefcase. "This is a MOA. It was approved. In order for us to get an MOA to you to sign, this went all the way up to the Director of Central Intelligence, who authorized us to work on the first MOA that was signed by then-Director Bush in August of 1991."

Director Bush, in 1991? Victor stifled a laugh. "Excuse me. What country are you referring to?"

"Pardon?"

"What country did you refer to when you said: 'then Director Bush'?"

"Then-Director Bush. He was then the Director of the CIA."

Victor was incredulous. "In 1991?"

"That's correct." She paused. "Excuse me. We're already getting off track here. Are you trying to tell me when Bush was Director of Central Intelligence? His name is right here." She stuck her finger on the signature line and read: "It says: 'Eighth of August, 1991, George Bush, Director of Central Intelligence.' OK?"

Victor cursed himself. *Idiot. She's handing you evidence of their crime, and you're trying to make a joke out of it? This is your break. Take it and shut up.*

Victor said mildly, "All right," and quietly took a deep breath.

To Victor's amazement, nobody else at the table seemed to have caught the significance of Amy's grossly erroneous admission. Victor guessed that they tuned Amy out whenever she spoke. Before them all lay a document forged by the CIA. Like a bad-luck-Charlie counterfeiter putting the portrait of a wrong President on an otherwise perfect twenty-dollar bill, the CIA had forged the signature of the sitting President of the United States. Although Victor had caught the CIA red-handed, and knew that proof of their crime was recorded on an official tape that would be held at the NSA, he felt no satisfaction over his victory. Rather, he was filled with disgust.

Wanting now to completely nail the CIA, Victor pushed his luck again a few minutes later. After a preamble as polite as he could muster, Victor asked Amy: "To your knowledge, have I ever been shown forged documents by the CIA?"

"Never."

"Never? Are you certain of that? I did say, 'to your knowledge'."

"Not only to my knowledge. I have reviewed your files. You have never been shown any forged documents."

"All right."

Victor took another deep breath.

Soon it became obvious that the meeting was going nowhere. But before Victor could call it off, Amy took another sheet of paper out of her briefcase. It was a response from the Inspector General, stating that Victor's complaint had been looked into and no reason had been found to proceed further. The "complaint" was Victor's notification that his pension had been cut off, contrary to the promises given after the IG investigation several years earlier. The IG should have responded directly to him, not through the object of the complaint. *So much for an independent IG. Or—is this another forgery?*

Victor returned the letter to Amy, who promptly said: "You have to sign it."

"Why is that?"

"To attest to the fact that you read it."

Victor inspected the paper again. At the very bottom of the page, with a couple of inches of white space above it, was a line for his signature. *Well, this is a bit too much. Do I look really that dumb? They obviously need a recent sample of my signature. The one they have is several years old, and they know that signatures change over time. So, they need to refresh their forger's bank.*

He refused, and was amused by Amy's ferocious pressure to change his mind. "You have to sign it, since you've read it." She was really shouting.

Victor just quietly said, "No."

Then Amy produced another paper from her magician's briefcase. This one listed references to government documents that described available medical services. Sure enough, the brief listing had nothing to do with Victor as the CIA had never provided any medical services beyond 1981, but mysteriously it was followed by three inches of white space and a line for Victor's signature.

This is getting really pathetic. "And you want me to sign it? Why?"

"Of course. You've read it, haven't you?"

It must be very hard to be that stupid. "I see no reason for that."

The meeting was over with no progress whatsoever, Victor and Robert promptly departed the suite leaving infuriated Amy with her armed entourage. Of course, Victor's pension payments stopped.

A few days later Victor dropped by the NSA office and verified Amy's statements with the transcript. Robert was laughing wholeheartedly. "I couldn't believe what I was hearing then and I am still startled when I look at the transcript." He paused. "Well, nothing can change the Coneheads." That was the nickname for CIA people that somehow stuck to them for years. To the best of Victor's research it was Victor Belenko, the pilot who flew a MIG-25 to Japan in 1979, who used it first. Victor used it routinely at the NSA and the FBI.

Although Chris, a friend, a PhD in physics who for some unknown reason briefly had been his official contact at the CIA following the

IG investigation, and his wife Lee had retired and moved to the West Coast. Victor had kept him apprised of developments from time to time. When he called Chris to brief him on the latest, he replied: "You know, Victor, I've been hoping all along that they'd come to their senses. Now I think that you should find a damned good lawyer."

"Chris, you know how things are if you try to sue the Company. Are you willing to testify? I don't want to jeopardize your pension."

"If things continue as they are, of course I will. Victor, I'll always testify to the truth, and I don't give a damn who says what about it. As to my pension, I'm not that easy to scare, you know. They'll have a hell of a time trying to take it away from me."

"Thanks, Chris. I have to think about it—it's so damn difficult."

Olga and Victor discussed the situation, and Olga summarized it. "Victor, I think the CIA is so bad for us that we should avoid any contact with them at any cost. I think that we're better off to forget about this money rather than dealing with them again. It's just too unpleasant. I hope they will leave us alone if they cancel your pension. You are making enough for us to live on. Let's just cut all ties with them. They're really bad people."

"I agree." The issue was settled.

PART III

38

The NSA project Victor was involved in was close to completion. Both he and Olga felt that it was time to start thinking about a different phase of their life. They discussed various possibilities. Olga asked if Victor was interested in going back to what was interrupted in 1989, investment banking.

Victor rejected the idea. "Well, if I have to I can do that, but it's really too late. During these years the business has changed so much that I wouldn't know where to start."

"Oh come on, you can catch up pretty quickly."

"Do you want to move to New York?"

"No."

"Well, most investment banking is there. If one's serious about it, that's the place to be. Besides, I'm not sure I want to do that anyway."

"What do you want to do then? How about writing books?"

Victor though for a moment. "Maybe. But I can do that later. Meanwhile I have a couple of pretty good technological ideas that may be marketable."

"You want to sell them to some company?"

"Possible, but maybe a better idea would be to open my own shop."

"You want to start a company?" Olga was clearly skeptical.

"Yeah, why not?"

"We don't have the capital. Can you use your old connections for that?"

"No. I was working there under a different name, remember? It would be a mess if I mix the two."

"Venture capitalists?"

"No way. Many people call them vulture capitalists. Years ago, at the university, I looked at their operations from the standpoint of financial operations. Guess what: essentially they operate exactly like pawn shops. I don't want to be on either side of that equation." He paused. "But don't worry, I'll think of something. Maybe the Government will help with funding."

A couple of weeks later he asked to present an idea to the NSA as a private endeavor. He presented it to a very impressive panel of top NSA scientists. The conclusion was positive, as much as it could be coming from the NSA: "We can see no technological reason why the concept could not be implemented. The implementation, if done properly, would add additional protection to systems you described." For funding NSA referred Victor to one of the Government programs. Victor did some research, and found that the bureaucratic process required would be too much for his psychological capacity. He went to an old friend, Donald. He explained the concept and the applications.

"Can you help me to get two million funding for this?"

"I doubt it. This isn't a top priority now." He chuckled. "However, if you solve the Internet hacking problem I can get you two billion–everyone is crazy about that problem."

Victor remembered how once in a casual conversation with some NSA scientists one of them lamented the problem of hacking. Knowing that several people there were working on solving the problem, Victor had teased, "Hey guys, look at the situation: it takes half a million bucks and half a year to design a decent firewall. But it only takes a PC, a pony tail, and a week to hack it. That's not a good equation. Aren't you ashamed of yourselves?"

They just laughed, but one of them said: "You know, if you're so frickin' smart, why don't you come up with an algorithm to fix it?"

It was a casual remark, but the challenge thrown at him got Victor's attention, and it got him thinking.

39

Bob Hanssen called Victor and asked him to come by his State Department office. At the time Bob was assigned as the FBI liaison to the State Department. Victor had been there before, and every time it was just for a short chat regarding Bob's current interests. This time Bob asked a few questions that clearly were not worth a meeting. Then he suddenly asked, "What are you up to with those guys from NSA?" That was unusual, since the unspoken rule had always been that Victor did not discuss with one agency what he was doing with another.

Surprised, Victor paused for an answer. Bob immediately understood that his question was inappropriate. "Oh, I mean do you discuss much counterintelligence stuff with them?"

"Not really. And I haven't talked to your guys much either since I talked to Jim Millhorn quite some time back, when he was lukewarm about what I suggested to him." Bob was still Victor's liaison with the FBI, with practically unlimited FBI clearance.

Bob changed the subject. "Let's take a look at what's happening operationally around here." Victor thought that he was trying to show that he was still in the Russian counterintelligence game. Bob logged on to a computer on his desk, and then logged on to some remote server. "Hmm, let's see if there have been any dead drops detected, say around my house." With a few keystrokes he made a query entry and turned the screen so Victor could see it. "None." Then he said: "How about the KGB guys showing up in the area?" A few more keystrokes. "None." He laughed. "Great, they stay away from where I live."

Victor said: "That's a great capability. Very convenient."

"Yeah. Anything you want to know from here?"

"How about the SSN of Y?"

Bob glanced sharply at Victor. "Sure." Victor gave him a name, and Bob made an entry.

"Here he is. By the way, he's been seriously investigated twice. Both times they couldn't come up with any proof. Probably somebody warned him." Again, it was 'they' as if Bob was distancing himself. He paused. "See, somebody also warned Felix Bloch, and they couldn't come up with any proof as well. They're just stupid."

Victor looked at the number. "It's not what I have. Can you trace a number?" Victor thumbed through his notes and gave him a number.

"Sure." He gave Victor a different name.

"Interesting. I'll have to work on this some more."

Bob logged off the computer. "So, what is it that Jim wasn't much interested in? He's pretty good, but he misses some clues too."

Victor showed Bob his graph of Cherkashin's in-out schedule marked with Martynov's and Motorin's recruitment. "See, Cherkashin knew about Motorin's recruitment practically in real time." Then Victor explained his theory that Ames could not possibly be the source for the KGB's roll-up of the whole CIA network.

Something changed in Bob–his face, his demeanor, his voice, but Victor couldn't put his finger on it.

"Victor, why are you doing this?"

Victor was surprised. *And you too don't want to see the inconvenient truth. It's pathetic.* He looked Bob straight in the eye and slowly and testily said: "Bob, I was hurt by the CIA. More importantly, my wife and even my daughter were hurt by them. A friend of mine was probably killed. And you want to tell me 'take it easy'?" The only reason for all this that I can figure is that the CIA is being manipulated by KGB moles. Because the CIA's culture is so rotten it's not too hard for anyone with bad intentions to manipulate it."

Bob didn't answer, and Victor said, "Everyone knows the CIA has a mole, but no one has the guts to do something about it."

Bob smirked with his dark sparkle in the eyes. "You're wrong. They have at least three moles, probably five or six. But how are you supposed to find them? The FBI is just not good enough for that. You need someone like Patton to head it, but we don't have Pattons anymore. All we have is a bunch of wimps."

Victor was stunned, and he knew how well informed Bob was and how much he could not tell Victor for security reasons. "What? More than three moles? That's practically impossible to catch."

In counterintelligence work it was well understood that one foreign agent can be detected if the breach is known. If one knows what information has been lost in his organization, one can deduce the perpetrator or, at least, narrow the circle of potential suspects. The more 'leaks' that are known, the narrower becomes the circle of the potential suspects. However, if the penetration involves more than one agent, the problem grows exponentially; and detecting three moles in one organization is almost impossible. The circle of suspects is too large. In other words, the more moles you have, the more information is leaked, the more difficult it is to pinpoint the source or, rather, sources. Too many suspects. Everyone's unspoken fear was that the CIA housed more than one KGB mole.

Bob smiled: "That's right. With more than two there is no hope." He made a pause. "Victor, look, you have to understand, the really important things in life are God and family. The rest is not." He paused again, and his voice turned icy. "Just stay away from this stuff."

"Bob, I'll try to finish this study, and I'll turn it over to you, and you do whatever the hell you want with it."

The meeting was over.

A few days later Bob called Victor. "I need to talk to you, what's your schedule for the next week?"

Victor looked at his calendar. "Tuesday morning's clear."

"Good. How about eleven?"

"Perfect."

Next Tuesday Bob called. "Victor, I don't feel very well, so I'm home. Can you come here at noon?"

"Of course. Are you sure you're OK to work?"

"No problem, it's going to be pretty short."

At noon Victor pulled in to Bob's house. Bob ushered him straight to the newly built spacious back porch. An odd choice on a very hot summer's day.

"I hope it's not too hot for you, I need some fresh air."

"It's OK." Victor had always been comfortable in hot weather.

"Anything to drink?"

"I'm fine, thanks."

The table was set so that they were sitting in direct sunlight, which struck Victor as a little strange.

Bob started with a small religious lecture, emphasizing the importance of confession. Victor was used to that from Bob, and was waiting for him to turn to business. Bob asked a couple of benign CI questions, so Victor thought that he would turn to the real business later. Some time later Bob asked, "Anything to drink?"

"No, thanks."

"Look, it's hot and you don't want to get dehydrated, you really need water. Let me bring you some." Bob left for the kitchen.

What the hell is wrong with Bob today? He's excited, almost agitated. He's probably is in some pain.

After a few minutes Bob emerged with a large full glass of water for Victor. Bob stopped in front of Victor and handed him the glass. Victor took the glass and put it on the table. Victor usually didn't need a lot of liquid, and he really wasn't thirsty.

Bob started talking about obedience in religion, how important it is to obey without question. Victor listened patiently, but by now he was slightly irritated. Bob said: "For instance, if tell you 'drink this water' you should do it without question or hesitation." It was hot, and Victor began to feel thirsty. Mechanically, he took the glass and raised it to his mouth. When Victor just wet his lip, Bob became really excited, and said in a commanding tone 'drink it!'. That really irked Victor. He deliberately and slowly put the glass back on the table and said nothing, clearly demonstrating disobedience.

"Why aren't you drinking?"

This is becoming bizarre. "Because I don't like being told what to do. Any other questions?"

Bob's face displayed a mixture of frustration, irritation and puzzlement.

Victor looked at his watch. "I really have to go now. I didn't think this would take this long. Let's meet some other time." He stood up. Bob had no choice but to see him out.

Victor went to another meeting, and grabbed a sandwich on the way. He was home for dinner.

That night he was very sick. It was obviously food poisoning. The sandwich was to blame. Victor was sick for several days. He couldn't work because of his extreme fatigue. Olga became scared when she saw that Victor started losing hair badly. In the morning there was a lot of hair on his pillow. Victor went to a doctor who found nothing, but ordered a toxicology blood test. On a follow-up visit the doctor said: "It's very odd, you seem to have some kind of hangover, pretty light though, from Thallium. I looked it up, and the only use of it I found is in the electronics industry. That could be pretty dangerous as an industrial hazard. Have you been anywhere where you could have come in contact with it?"

Victor knew another use of Thallium: poisoning. He had to think quickly. "Yeah, I've been abroad to some Godforsaken places lately. I have to think about it."

"So, you don't think it's in this country?"

"Definitely not."

At the NSA Victor told Robert about it.

Robert took it seriously. "Can you fully recollect that day you got sick?"

"I already have. I didn't eat out anywhere where I was known. So, I can't imagine anyone knowing where I would get a drive-by sandwich."

"Where else did you go that day?"

"Home, XYZ, a Government contractor that you know, and Bob Hanssen's. I didn't eat or drink anything at either place."

Robert just shook his head. "Odd."

A few days later the Hanssens came over for supper, scheduled long before. Bob brought Victor a book, *Transformation in Christ* by Dietrich von Hildebrand, a heavily religious book which Victor understood to be about spiritual instructions for preparing to die, and a wearable cross. Bob gave him the book saying as he always did, "God loves you."

Victor casually replied: "God loves everyone."

Victor turned away, but Bob took him by the arm. That was highly unusual since Bob always avoided even the slightest physical contact.

He gave him a smile with a dark sparkle in his eyes and emphatically said: "No. God loves *you*." Victor nodded; he did not know what to make of this. At the time.

Victor was able to perfectly correlate postings of one senior CIA officer, Y with all the CIA assets lost in the Soviet Union and Russia. The losses occurred shortly after he left every post. However Victor was not satisfied. Everything Victor researched pointed to Y. But there was a major hole there. Y has not been stationed in India at the time that Cherkashin was. Olga searched the State Department records, and there were no records of Y at the time. So, he could not connect Y to Cherkashin.

Soon Victor completed his search for the CIA mole. The major break came quite unexpectedly.

One day Victor was having an early dinner with an old friend who was working very close to Y at the CIA at the time. After a lot of other discussions Victor casually asked: "By the way for some reason I thought that Y was stationed in India, but apparently he was not."

"Yes, he was, for sure. He was only posted outside of the diplomatic quota. His status was temporary and renewed all the time, you know how it is."

Bingo! I just wasn't smart enough to think of that. It's a common practice for bureaucratic diplomatic reasons to keep people on a temporary status for a long time. This way they are not on the diplomatic rosters.

"Are you sure?"

"Absolutely. He played a lot of tennis there. Good for contacts."

"I know."

The dinner was soon over, and Victor was excited. Now it all clicked, All the dots connected.

Victor completed the memo very quickly, and called Bob for a meeting.

In Bob's office Victor said: "Bob, one mistake the FBI made when they were looking for the mole was in assuming that the timing was related to the beginning of the suspect's access to information. I mean fundamentally sensitive information, not perishable. A careful mole would pass such information only when he was losing the access."

Bob suddenly turned to Victor. His demeanor was stiff and unfriendly.

Victor took a paper out of his briefcase. "This is my memorandum to the FBI on the matter of the moles. It shows that, one, neither of the known KGB moles in this country nor all of them together can account for the losses of the CIA network. This includes Howard and Ames. Two, the marines at the US Moscow Embassy cannot account for that. Three, Y is a likely suspect who can account for all the losses. Four, Y's payments may have been hidden in other identities that are listed here. Five, there may well be other moles operating in the US intelligence community, most likely at the CIA."

For the first time in the decade that Victor had known Bob Hanssen his face was very pale, much paler than usual, Bob took the 16-page memorandum, and started reading. Victor watched him reading. Bob's face turned ashen. He stopped reading about two thirds of the way through. His voice suddenly cracked. "Have you shown this to anyone?"

"Yes, Robert Holderman has a copy." What Victor did not realize was that he just saved his own life. Again.

At the time, however, he figured that the memorandum was an inconvenient truth, and that Bob was intensely uncomfortable about the risk the information posed for his career. Victor just felt pity. "Well, I guess I'd better go."

Bob barely nodded, avoiding Victor's eyes.

About two weeks later Olga came home saying that she'd been followed from her TV studio.

"I noticed that, and went to the Home Depot Store nearby. There, I saw the man again. There was a woman with him, but she stayed a bit away."

"What did he look like?"

"About sixty, maybe a little more …"

Victor interrupted: "Sixty? That's a little old for that job. Are you sure?"

"Yes." Olga described the man. Victor instantly felt uneasy. He dug into one of his files, and took a picture out.

Olga just glanced at the picture. "That's him, for sure." It was the picture of Y.

"Was the woman with him tall, kind of blond, pretty, much younger?"

"Yes."

"Did they follow you further?"

"I didn't see them. But in the store I felt that he wanted me to see him. He didn't avoid eye contact."

"Intimidation?"

"Maybe, I don't know."

Victor immediately called Bob. "Oh, Victor, I was just about to call you. Can you come to Headquarters tomorrow, they want to talk to you about your memorandum."

"Sure." *It would be better to talk about this surveillance incident tomorrow.*

The next day at Headquarters Bob met Victor and escorted him to a conference room. There was a kid in his early twenties in the central chair, and Jim Millhorn sat at the side of the table . The boy was obviously fresh from the introductory course at the FBI Academy. Bob Hanssen also took a chair to one side, clearly showing that he was not running the show.

Victor was a little puzzled and thought the guy was just a junior agent gathering more information for the complicated investigation. After an introduction Victor began with small talk. "Is this your first investigation since the Academy?"

"Yes."

"You're lucky, this is an interesting one."

The guy did not reply. "Well, Mr. Sheymov, we investigated the matter you brought to our attention. Your accusations turned out to be false. We went to Florida to brief Mr. Y of your accusations. That's about all I can tell you."

What? You already finished this investigation that should take probably a year at best? You informed the subject of the investigation?

"I see. May I ask who actually performed the investigation?"

"I did." That was like an April Fool's joke; there were very few investigators in the country qualified to do that. Folks like Robert Holderman, Bob Hanssen, Jim Millhorn and such, but not a chick out of the Academy.

Victor looked at Millhorn. Jim was staring at the opposite wall, carefully avoiding Victor's yes. *What a disgrace. Out of all people you know what's going on here. Do you have any sense of dignity at all? I feel sorry for you.*

Victor turned to Hanssen. Hanssen seemed to be saying, "Not my department at this time, you know."

"Well, thank you for the information."

Victor left. On the way out neither he nor Hanssen said a word to each other.

Back home Victor told Olga what had happened. At the end he said: "You know, if the FBI doesn't give a damn, why should I? I did all I could, and that's it. But I really feel sorry for Bob Hanssen and Jim Millhorn. They are so worried for their careers that nothing else matters. Don't invite the Hanssens anymore. If they invite us, I have a prior engagement." He paused. "I'm sick of these guys."

40

Along with the leading NSA computer security experts Victor realized that the legacy methods of protection cannot work. The firewall approach was fundamentally flawed. It had been mathematically proven that any firewall can be defeated in an unlimited number of ways—the ultimate flaw.

Victor realized that the basic problem was that the legacy systems were based on methods appropriate for physical space. They all tried to fortify a protected computer. Fortification works to some extent in physical space, but it is worthless in cyberspace. Cyberspace is different from physical space.

Having clearly understood that fundamental principle, Victor came up with the idea of protecting computers not by fortification, but by dynamics. This means that the computer's IP address, i.e. its location in cyberspace, can be made known only to authorized computers, leaving the hackers in the dark. Furthermore, these locations can be changed frequently enough so an adversary cannot follow the process. Further yet, by making replies selective, the computer can be made *cyber-visible* only for authorized computers, and remain *cyber-invisible* to all others. How can you attack something that you cannot see and don't know where it is? The dynamics concept could be expanded to other communications parameters that essentially represent cyber coordinates, that is, the coordinates of a computer in cyberspace.

The concept was simple, but the implementation would be far from trivial. Essentially the book of communications would have to be rewritten.

One evening Olga and Victor went to Jim and Jean Dwyer for supper at their Laurel home in Maryland. After supper Victor described the idea to Jim. It took Jim less than five minutes to understand it. He just said: "Yes, this would work. Pretty good idea. This is a new method of communications; they come about once in a quarter of a century." That was the highest praise one could get from Jim. With his legendary achievements a remark like this would put any NSA scientist in nirvana.

"Yeah, as an inventor I have the traditional right to name it. I'll call it the Variable Cyber Coordinates method of communications, VCC."

Jim chuckled: "Sounds good."

After a few weeks Victor took this idea to some scientific-engineering -administrative types at the NSA.

After describing it, Victor concluded, "It looks like this would work. My hunch is that it should be classified. Can you fund the development?"

The response was lukewarm at best. "Victor, this is way over the top. It's not gonna work. If you want some advice, forget it. Don't waste your time."

Obviously, Victor was disappointed, but he knew better than to argue. "Well, do you mind if I try it commercially?"

Promptly, the response was shrugged shoulders. "Go ahead, if you want."

Victor started working on the idea, and tried to find funding for it. After a few months he still could not find any investors. He went to Donald, remembering his remark that he could get a couple of billion for the hacking solution, but Donald was not really interested; he thought the idea was too unconventional.

When Victor discussed the problem with Olga, she said: "But you've been raising a lot of money for other companies when you were in the investment banking business back in the South. Can't you use your connections now?"

"No way. I was working there under a different name, remember? It would mean a lot of questions like 'who are you, really?', and a lot of hesitation."

Then Olga said, "You know, when the CIA cancelled your pension we decided just to avoid them like the plague. However, can you demand that they pay you a lump sum? After all, the pension was set by the congressional committee."

Victor thought for a moment. "You know, that makes good sense, but there's no way they'd agree, and the process of arguing with them would be very unpleasant."

"Can you sue them?"

"Maybe, but you know how difficult that is. Let me think about it."

Victor started looking around. A friend suggested talking to Jim Woolsey, a former Director of Central Intelligence, currently a lawyer with a venerable Washington firm.

Victor met with Jim Woolsey and briefly described the situation. Woolsey was skeptical when Victor described the actions of the CIA, but having heard of Victor's reputation in the Intelligence community, he did not dismiss the case out of hand.

The next time they met for a serious discussion, Victor brought many documents as evidence of what the CIA had done. Jim could not believe what he read. As a former DCI, he had easy access in the CIA. He decided to verify what Victor told him. Victor wasn't surprised to receive a phone call from him suggesting another meeting.

Woolsey was outraged. "I apologize for the Agency I once headed." He paused. "I will represent you *pro bono*."

It was not a simple matter for Jim Woolsey for many reasons, one of them that for such a representation he had to obtain a personal release from the President. President Clinton granted it, and Victor thanked the President in a letter.

Woolsey's representation was very effective. In a few months the CIA had no choice but to agree to arbitration by Bill Webster, a judge who was the only person that had been head of both the FBI and the CIA. The CIA hated the process, but as always they never showed any remorse for their crimes, but only strongly resented being caught. The settlement imposed by Webster provided Victor with enough money to start the development of the new dynamics technology. Victor demanded that the settlement include a provision that the CIA must never interfere with the Sheymovs' lives and interests, and must never again make any contact with them.

41

Victor quickly discovered that finding a scientific solution to the hacking problem was only part of the challenge. He went to see Jim Dwyer. After a quick review they came to the conclusion that the problem involved not just developing a system, but also a totally new technology. In addition to numerous scientific uncertainties to be resolved, there was a formidable engineering task to be addressed. Even if all the necessary algorithmic solutions were found successfully, implementing them in an electronic system would be challenging at best. At the end of the discussion Jim quipped, "If anybody can pull it off, you can." That wasn't too encouraging.

Victor applied for a patent for VCC, incorporated Invicta Networks, and started looking for people. The huge difficulty was that, due to the complexity of the problem, it was next to impossible to find people with the necessary skills, and especially with the necessary high level of those skills. His NSA connections were crucial, because at the time there were no such talents available outside the NSA. Eventually Victor was able to find a team that included three Distinguished Members of the Cryptos Society. No more than two dozen of them were still active. No company in the world had two of them under one roof. Having three Distinguished Members associated with one project was unheard of. The flip side of that was that Victor had to manage a pack of alpha dogs, a quite interesting task.

Victor went around trying to recruit the team he needed. With the high-tech boom finding even a mediocre programmer was not too easy. However, a few NSA heavy-hitters were interested, mainly for the intellectual adventure.

Under normal conditions a project of such complexity would require tens of millions in funding, and a good technological base of hardware and software. Victor had neither, so he tried the traditional high-tech startup approach, with core participants pulling together some resources and working for nominal pay until the next round of financing was obtained. There were no takers. Victor discussed this with Olga. She enthusiastically agreed they should provide their own available capital, taking on all the initial financial risk, always the highest. Victor then tried to supplement their funds, asking prospects to work for a reduced rate in exchange for generous stock options. But by that time many high-tech startups had gone sour, making stock options a useless incentive. There were no takers at all. Everyone wanted full pay appropriate to their expertise, and they didn't come cheap. Victor talked to Olga again, explaining that the risk level had increased.

"How long will our money alone last?"

"About six months, maybe seven." Victor paused. "In order to persuade potential investors to put in the next round of financing we have to prove to them that our approach is valid, that it's not just an idea. This is called the 'proof of concept' stage. There would be risk after that for sure, but it would be much, much lower than it is now."

"How long will that stage take?"

"Nobody knows. That's why I couldn't find any investors, and I don't want you to have any illusions."

Olga persisted. "But this is your field, you should have an idea?"

"Well, my hunch is about four months, my hope is three. But there's no way I can guarantee it." He paused. "I can pull together a lot of skills, but it will take a lot of luck too. Some pretty smart folks think it's a dumb idea, and that it will never work."

Olga was silent for a while, then suddenly said: "Go for it."

Victor rented a small office in Laurel, Maryland. The choice was deliberate–that's where the talent base was. Some people he hoped to get had just retired from the NSA, others would be quitting very soon, and Victor had quite a few leads. But these people knew their value well, and he had to cater to them, at least for the time being. Victor realized that if the company succeeded, he would not be able to rely on only former NSA guys in it, for a variety of reasons. The non-NSA, more general pool of talent was in Reston, Virginia. But that was a big and remote "if."

The company began functioning right after the New Year, hiring people one by one. Some in the initial group did not quit their jobs right away, but worked two jobs and utilized their accumulated vacation time, in some cases taking unpaid leave. Needless to say, Victor was leaving home early and returning late. Weekends were nominal. Olga helped as much as she could. The race was on.

Victor retained one of the two top firms in the country that specialized in independent evaluation of companies, mainly large publicly traded corporations. He would need their rating of Invicta to attract potential investors. Their service in itself cost about half of what the company had in cash. Stressful, but unavoidable.

Out of the first group a few people fell away very quickly. Victor learned to recognize that look of a deer in the headlights when he tasked them. Sure enough, in a week they were gone. The rest worked very hard and the level of enthusiasm was tremendous.

By mid-March their server contained an embryonic model of the new system. The concept worked! At least in the model. By mid-May another server was programmed to imitate the hardware component that each protected computer would be equipped with. That also worked. There was a tremendous sense of accomplishment within the team. The next task would be to reduce one server to the size of a regular PC, and another server down to the size of a small computer card. These were not trivial tasks by any standard, but the team knew they could do it. Now they had to convince potential investors.

Victor went back to the valuation company. Victor was pleasantly surprised by their response. They estimated that the value of the company had grown about four hundred times from their initial valuation. However, the timing for raising money could hardly be worse–the hi-tech bubble had just burst, and the last thing most investors were interested in was another high-tech startup. An old New York friend helped raise enough funds for the company to last for about a year, maybe till the end of 2001. By then they had to have in place a lab prototype of the first system that could actually be installed to protect real-life computers, and that could be demonstrated to anyone. To get that done the company needed to move to larger space.

Finding suitable office space in Virginia at the time was difficult. They were lucky to sublease offices in Herndon from a small airline that had moved to Atlanta—virtually the only such space available in the area. The office was on the fourth floor of a wing of a drab old building adjacent to the Hilton hotel, located on Route 28, over-looking Dulles International airport. The space was larger than the company needed, but there was no choice, and Victor anticipated an expansion of the company soon.

Victor's own office was large and bright, with two glass walls. His outside wall faced the airport. The view of planes taxiing, taking off and landing was mesmerizing, so he had to put his desk with his back to the view. There was a coffee table with four chairs for informal discussions. He faced a tinted interior glass wall, which looked across a large atrium to glass elevators connecting the floors to the spacious entry foyer below. The elevator doors opened to a narrow balcony on each floor, leading to the offices. On the Invicta floor the other wing was occupied by the remaining offices of the airline. Locked and secured doors were the only way from the elevator to the Invicta wing. It was hard to see into Victor's office through the tinted glass, but he had a clear view of the elevators and the balcony between the two wings.

Victor was lucky. Throughout his career he had worked with world-class experts. He had met many very talented people. The sheer scale of his projects usually required the best teams an organization could put together. But Invicta Networks was something else again. The company's technical staff had the highest concentration of experts in several different fields that Victor had ever witnessed, and he was proud of it. Somehow, they worked together with an eagerness bordering on obsession. Quite often, before going home around eight, Victor had to go round the office and the lab kicking people out.

Sometimes personnel recruitment took an unusual turn. One day Victor was invited to the NSA Counterintelligence for consultations. He arrived at the parking lot of the nondescript old Security Building and parked in the visitors section. Walking to the building he saw a shiny, meticulously detailed BMW smartly pulled into one of the few slots reserved for executives' parking. He knew almost all the cars that were usually parked in those spaces. Like the rest of the cars in the parking lot, they were modest cars and pick-up trucks that would be seen on any rural road anywhere in the US. The BMW really stood out. Victor just smiled—a cocky visitor obviously had no clue what he was doing. Suddenly, a sleek black woman who looked about twenty-eight, in a tightly fitting pin-stripe business suit and high heels, popped out of the car and walked briskly and confidently to the entrance. Victor was expecting her to come back quickly to re-park the car. However, when he entered the building she was gone. The Counterintelligence section looked the same: a drab, poorly lit, partitioned space tightly packed with working people, a government version of a beehive.

There, he laughingly said, "Hey guys, I just saw a cute chick parking her BMW in the executive parking and cat-walking to the building. So out of place, really funny."

The response was an awkward silence. Then one of the guys said: "Victor, that's our new Deputy Director."

"What?" Everybody knew that security and counterintelligence is not a simple business. It takes many years of education, training, and at least twenty years of successful hands-on experience to be qualified for any managerial position. Victor paused. "She must have done something extraordinary to be appointed like that."

"Well, she worked in Personnel, and most of her activities were in some kind of racial equality and affirmative action committees."

That was truly offensive, an open slap in the face to professionals who worked so hard and for so long in an area in which they were experts, only to be bypassed by some clueless sleek ideological appointee. It was common knowledge in Security that Robert Holderman was the most qualified person for the job as the next Deputy Director. And there were several highly qualified guys right behind him.

Victor was about to express his unsolicited opinion, then quickly realized the guys understood the situation probably better than he did, but there was nothing they could do about it. Besides, they were a part of the DoD, and that implied strict discipline—you keep your opinion to yourself.

Victor shook his head. "She's probably just 'punching her ticket', and I hope she'll be out of here soon."

"Yeah." The damage to their morale had already been done.

Victor did not discuss the issue with Robert, but he kept his ear to the ground. Not long after, he received an invitation to Robert's retirement party. Victor offered Robert a job at Invicta, and he agreed.

The very tough budget made the technical development especially challenging. It was agreed they should proceed by developing the core system software simultaneously with the hardware components, significantly shortening the design cycle. The team recognized the risk, but confidently decided that they were good enough to succeed regardless. By the fall of 2000 the commercial prototype of InvisiLAN, as they called the system, was ready for demonstration. Victor invited several top hacking teams in the country to break it. None of them were able to. That was unprecedented, especially for a prototype. The surprised NSA experts asked only one question after testing the prototype: how was the company going to solve the scalability issue, so that the system could be deployed on the scale of millions of computers? That was a legitimate question, and the company scientists went back to the drawing board.

Overall, by the end of 2000 the company felt a great sense of accomplishment and was proud that it had achieved an extraordinary technological breakthrough. However, there was still some way to go for the commercialization of the system. Investors were licking their wounds after the high-tech bubble burst, so despite Invicta's technological success funding was still a challenge.

Management did not always go smoothly; once in a while Victor faced some unexpected issues. One day a woman in charge of purchasing for the company came to see him. After a short chat she asked for "preferred" status for one of the suppliers. That meant that sometimes the company would be paying more just to buy from that company. When Victor asked why she wanted to make them a preferred supplier she replied, "Well, they're friends of mine." That was obviously less than convincing. The woman added, "See, they're a homosexual couple, very nice people. Also, they are godparents of my dog."

Victor was aware of changing social values, but he was perplexed. To buy some time, he inquired with a straight face: "Is your dog also homosexual?"

The woman stared at Victor for a second, then burst into tears and dashed out of his office, startling his secretary. A short while later the woman's supervisor came in and suggested that Victor had been "insensitive," and hinted that Victor should apologize. Victor just shrugged it off, saying, "To whom— to her, to the homosexual couple, or to the dog? If someone doesn't have a sense of humor, I can only state that I cannot allow the sexual orientation of employees, suppliers, and their dogs to interfere with our purchasing policy." The socially conscious supervisor retreated.

Olga and Victor decided to go to Whistler, British Columbia for Christmas and New Year's vacation. Shortly before the trip Victor discovered that his passport had expired. It was already evening and all the travel agencies were closed.

Suddenly Olga came up with an idea. "Victor, is Bob Hanssen still at the State Department?"

"As far as I know." Victor still had a bad aftertaste after that FBI flop over his Y memorandum, and he hadn't seen him in a while. Not that he felt any great animosity towards Bob, but he had lost all respect for him, attributing Bob's position to career considerations.

"Look, I know you aren't keen on meeting him, but he's still a friend. Why don't I call him? This is nothing for him." Victor reluctantly agreed. He found some reserve passport photos, and Olga called Bob.

Bob was delighted to hear from Olga, and he suggested that she bring the old passport and the photos to him. Olga put it all in an envelope and was gone in a few minutes–she remembered the Hanssens' restriction: Bob was unavailable after about eight, dedicating that time to the children.

When she came back, she said, "You know, Bob said that Bonnie was already sleeping, so I only spent a few minutes there. He got very excited after what I told him about Invicta's success. He asked if you could come by tomorrow morning to get your passport. I guess he also wants to talk technology.

Victor went to see Bob to pick up his passport, just in time for the next day's early morning departure. To his surprise, Bob was extremely interested in the Invicta technology, and asked a lot of questions. He noticed Victor surprise, and said: "See, I'm going to have another job very soon, as head of the FBI computer systems. Naturally, security is my Number One priority."

"Oh, that's interesting. Can we show you our system?"

"Of course, and very soon."

42

After their Whistler vacation Olga and Victor felt refreshed. With all the holiday festivities behind, everyone was eager to get back to work. The next phase would be the development of a commercial prototype of the InvisiLAN. There were now sixty people including those working on administrative and other nontechnological functions, which were now taking more and more of Victor's time. Without any sign of animosity the technical people generally tried to stay away from the marketing and sales departments. Victor recognized that combining the two distinctly different cultures was not feasible, so he had to adjust his management style to the different cultures, while still maintaining the integrity of the company.

One day Victor got a call from Bob Hanssen. Victor was surprised at how pointed his technical questions were. After some discussion, Bob said: "I want to bring a very high-level FBI team to your company. Can you give them a good technical briefing and demo your system?"

"Absolutely, we'd be delighted to."

The team, headed by the FBI Chief Scientist, was impressive. Only one participant seemed a bit out of place. Victor could not figure out what he was doing there, but that was not really unusual and he dismissed it. The briefing went very well. At the end the CTO said that they were very interested in the technology, and would like to install the system on the executive seventh floor of the Headquarters building as soon as it was available as a commercial product. That would be a very prestigious sale for the company. Everyone was pleased and excited by the prospect.

After the meeting Victor went back to his office. Olga came in still wearing her coat, without even dropping by her office. She had a number of roles at Invicta, but her main job was the development of external communications for the company, including designing graphics and other promotional materials.

"How did it go?"

"Very well. They want to buy InvisiLAN."

"Great!" She paused. "You know, I just met Bob with the other guys in the corridor—I was just walking in when they were leaving. Strange, Bob looked so excited, not his usual self. He hugged me tightly–kind of demonstratively. Unbelievable—you know how Bob avoids physical contact at all costs."

Soon Bob called again and suggested lunch. Victor knew that personal relationships are treacherous ground when dealing with the Government on a commercial basis. You really have to avoid any appearance of impropriety. The solution was simple—he invited Robert Holderman to participate.

When Bob arrived, the three of them went to the adjacent Hilton hotel restaurant. The restaurant was almost empty. Victor noticed that there were many available tables, so it was a little strange that the waiter placed a group of about six at the next table. The group looked pretty normal if a notch too loud. Victor was facing the group and Bob Hanssen was across from him, with his back to them, and Robert sat at the side. Victor noticed that the guy at the next table sitting back-to-back with Hanssen was leaning back a little too much, like he wanted to hear better. It's common knowledge that a person in such an environment hears better what is behind than what is in front. Victor quickly dismissed that as either a casual curiosity or just his having been in the intelligence business for too long.

Bob, Robert, and Victor chatted casually for most of the lunch, and Victor only mentioned that it would be great if they could supply security equipment to the FBI.

Then Bob suddenly said: "I really like your technology. It has a great potential. I'd love to work for Invicta." All three of them were well aware of the Government ethics standards; any mention of employment with a potential vendor was taboo. So for Victor and Bob this was a bombshell.

Victor could not believe his ears. He glanced a Robert, and saw the same reaction in his eyes.

The ball was in Victor's court. "Well, we can discuss it after you retire, which I'm sure isn't happening soon–since you just got a promotion."

Victor almost felt Robert's relief. "Yeah, that's right."

Victor sensed that Bob might persist, so he called a waiter and started some discussion with him, and then he realized that he had a meeting coming up in a couple of minutes. Robert played along, changed the subject, and they left the restaurant soon after.

They parted, and Robert and Victor went to Victor's office. Both were dumbfounded.

Robert said: "I couldn't believe it. At the time when we are talking commercial business with the FBI he's asking for a job! It's not just unethical, it's illegal as hell!"

"I couldn't believe it either. He should know better than that. He's a smart guy, an FBI senior supervisory agent. He really put us all in a terrible position. I just can't understand why he would do something like that."

Both were silent for a while, then Victor said: "Do you think that's the end of it, or could it pop up again?"

"I hope not." Robert paused. "But you know what's also strange? Bob looked really tired, almost exhausted, worn out."

"Yeah, I noticed that too. Could it just be burnout, so that all he wants right now is to get the hell out of the Bureau?"

Robert chuckled. "Not with his last job at the State. You don't get burned out there."

"All right. Let's just wait and watch."

Victor didn't have to wait too long.

February 16, 2001. It was one of those once-a-month afternoons that everyone has some urgent thing to do, and, magically, you can't find anyone after lunch. Victor was sitting alone in his office waiting for Bob Hanssen to drop by for a visit, which Bob had requested on very short notice.

Through his glass wall across the atrium Victor saw Bob with another man. He was a little surprised to see Bob with someone else, and went up front let the men in, and ushered them to his office.

Bob said: "Victor do you remember Richard, my son-in-law?"

"Of course, I remember that wonderful wedding." Actually, that was a white lie. Victor had seen the guy only once, at the ceremony in the church, after which he and Olga had had to bolt, and they didn't attend the reception. "Coffee, tea, anything else?"

Both men declined. They sat down at the coffee table. Victor's chair was closest to his desk so he could quickly get there if needed. Bob took the opposite chair with his back to the glass wall into the atrium, and Richard sat to one side.

Bob said: "Richard is a lawyer, he's flying to New York on a business trip, and I'm going to give him a ride to the airport."

Business trip to New York on Friday afternoon? "Sure, I understand."

Bob looked really exhausted, with circles around his eyes. He looked like he'd aged ten years in less than two months.

"So, what kind of law do you do, Richard?"

Richard started explaining his work.

At that moment Victor saw a guy exiting the elevator on their floor. He seemed confused and trapped. Obviously, he didn't realize that anyone was watching him through the tinted glass. He sat on a small bench and pretended to wait for somebody. That was a little silly since he hadn't rung any doorbell. In fact the opposite wing had been closed a few days before, and the last of the airline people had left. The doors to both wings were locked. Then he started nervously walking back and forth on the balcony. This was becoming hilarious. *This is like a surveillance in a bad movie.*

Victor decided he'd make a joke of it and ask "Bob, is that your tail?"

By then Richard had finished his explanation. Victor nodded, and started to say, "Bob, is that..." Bob interrupted: "Victor, I've decided to retire soon, in April."

Victor knew what was coming and tried to evade the danger. "Oh, really? What happened?" *Must be a really bad conflict with the new boss.* He saw the guy on the balcony board the glass elevator and go down to the lobby of the building.

Bob was irritated. "Nothing, I'm just tired of all the bureaucracy. Besides, I see a great opportunity with Invicta."

That was really pushy, very atypical of Bob's usually very smooth way of talking.

"Well, conceptually it's great, but we're not hiring right now."

"Victor, you don't understand, I can be a great asset to you."

Victor new that Bob was pretty good with computers for an amateur, but he had nowhere near the expertise level required for Invicta. Victor decided to play that card. "Bob, there are many aspects to hiring here. We have a specific list of specialties that are urgently needed by the development department, and I don't see how you can fit any of them."

"I am not talking about a technical job."

"Well, we're not going to be able to hire anybody in an administrative job for a long time; we have to get a lot of funding for that, and getting funding now is a killer."

Suddenly, Bob went to the whiteboard on the wall and drew a diagram. Victor was surprised at how accurate it was. Bob made a quick review of the Invicta technology and outlined the huge potential. He really understood the basics and applications of the new technology. Now Victor understood why he was so enthusiastic to get in early in the game; it could be very lucrative for him.

Suddenly, things turned weird. Bob asked: "Do you know really why Julius Caesar was so successful?"

Victor was taken aback and was becoming irritated. "No idea."

Bob's eyes sparkled as they did during his religious lectures. "It was because he had perfect internal intelligence. He had his agents report to him everything his subordinates were up to, so he could ask very penetrating questions."

This was really bizarre. "Bob, this is very interesting, I never heard of that before. I think I need to digest it." Victor paused. "Meanwhile, no matter what, I cannot even start thinking about hiring before we get the funding. Unfortunately, I don't even have a good lead for now."

Suddenly Bob's demeanor completely changed, now strictly businesslike. "How much money do you need?"

"A few million, at least two in the short term."

"Do you have any restriction on foreign ownership? Without losing control, of course."

Victor laughed: "None. When we applied for the export license the Commerce Department told us that we don't even need the license. Just sell the products to anybody except terrorists."

"You must be kidding. They are so stupid that they didn't want US control of this technology?"

"Whatever the reason, we have practically no restrictions."

Bob thought for a second. "I can get you funding from Switzerland."

Victor chuckled. "You never mentioned you have a Swiss account."

"I don't, but I know some people who do."

"Well, there's no substitute for good connections."

This discharged the atmosphere and gave Victor an out, so he could avoid any discussions of employment, at least for the moment.

"All right. Why don't you check it out with your Swiss investors, and if they are interested, we can discuss particulars."

"OK."

Victor saw Bob and Richard to the door.

The following Monday Victor was coming downstairs for breakfast when the phone rang. It was Robert.

"Have you seen the news?"

"No, not yet."

"Good, I don't want you to get it from CNN. Bob Hanssen was arrested last night."

"My God, what for?"

"Espionage."

"What?"

Robert did not reply.

"For whom?"

"Russia."

Victor couldn't believe it. Olga turned the TV on. They saw a large image of Bob Hanssen.

"Could it be some sort of a game?"

"No." Robert paused. "I'm not coming to the office today."

"Sure."

Victor's brain had a hard time accepting the news. If it was true, this was devastating for the entire American Intelligence community, particularly the FBI and the CIA.

Together with Olga, he was flipping channels. Anchors were hectically reciting the FBI court affidavit, a lot of people were talking, with very little real information emerging.

Olga was devastated. "Victor, I just have a hard time accepting this." She paused. "Poor kids and Bonnie. The media will tear them apart. Let me call her to see if we can help. Can we hide them here?"

"Sure. The media don't know our address. Should work for a while."

Olga tried to reach Bonnie at all the numbers she knew, but to no avail. When Victor came to the office, the company was a beehive.

Everybody knew that he and Robert knew Hanssen. Victor fended off a few attempts to talk, just saying that he needed to know a lot more before he can say anything. Olga called. "Victor, your name is in the affidavit, just want you to know." That explained a large and growing pile of notes to call from the media. Victor's secretary had a hard time keeping up.

Victor was wondering why his name showed up there. On the other hand, he was wondering about the whole thing. After a short while Victor figured that he couldn't concentrate on his work, and left for home.

He was trying to reconcile everything. A lot of small pieces accumulated over the years suddenly came together, and fit perfectly, but the overall picture just did not make sense.

The biggest unanswered question was: WHY?

43

For immediate Release	Washington D.C.
February 20, 2001	FBI National Press Office

Sunday night the FBI arrested Robert Philip Hanssen who has been charged with committing espionage. Hanssen is a Special Agent of the FBI with a long career in counterintelligence.

The investigation that led to these charges is the direct result of the longstanding FBI/CIA efforts, ongoing since the Aldrich Ames case, to identify additional foreign penetrations of the United States Intelligence Community. The investigation of Hanssen was conducted by the FBI in partnership with the CIA, the Department of State, and, of course, the Justice Department.

The complaint alleges that Hanssen conspired to and did commit espionage for Russia and the former Soviet Union. The actions alleged date back as far as 1985 and, with the possible exception of several years in the 1990s, continued until his arrest on Sunday. He was arrested while in the process of using a "dead drop" to clandestinely provide numerous classified documents to his Russian handler.

It is alleged that Hanssen provided to the former Soviet Union and subsequently to Russia substantial volumes of highly classified information that he acquired during the course of his job responsibilities in counterintelligence. In return, he received large sums of money and other remuneration. The complaint alleges that he received over $600,000.

The full extent of the damage done is yet unknown because no accurate damage assessment could be conducted without jeopardizing the investigation. We believe it was exceptionally grave.

Olga and Victor were jolted by Hanssen's arrest. It wasn't that the event in itself was unimaginable, but the fact that neither of them had noticed a single clue during a decade of friendship was profoundly shocking.

The details that trickled through the media did not add any clarity. Some of them were very surprising, while others Victor and Olga knew were totally wrong. They discussed these new details, but neither of them could comprehend the main fact.

It took a couple of weeks for them to bring themselves to a real discussion of the event.

"Victor, we were both surprised and shocked, and it's been difficult for me to accept what Bob did, but now I think it's beginning to sink in. How about you?"

"Well, I don't know. I accept it as a fact, but I still don't understand it. It's funny how all the details dovetail. Many small things that didn't make sense before are perfectly understandable now. The irony is that while all the details come together very well to make the whole, that whole doesn't make sense to me."

"Yeah, I have the same feeling." Olga paused. "What really surprised me were the other sides of his life we had no idea about. For example, all that sex stuff, assuming that's true of course. Bob was so prudish that," she chuckled, "I even wondered how they managed to have six children. He never ever gave out the slightest sign of that side of him."

"That's true. Actually, that's what looks like a common thread through many of the details we know about Bob. He was consistent in what he showed of some sides of him, and he hid the others perfectly."

"Precisely. The Hanssens didn't have too many friends. Apart from a few relatives like Bonnie's sister, over the years we probably had more social contacts with them than others. If we never noticed anything suspicious, I think most people wouldn't have."

"I agree. Bob has an almost unnatural ability to compartmentalize everything. Most people cannot compartmentalize two things. Look, he never ever mentioned that he owned many weapons. Even when we went to the FBI Academy's range with him, he didn't shoot. We did, he didn't. He even complained that he sometimes had to carry his little service revolver. The perfectly peaceful intellectual. It turned out that he had a dozen weapons in his house, including an AK-47." Victor took a breath. "He would never go to a bar with the Intel community boys— forget any strip club. Yet it turned out that he was doing that porno stuff and posting it on the Internet. He bragged that he was studying Japanese, but never mentioned that he'd studied Russian, never tried to say a word in Russian. That's quite remarkable. Sooner or later everyone makes a mistake, mixing up compartmentalized things. He never did."

Olga sighed. "You know, I shiver when I recall things that happened around us. Now I know who killed our dog, Tim. Now I know who tried to poison you. It's so obvious now."

"Well, it's not so obvious. There's something strange there. I can tell you for sure that if the KGB or SVR had wanted me killed, they could have done it easily, especially with Hanssen providing them with information about me and even a good opportunity. He would have a perfect alibi. It tells me that whatever he did, he did on his own, it was personal. And that doesn't make sense at all. It baffles me.".

They were silent for a while, then Victor said: "The biggest question for me is still WHY? I'm beginning to appreciate the American courts' obsession with identifying a motive for every crime."

"I can tell you one thing for sure, for Bob it wasn't money."

"Of course not. All that media stuff about his greed is just garbage based on ignorance and a bunch of speculation. The family lived very modestly, we know that better than anyone. He never bought a new car. He gave all the insurance payment from his car accident settlement to the Church. He made donations to the Church and the kids' schools, just to mention a few things. He also rejected a career as a dentist after all the training, and only five minutes before graduation."

"Yes, and remember, Bonnie refused any customary money for her blood donation for my surgery; I had to give her a modest gift instead, and even that took a lot of persuading to get her to accept it. And remember the other business, about the power of praying?"

"What was that?"

"Do you remember Bonnie's sister with, I think, eight children? When they had financial troubles, and had to sell their house, and rent a smaller one?"

"Oh, yes. Bob told us that the family couldn't afford to pay the rent. Bonnie was upset, and she prayed very, very hard."

"Of course. And then, magically, the woman who owned the house just decided to gift it to the family. Now I am wondering if Bob had anything to do with that minor miracle."

"You're right. Whatever his motive was, it wasn't money. At most, it was a secondary consideration. He didn't ask for what he could have gotten. He probably viewed that money as a retirement pension. As for the diamonds he asked for, I think that was some kind of a game for him, justified by their being easy to carry in an emergency."

Victor paused, and then said: "In fact I think it was some kind of a game for him. He probably felt like a puppet master playing everybody around him. In fact, I remember one pretty funny story. Do you remember when Ian came here?"

"Sure."

"Well, I told him at the time that I felt that I was walking very close to something very big and very ugly. The ultimate irony was that shortly thereafter Bob gave me some caricature, you know, one of those printed on three-by-three sheets of paper stacked like Post-Its."

"Oh, yes, I've seen those. Some doctors stick up their favorites in their patient rooms."

"Yes. So, that was a drawing of two penguins, one saying to the other: 'first, it was Joe, then it was Bill, and now it's Bob. Something's going on here. The funny part was that between them, a foot behind, was standing a huge polar bear with a fake penguin beak, supposedly camouflaged as a penguin."

"This sounds like an intelligence joke."

"Absolutely. Bob was laughing at it in a way I never saw him laugh before. I also found it funny at the time. But now it looks like it was a professional embarrassment for me. He was having fun at my expense."

Olga shook her head. "Yeah, it sounds like he was looking for excitement and took intelligence and his job as some game."

After a short pause Olga said: "But why was he trying to kill you and when he failed, never tried it again?"

"The only explanation I have is that when I told him that Motorin and Martynov could not have been betrayed by Ames, that this must have happened well before Ames. He felt threatened and panicked thinking that this exposed him and put him in the suspect circle. At the time he probably did not remember that he re-established his contact with the KGB a few months after Ames disclosure. Later, I guess, he realized the mistake. Besides, with my memo out, the situation was not in his control and there was nothing he could do. So, he told me that God loves me, gave me that book and a cross as presents."

After a while Victor said: "Well, anyway, if it wasn't money, what was it? The other common possible reasons are ideology and job dissatisfaction. Bob was certainly ideologically very conservative. Given his religious beliefs that virtually rules out that cause. He despised communists, despised a 'godless society'."

"Yeah, I think he was very genuine in that."

"He definitely didn't join Opus Dei for spying–I wouldn't be too surprised if he spied for it, but not against it."

"All right, so it's not money, nor ideology. How about his job?"

"Not that I can see. As far as I know he had a good career. I suppose he could have done better if he wanted, but I don't think he cared that much about it."

"The whole thing's crazy."

"Well, that actually may be the only viable explanation. Once in a while he had that kind of dark sparkle in his eyes, remember?"

"Yes, I was always uncomfortable when I saw that."

"Also, he and Bonnie met 'in a madhouse'. Remember?"

"That was a good laugh at the time. But come to think of it, Bonnie said he was doing some gardening work there. What I didn't catch at the time was that interns, as he supposedly was, don't do gardening work, though some patients do."

"That may be it. Probably nobody checked the place. Even if some-one did, Bonnie's father ran it, so Bob could have had enough access to fix the records to show Bob had never been there, or if he was there, he was there as an intern from a medical school. A theory, but maybe worth considering."

"The bottom line is that we just find it difficult to believe he did what he did. The only member of our family who had as little contact with him as possible was Elena."

"Yes. She felt that something about him was very wrong. Obviously, she has great instincts."

44

Victor called Joe, the Chief Scientist of the FBI who headed the FBI team for the presentation of the InvisiLAN technology.

"Hi, Joe, how're you doing?"

"You can guess, the mood is really bad here. How about you?"

"All right, I think. Under the circumstances." Victor paused. "With all that unfortunate stuff, we still have to work. You mentioned that you wanted to try InvisiLAN on one of the networks at Headquarters."

Joe mumbled, "Victor, that's a political impossibility now."

"Why, just because Hanssen liked it? His case has nothing to do with our technology."

"Right, but also because of his connection with you."

That really stunned Victor. "Joe, wait a second. I'm the one who the Bureau jeopardized by introducing Hanssen as a completely trusted liaison with practically unlimited clearance. I understand, and I'm not complaining, but somehow blaming me is just crazy."

There was a long pause. "Victor, I understand; it's probably just guilt by association. All I can say is that it's just a political impossibility. That's all."

That was the end of the conversation. They parted on personally friendly terms, but never spoke after that. Victor knew that many people in the FBI had also been hurt by their association with Bob Hanssen.

A few days later Victor talked to Robert. Both had needed time to digest the event and for a few weeks they barely mentioned it.

Victor started the conversation. "So, what do you think?"

"I'm really angry. He did so much damage to everybody: the country, the Bureau, his family, you and me, our company. How about you?"

"No. Not yet anyway. I just don't understand it, I'm baffled."

"What's not to be understood?"

"The Why? It's hard to accept what happened until we answer that question."

"You know about the money and the diamonds?"

"Yes, and that's garbage. I'm sure that was not his main motivation."

"Why?"

Victor told Robert about his observations of Hanssen over the years. After some thought, Robert said: "Well, it's a puzzle, definitely."

"All right, let's go down the usual list. Ideology? No way. I'm sure he was genuinely conservative, an anticommunist. I'm very sensitive to that, and if he had had any sympathy for that system I would have felt it."

"I also didn't notice any warning signs of ideology."

"All right, career? Pissed off with his boss, the common excuse? Did he have any problem like that?"

"Not as far as I know."

"Well, then what?"

Robert just shook his head. "Good question."

"How about insanity?" Victor told him some of the ideas he had discussed with Olga.

Robert was unconvinced. "I don't now. We have good psychiatrists. I never heard that they found anything."

Victor chuckled. "With the pressure on the Bureau now? It's probably politically impossible to consider that." He smiled at the irony of using the phrase he'd borrowed from the FBI CTO.

"Oh, come on. "

"Oh, sure. Can you imagine the fallout if he was declared insane after a long career at the FBI, and they didn't know it when they hired him, nor noticed it during his entire career? A lot of folks would demand that they test all the other FBI guys. An unbelievable scandal, and the Congress would demand scalps."

Robert laughed. "OK, let's think some more about his motive. I must admit it's a more interesting subject than I realized."

"Yeah. The man risked everything he had and loved: his family, his beliefs, his standing in the Church, his job, his pension, and his freedom. For what? For the money that was probably less than the value of his pension that he'd already earned, the money he did not and could not use and was partially giving away? I find that very hard to believe."

The conversation turned to Hanssen's actions.

Robert said: "Actually, tradecraft-wise, I assumed he was better than that. What he did wasn't topnotch at all. I wonder why? He certainly knew all the most sophisticated tricks of the trade."

"I was wondering about that too." Victor paused. "By the way, do you believe that the KGB/SVR didn't know his identity?"

"Not really. I think they knew, but just played along. What do you think?"

"I think they knew. There's no way that they'd resist the temptation to take a look at him. At his insistence they used the same dead drop site and signal site, at the same location for both, leaving and retrieving parcels by both parties within minutes of each other. Very dangerous too, you know."

Robert just nodded, and Victor continued: "Besides, did I ever tell you about Bob and the concert at the Wolftrap?"

"No, what was that about?" Victor told Robert the story and finished by saying: "See, he was parading me alongside of him to the whole Russian Embassy and the whole KGB station there. He was exposing me, but he was exposing himself as well."

"Unbelievable. Why didn't you tell me this back then?"

"I thought it was some kind of FBI game. After all, he was a Supervisory Special Agent, the official FBI liaison to me, with a lot of clout and full clearance."

"By the way, he was the only one who encouraged me to go public, back in 1990"

"He did?"

"Yes. I was grateful at the time, but now I understand why–he just wanted to enlarge the circle of people who knew about me. Now I understand why he wanted us to move to New York–to degrade our security."

Robert just shook his head.

After a silence Victor said: "Robert, the whole thing is really crazy. Just think about when he reinstated his contact with the KGB, in 1985. That was at a time when the whole USSR started to fall apart. He knew that. He knew that massive defections from the KGB were likely to follow. The risk, high enough already, was growing drastically, and he still re-engaged them. It looks like he was playing some kind of a game for a thrill that he couldn't get in his life otherwise."

"Yeah, the timing is odd. Everything is odd."

"Precisely. As far as I observed, Bob never did anything without a reason. He wasn't an emotional guy, nor an extrovert. Besides, he had an MBA in accounting, he was a CPA. He surely understood that the value of what he might get at such great risk was much less than what he could get without any risk—i.e. his salary, his pension. If he really needed money, he could easily moonlight for a hundred grand a year just doing taxes. So the money could not have been his main motivation. The real reason was something else—some kind of inner, self-contained psychological compulsion."

Robert just sighed.

Victor continued, "But the really funny story happened right here, in my office, when he came by just two days before his arrest."

"Yeah, you told me he came here. What happened?"

He asked me again for a job at Invicta. He proposed running an internal security system, reporting on everyone to me.

Robert stared.

"Of course I was shocked, and put him off immediately. But wait, there's more." Victor nodded toward the tinted glass wall behind Robert. "See that elevator balcony there?"

Robert glanced back and nodded.

"Well, Bob was sitting in the same chair you are now." Robert jokingly shuddered. "I noticed a guy coming out of the elevator, then just loitering on the balcony between the two wings of the floor. I almost laughed, thinking that it looked like a really clumsy surveillance. Now we know that's exactly what it was. So, I wanted to make a joke asking Bob if that was his tail. I got as far as saying 'Bob, is this …'. when he interrupted me, started talking intensely about something, obviously stressed, so I dropped the joke. Then I saw the guy taking an elevator back down to the lobby."

Robert was shaking his head, and said, "If you had actually told him, it could have been disastrous. How do you think he would have responded?"

"He had any number of options, and I would probably have helped him in many ways if he asked. As all visitors, he was parked in the lot outside. If he'd asked, I would have taken him to our internal elevator, which isn't accessible to outsiders. He could easily have gone to the first floor of the building. That elevator opens into a corridor next to the Hilton, which the surveillance was unlikely to cover. He could then take a taxi or the Hilton shuttle to Dulles, and could have been on a flight to Canada very soon after. Apparently, he always carried his passport, money and a gun in his briefcase. If he had decided to be more careful, he would have taken the same internal elevator to the basement garage with restricted access that we shared with the Hilton, and then got either a taxi or the Hilton shuttle to Dulles. He could also have borrowed my car or asked me for a ride and I'd have been happy to oblige. That's what I see. He might well have had other options too."

Robert just said: "Unbelievable. And you are saying that you'd have helped him?"

"Of course. He was a senior FBI man, and for years my closest official contact with the FBI, remember? My assumption would have been that drug dealers or some kind of thugs were after him. If he'd asked, I'd even have given him a ride on the floor of my car, to beat the surveillance, and I'd have dropped him off anywhere he wanted."

Robert suddenly laughed. "So, point one is that the Bureau got a really lucky break here. Point two is that he's going to do life in prison for interrupting you." He paused. "I don't even want to think what would have happened if you'd got him out of here and he had fled."

"Neither do I."

After a pause Victor added: "By the way, remember that copy of my memo to the Bureau on the Y case?"

Robert nodded, and Victor continued: "so, once again, some folks start declaring a victory in the CI war: Bob Hanssen could not possibly have known the identities of the CIA networks in Russia."

"That's correct. He only knew about Mororin and Martynov because both were recruited by the FBI."

"Well, neither could Ames have been the first to give out at least the three major losses: Gordievsky, Motorin and Martynov, just based on the precise timing analysis. And, personally, I doubt that he knew all the rest of them, maybe just some of them. The CIA still has some compartmentalization, you know."

"So?"

"So, the CIA is still penetrated, and badly. By the way, I heard through the grapevine that the Bureau started another investigation of Y the next day after Hanssen's arrest. But I really doubt that it can be successful. Too many warnings, too much time to get rid of all the evidence."

Robert did not say a word.

Both Olga and Victor felt that they really needed some kind of a closure to the Hanssen saga. When Victor told Olga that the FBI was refusing to go further with the InvisiLAN technology because of Hanssen, Olga said, "He did so much damage. To everyone. I'm not sure his kids will ever recover."

"That's true. But the Why question has still not been answered with certainty."

"I don't think he was a psychopath, somebody who doesn't know right from wrong, doesn't understand what is real and what is not. He certainly wasn't like that. It looks to me he was more like a split personality, like Jekyll and Hyde."

"Come to think of it, that may be the only true answer. In fact, I have a theory that could explain Bob's behavior. People in Intelligence deal with compartmentalization all the time. Psychologically, this requires the ability to concentrate on one issue at a time and disregard all the others. When you work on classified matters and come home, you have to turn off the job side and turn on the family side. Some people cannot compartmentalize at all. Others do it very well. An extreme example is a concentration camp guard coming home after killing people at work, clearing his mind and playing with his kids as a great father, as though nothing had happened. At the other end of the compartmentalization spectrum is the multiple-personality disorder, when memory is not shared by the different personalities."

"I hope you don't develop this theory any further. It sounds like we all have different gradations of the disorder."

Victor laughed. "That may be right, at least to some degree. It also relates to what's happening in electronics now."

"What do you mean?"

"Well, we are perfecting computer virtual reality games to such an extent that it is becoming more and more difficult to decide what is real and what is not. But the inability to detect what is real and what is not is a practical definition of insanity."

"Victor, just stop it."

"Well, joking aside, I think we should put it behind us and just move on."

"I agree."

45

The development of the new system at Invicta was going at breakneck speed. As if other challenges weren't enough, the industry rumor mill brought news that a very large company was budgeting about fifty million for a similar project. Victor had applied for a patent long before, but until the patent was issued or denied, one never knew. But one of the Invicta developers mentioned that he knew the competitor, and assured everyone that they didn't have the talent needed for the job, though this brought small comfort. Victor was concerned about the developers' workload, and made a point of doing the rounds every evening, grumbling, "I need you healthy and in good sprits. Besides, I don't want any divorces here. Go home." Often the response was "OK, OK. I need just five minutes to finish this thing." Sure enough, thirty minutes later the guy was still there.

Despite all the daunting technological obstacles the development of a commercial prototype was going well. Close interaction between the software and hardware teams was a crucial key to success. Usually a challenge, this interaction was working well. Morale was high—Victor knew that complex development always hits a snag once in a while, and he was very happy to see that whenever that occurred he never saw any blame-shifting or finger-pointing.

At the company the Hanssen debacle was largely forgotten. Personally, however, despite Olga and Victor's best efforts, intelligence issues kept coming to mind. One Sunday while they were enjoying some nice weather in their backyard, Olga brought up the subject.

"Victor, I still can't put all those things related to the CIA and Hanssen behind me. Can you?"

"Not completely. They do keep coming back from time to time. I don't like it, but it's still the case."

"You know, I really want to let go of all of it. The only way I know to do that is to discuss it. When can we talk about it?"

Victor chuckled. He knew that if Olga wanted to discuss something, they would. "All right, now is as good time as any." They sat down on the porch.

Olga said: "After all that's happened, what do you think of the CIA?"

Victor laughed: "For a brief chat on that issue we'd need about two weeks."

"No, I'm serious. In a nutshell, what do you think of them?"

"Well, first of all, the CIA is a huge behemoth. Initially their task was to provide clandestine services for the country, but over the years they acquired many other functions. I don't know if that was just a routine bureaucratic power grab, or an attempt to dilute the impression of their subpar performance in clandestine operations. Whichever,

I'm only familiar with one part. So, when I say 'CIA,' I really mean only their Operations, Resettlement being a logical part of that."

"That's exactly what I mean by 'CIA'. I don't even know about the other parts."

"OK, with that understood, the OSS, the CIA's predecessor during the WWII, was an extraordinarily successful organization created in an extremely short period of time with heavy help from the British. There's one very important aspect here. It was a thoroughly apolitical organization, as an intelligence service must be." Victor took a breath. "Later on, it gradually became increasingly political. Now the transition is complete, and it's become mostly political. This is not good, because by definition a political organization cannot be objective."

"What do you mean by that?"

"An apolitical organization is blind to what the 'customer', that is the boss, wants to hear. But a political organization's first priority is the opposite: to find out what the boss wants to hear and then to tell him what he wants to hear. Remember, when I told them that Andropov was going to be the next Head of State in Russia, they didn't even want to hear how I knew that. They dismissed it right off the bat. Why? Because that was their superiors' political opinion at the time. From an intelligence standpoint, that's a disaster. But that's just the beginning of the CIA's troubles." Victor paused. "In any organization, its people are the key to success or failure. Contrary to the occasional propaganda praising 'men and women without uniforms'."

Olga laughed. "Victor, stop it."

"Well, every politician suddenly stopped calling the military military, and started calling them 'our men and women in uniform'. It's laughable and, actually belittles the military. I guess the logical extension for the CIA is 'our men and women without uniforms'."

Olga just shook her head.

Victor continued. "In countries with the best professional intelligence services like Britain and Russia, Intelligence is considered a very prestigious, very honorable profession. Consequently, year after year these services get top graduates from the best universities. Now, take a look at this country. The CIA keeps popping up with embarrassing scandals, and is certainly not a desirable place of employment. If you try to recruit a top graduate from a top university to the CIA, he'll just laugh at you. The result is that the labor pool they have to work with is a small number of misguided idealists and a large number of people who either could not find a decent job or think that they can get ahead by their manipulative political skills and the power of Government authority. The CIA has no hope of getting the best graduates. I can assure you I never heard anyone saying proudly that he works for the CIA, I mean within the intelligence community where that can be said openly. In my experience, they admit it in a way that you can see that they are almost ashamed of it."

"Is it really that bad?"

"Maybe I am exaggerating a bit, but essentially this is the case. As one of my British friends once jokingly said, 'We recruit honest people and teach them to cheat when absolutely necessary; they recruit dishonest people ant try to teach them to be honest when it is absolutely necessary.'"

"Victor, all this is on a very high conceptual level. How does it relate to what the CIA did to us?"

"These are the fundamentals. When you get the fundamentals wrong, you don't have to look for troubles, they'll find you."

"But why were they were so vicious to us?"

"Because the fundamentals set the cast of characters, and the modus operandi. The culture within the CIA basically is about competition for who can outcrook whom, for who is the most successful crook. That's also their idea of clandestine operations. I think that they genuinely do not understand that intelligence, in a real sense, is an honest business. Whatever you promise, you must deliver."

Victor paused. "Let me give you one more fundamental. Contrary to popular belief, The CIA never recruited anybody abroad."

"Oh, come on."

"It's true. They don't need to. People come to them, people volunteer. Why do they do that? Because of the image of this country, of the United States. So, the CIA people don't have to work as hard as their counterparts in other countries. Essentially, they live off the image of the United States."

"Well, that sounds right as far as I know. That's why we ourselves volunteered to defect to the CIA."

"That's the good news. The bad news is that the CIA is squandering the good image of this country with their blunders. That also gives a lot of fodder to the country's adversaries, and enables them to inflict more propaganda damage on the United States."

"I still don't understand how all this relates directly to what happened to us."

"Well, the rest is logical. Everything I've described creates an unhealthy culture within the CIA. Just read a few accounts of what's going on there. Ames' confessions are a good place to start. That culture makes it easy to manipulate the organization into doing something bad. The reason is very simple: according to their morality, doing something bad is normal. For example, remember when Elena was expelled from her school for no good reason?"

Olga nodded, and Victor went on. "In an organization that had any decency, if such an action was proposed, someone would certainly say: 'We don't do this kind of thing, sir.' In the CIA, however, it was normal." Victor took a breath. "In an organization with a moral code that low, one can get away with anything. This attitude is at its worst in Resettlement. When I complained to Donald about Resettlement, you know what he told me?"

"What?"

"He said, 'Victor you know how demanding operations are, especially against the KGB. We don't have enough good people to fill those jobs—and they are a top priority. Resettlement is at the bottom of the heap. Those are the people that aren't any good anywhere, only just a notch above being kicked out."

"Well, I understand this, but why go after us in the first place?"

"That's where all the weaknesses of the CIA come together in a gaping hole in their security. What do you think is the biggest danger for a KGB mole within the CIA?"

"A defector from the KGB?"

"Precisely. A mole would dread the possibility that someone with knowledge dangerous for him would defect. Logically, he would fear all defectors, and try to do whatever he could to give them a hard time, to discredit them, destabilize them psychologically, make them drunkards, real or rumored, make them so frustrated that they go back and discourage other defections."

"I must say, this seems to be precisely what is going on now in the CIA. But, even with a CIA culture that encourages and enables manipulative behavior, how can one mole manipulate so much?"

Victor chuckled. "First, that depends on how high the mole is in the CIA bureaucracy. Second, who said that they have only one mole?"

"Do you really think that they have more than one?"

"Bob Hanssen told me that the CIA had at least three moles, maybe five or six."

"Come on, how would he know?"

"Well, for sure he was in an ideal position to know. Moreover, I learned a long time ago that, if you know your field very, very well, you can learn more from the questions asked than from the answers given."

"I remember, you mentioned that during our debriefings in 1980. But the questions can be misleading, and one can also ask a question already knowing the answer. That's standard operating procedure for interrogators, lawyers, or journalists."

"True, the questioner can try. But, if you know your field you can judge by the follow-up questions or lack of them. For instance, if the answer is already known, you rarely get a follow-up question, even at the first level of follow-up. You can also gain a lot of insight from the way questions are worded too, and so on."

"Interesting, I never thought of that."

"So, Bob Hanssen was in a good position to know. He had extraordinarily broad access to information, and he knew generally who could have access to different parts of every national security issue. Also, over many years he got a lot of questions from the KGB. He could judge what they didn't know and what they already knew. From what they didn't ask him he could deduce the areas they already knew. Then, he could estimate how many different separate areas this represented, that is, how many sources they must have had in different areas."

"Wow! Do you think he ever told that to the FBI?"

"I doubt it. He's not the volunteering type, as you know."

"So, you think the CIA was manipulated by the mole or moles to treat us and other defectors badly?"

"Yes, I am absolutely convinced of that. The only beneficiaries of the bad treatment of defectors are the KGB and its moles. This country and the defectors are the injured parties. And I'm pretty sure that one of these moles had something to do with Jack's death."

"Do you want to talk to the FBI about it?"

"No, thank you."

"Do you think that the FBI understands this?"

"I did suggest it formally in a memo a couple of years ago, and they rejected the idea out of hand. At the time I thought they were worried that challenging the CIA would harm their careers. Remember? I was so disgusted that I said we should stop seeing the Hanssens socially. However, I heard through the grapevine that they re-opened the investigation of Y the very next day after Hanssen's arrest, based on my memo, and a lot of other things they have on him."

"Will they succeed in getting him?"

"I doubt it. They were duped by Hanssen into warning him and thus allowing him to destroy a lot of the evidence. They also have a record of two previous investigations of him, and we don't know why they were not successful. By now they probably can't put together enough evidence to convict him."

"Are you saying they're going to let him get away with it?"

"Probably. That's one of those things we have to pay for that makes this country as great as it is. You have to have real evidence to convict people. Knowledge alone is not enough." Victor paused. "Felix Bloch is a classic example. They knew for sure he was spying. But Hanssen warned Bloch, allowing him to destroy enough evidence to prevent prosecution. Nothing they could do."

After a while of silence Olga said; "Victor, we've been hurt and frustrated by the CIA's treatment. At the same time, we have to reconcile it with the fact that they actually brought us here."

"Yes, that's true, and such reconciliation is not easy. Funny, this question came up once in my discussions with NSA Counterintelligence."

"What did you say?"

"I said that we are alive and here by God's grace. He wanted all five of the good CIA people to be in that operation, and all five of the really bad ones out."

Olga laughed. "You're impossible."

"Seriously, I never said that there aren't any good people in the CIA. The problem is that they are few and far between." Victor paused. "In fact, if the CIA had had its way, I'd be long dead. They first wanted me to work 'in place for a couple of years', and that would have been a death sentence for me and probably the Gulag for you. The NSA was the decisive factor. Admiral Inman insisted that we had to be brought here immediately. If we had stayed, Y would have learned about me by the end of 1980, and that would have been the end of the game."

"Did you ever talked to Bob Inman about it?"

"Yes. On one of my trips to Texas I visited him in Austin and conveyed our gratitude."

"What did he say?"

"He is a very intelligent man. He just smiled and said 'Yeah, not everyone understood the situation and the urgency. It was the right decision.'"

46

The development of a commercial prototype for the InvisiLAN technology was advancing well, but business realities assured significant stress for the company. One New York investor was very interested, and Invicta was comfortable with their pre-negotiated terms. However, the investor understood the complexity of the fundamentally new technology, and understandably demanded an independent test of a commercial prototype as a condition of his commitment. Everyone went into overdrive.

Testing would take time, and the company had modest funding that would last just until the end of the year. At a company meeting the developers discussed how they could accelerate the testing. It was decided that the best way would be to rattle the industry, so they planned to test vigorously, and quickly.

The latest trend in the computer security industry had borrowed from the politicians' playbook: spin. More and more industry leaders were saying that computer security as such was not achievable, so the task of the industry was now to "manage risk." It was a really nice approach that relieved the industry from the responsibility for actually securing their customers' computers. "Nothing is unhackable" almost became a slogan, endorsed by the testing teams who were now saying that given current expertise, "There's nothing we cannot hack."

Victor suggested attacking exactly that premise. No true cybersecurity expert was comfortable with the term "unhackable"— the technical term was, "unauthorized access to a computer over a network is computationally infeasible." So, Victor suggested deliberately using the word "unhackable." "This will wake everybody up. If we're wrong, and someone can hack the system, we'll find out really fast."

The response was cautious.

"Victor, are you willing to risk your reputation with that?"

"Sure, why not? If we can't hack it, no one can. Any doubts?"

The guys were hesitant. "Well, not really, but it's still scary."

It was decided to ask James Dwyer, the legendary ex-NSA cybersecurity expert, to test the system first and, unprecedentedly, with full internal access to the system, as well as the source code. No other security system had ever cleared that kind of testing. The secret was that InvisiLAN protected not by "fortification," i.e. how good its keys were, but by dynamics, by how often the keys were changed.

Everyone agreed that if James Dwyer couldn't hack it, no one could. James agreed to do the testing. The team held its breath. Victor had never seen these topnotch experts, usually professionally pretty cocky, and justifiably so, looking as nervous as college freshmen before their first exam. Victor noticed a significant drop in company productivity, but there was nothing he could do about it. Everyone was on tenterhooks. James took his time.

After about two weeks, James declared: "Nope. Nothing to cling to. I don't see any way to do it."

That verdict spread like wildfire through the company offices. There was a roar and, before Victor knew it, an unauthorized party exploded, which he was happy to participate in.

They continued to debug and polish the system before submitting it to an official testing.

Then came 9/11. The event shocked the country, and Invicta was no exception. Work productivity declined. One of the developers was badly needed at his old NSA job, and he agreed to go back, even with a significant loss of compensation, purely out of patriotic considerations.

In the chaos of the immediate aftermath of 9/11 the company managed to finish the commercial prototype of InvisiLAN. The system was submitted for testing to the NSA as well as to one of the best commercial testing teams in the country, PriceWaterhouseCoopers, PwC.

This time the developers were not very nervous. James Dwyer's test had given them real confidence. The PwC team was stunned by the fact that they could not hack the system, the first such instance in their team's history.

The NSA team could not hack InvisiLAN either, and raised only one concern: scalability—could the system be developed for millions of computers? The Invicta developers immediately set off to solve that problem. However, that was an easier problem than those they had already solved.

The tragedy of 9/11 was still on everyone's mind. It became clear that everything had changed: the security industry, the country, and the whole world. Drastic changes were taking place on a massive scale.

For the security industry physical security became by far the top priority. Anti-terror efforts overshadowed everything else, including cyber security. Understandably, the war on terror demanded huge resources. For Invicta this brought an unfortunate change in the financing environment. Interest in investing in cyber security shrank dramatically.

Victor was hoping that the CIA would finally leave him and his family alone. After all, most people that he dealt with were gone, and the new ones had enough other problems to deal with. However it was not to be.

After several presentations of InvisiLAN to major Government contractor companies Victor noticed a disturbing pattern. Every presentation was initiated by Invicta, and Victor's name was usually not mentioned. Most presentations were conducted by Victor, and were received very enthusiastically. The experts were really impressed and promised to start cooperation very soon. However, almost all of them disappeared soon after, and follow-up calls were not returned. People at Invicta were puzzled.

Then, by sheer chance, and old friend who was retired from the Government and was working for a government contractor called Victor. After a brief greeting he said, "Hey, Victor, what's going on? What's this 'no contact' business about?"

"What no contact business?"

You mean you don't even know? When I punched your name into our classified computer— which isn't too sensitive, just the general stuff that's shared by the Government with all cleared contractors—a very short note came up: 'NO CONTACT."

"What?"

"That's right. It's a very curt instruction to avoid any contact with you, no explanations. The source is the CIA."

Now it dawned on Victor why all those companies disappeared. They were reacting to the CIA command, having consulted the classified network after the presentation as a security routine."

Talking to Olga that evening Victor said: "Do you know what's my greatest scientific achievement so far?"

"What?"

"I discovered that everything in this world, at least on this planet, has it limits, except in three things: human stupidity, human indecency, and human greed."

"Stop it, Victor. You are not that cynical."

"Maybe, but it surely seems to be true."

Victor called Jim Woolsey and told him the story. Woolsey was incredulous: "Are you sure?"

"Yes, you can check it yourself. And I know what it's about. It was I who demanded that they leave me alone, and they promised to do just that. *And how—they did it with a vengeance, used my own demand against me.* But instead of posting that just for every CIA man in their internal operational database as they were supposed to do, they posted it for all Government contractors. That's called sabotage. It incidentally also hurts a new technology important for the security of this country."

"This is incredible." Woolsey paused. "All right, I'll go see Mike Hayden personally as soon as he can meet."

In a few days Jim Woolsey called. "Victor, I talked to Mike Hayden. He made a quick inquiry and told me: 'If anyone says anything derogative about Victor Sheymov, he does not speak for the CIA or for the Intelligence community.'"

"Thank you. Anything I can get in writing?"

"It wasn't a convenient time to ask. I'm sure they removed the damn thing."

Some time later, at a meeting that included General Hayden, during the few minutes that they were alone in the room, Victor thanked him for the kind reference. Hayden just smiled and nodded.

THE END

ABOUT THE AUTHOR

Victor Sheymov is a computer security expert, author, scientist, inventor, and holder of multiple patents for methods and systems in cyber security. He is the inventor of the VCC – Variable Cyber Coordinates method of communications.

He worked for the National Security Agency (NSA) for a number of years and was a major contributor to the intelligence community of the Western nations. He is a recipient of several prestigious awards in intelligence and security.

Victor Sheymov is the author of *Tower of Secrets: A Real Life Spy Thriller*, a book that describes his experience in the Soviet Communist political system and its repressive apparatus in the context of his career in scientific research involving guidance systems within the Russian "Star Wars" missile defense program, and then as one of the youngest majors in the Russian equivalent of the NSA, responsible for coordination of all security aspects of the Russian cipher communications with its outposts abroad. He and his wife and daughter were exfiltrated by the CIA in 1980.

Since finishing his work with the NSA, Victor Sheymov has been active in the computer security industry as the head of Invicta Networks, Inc., a northern Virginia-based developer of advanced cyber security technologies that address the protection of cyber systems, as well as programs to protect children and teens from Internet predators.

He is the author of the recently published *Cyberspace and Security: A Fundamentally New Approach.*

Victor Sheymov has testified before the United States Congress as an expert witness. He has been a keynote speaker at major government and private industry events like the NSA OPSEC Awards conference, a National Defense Industry convention, a National Science Foundation symposium, and has been a guest lecturer at a number of universities. He has also authored articles in the *Washington Post, Barron's, World Monitor, National Review* and other national publications. He has appeared on many national news programs including *Larry King Live, 48 Hours, Dateline, McNeil-Lehrer News Hour, Charlie Rose,* and the *McLaughlin Report.*

Victor Sheymov holds an Executive MBA from Emory University and a Master's degree from Moscow State Technical University, a Russian equivalent of MIT.

He is the author of *Party Gold: A Cyrus Grant Novel of Suspense.*

Made in the USA
Middletown, DE
03 July 2023

34462346R00176